"The placebo effect—our response to the belief that we've received a catalyst for healing—has long been studied in medicine as a curious phenomenon. In his paradigm-altering book **You Are the Placebo**, Dr. Joe Dispenza catapults us beyond thinking of the effect as an anomaly. Through 12 concise chapters that read like a true-life scientific thriller, Dispenza gives us rock-solid reasons to accept the game-changer of our lives: that the placebo effect is actually us, proving to ourselves the greatest possibilities of healing, miracles, and longevity! I love this book and look forward to a world where the secret of the placebo is the foundation of everyday life."

— **Gregg Braden,**
New York Times best-selling author of
Deep Truth and *The Divine Matrix*

"Dr. Joe Dispenza is a master teacher who has the ability to explain science at a very simple level so that everyone understands."

— **don Miguel Ruiz, M.D.,**
author of *The Four Agreements*

"**You Are the Placebo** is a must-read for anyone who wants to experience optimal health in mind, body, and spirit. Dr. Joe Dispenza dispels the myth that our health is out of our control and restores to us our power and right to expect wonderful health and well-being throughout our lives by showing us the way to create it. To read this book is to subscribe to the absolute best health insurance available in the world."

— **Sonia Choquette,**
six-sensory consultant and
New York Times best-selling author of *The Answer Is Simple*

You Are the

PLACEBO

ALSO BY DR. JOE DISPENZA

Books

EVOLVE YOUR BRAIN:
The Science of Changing Your Mind

BREAKING THE HABIT OF BEING YOURSELF:
How to Lose Your Mind and Create a New One*

CD Program

MEDITATIONS FOR BREAKING
THE HABIT OF BEING YOURSELF*

*Available from Hay House

Please visit:

Hay House USA: www.hayhouse.com®
Hay House Australia: www.hayhouse.com.au
Hay House UK: www.hayhouse.co.uk
Hay House South Africa: www.hayhouse.co.za
Hay House India: www.hayhouse.co.in

You Are the PLACEBO

making your mind matter

Dr. Joe Dispenza

HAY HOUSE, INC.
Carlsbad, California • New York City
London • Sydney • Johannesburg
Vancouver • Hong Kong • New Delhi

Published and distributed in the United States by: Hay House, Inc.: www
.hayhouse.com® • *Published and distributed in Australia by:* Hay House Australia Pty. Ltd.: www.hayhouse.com.au • *Published and distributed in the
United Kingdom by:* Hay House UK, Ltd.: www.hayhouse.co.uk • *Published and
distributed in the Republic of South Africa by:* Hay House SA (Pty), Ltd.: www
.hayhouse.co.za • *Distributed in Canada by:* Raincoast Books: www.raincoast
.com • *Published in India by:* Hay House Publishers India: www.hayhouse.co.in

Indexer: Jay Kreider
Cover design and interior illustrations: John Dispenza
Interior design: Pamela Homan
Brain-mapping graphics: Jeffrey L. Fannin, Ph.D.

The material in the color insert was made possible with the help of Jeffrey Fannin,
Ph.D. Special thanks to Dr. Fannin for providing the color brain scans and for
contributing to their interpretation.

Library of Congress Cataloging-in-Publication Data

Dispenza, Joe, date.
   You are the placebo : making your mind matter / Dr. Joe Dispenza.
      pages cm
   Includes index.
      ISBN 978-1-4019-4458-2 (hardback) -- ISBN 978-1-4019-4459-9 (paperback) 1.
Mind and body. 2. Attitude (Psychology) 3. Attitude change--Health aspects. 4.
Placebos (Medicine) 5. Change (Psychology) I. Title.
   BF161.D55 2014
   158.1--dc23
                                    2013045516

Hardcover ISBN: 978-1-4019-4458-2
Tradepaper ISBN: 978-1-4019-4459-9

17 16 15 14   4 3 2 1
1st edition, April 2014

Printed in the United States of America

For my mother,
Francesca

CONTENTS

Part I: INFORMATION

Part II: TRANSFORMATION

FOREWORD

Like most of his fans, I look forward to Joe Dispenza's provocative ideas with relish. Combining solid scientific evidence with stimulating insights, Joe stretches the horizons of the possible by extending the boundaries of the known. He takes science more seriously than most scientists, and in this fascinating book, he extrapolates the most recent discoveries in epigenetics, neural plasticity, and psychoneuroimmunology to their logical conclusion.

That conclusion is an exciting one: You, and every other human being, are shaping your brain and body by the thoughts you think, the emotions you feel, the intentions you hold, and the transcendental states you experience. *You Are the Placebo* invites you to harness this knowledge to create a new body and new life for yourself.

This isn't a metaphysical proposition. Joe explains each link in the chain of causality that starts with a thought and ends with a biological fact, such as an increase in the number of stem cells or immunity-conferring protein molecules circulating in your bloodstream.

The book starts with Joe's account of an accident that shattered six of the vertebrae of his spine. Suddenly, in extremis, he was confronted with the necessity of putting into practice what he believed in theory: that our bodies possess an innate intelligence that includes miraculous healing power. The discipline he brought to the process of visualizing his spinal column rebuilding itself is a story of inspiration and determination.

We're all inspired by such stories of spontaneous remission and "miraculous" healing, yet what Joe shows us in this book is that we are all capable of experiencing such healing miracles. Renewal is built into the very fabric of our bodies, and degeneration and disease are the exception, not the norm.

Once we understand how our bodies renew themselves, we can start to harness these physiological processes intentionally, directing the hormones our cells synthesize, the proteins they build, the neurotransmitters they produce, and the neural pathways through which they send signals. Rather than possessing a static anatomy, our bodies are seething with change, moment by moment. Our brains are on the boil, teeming with the creation and destruction of neural connections in every second. Joe teaches us that we can steer this process with intention, assuming the powerful position of driver of the vehicle, rather than the passive role of passenger.

The discovery that the number of connections in a neural bundle can double with repeat stimulation revolutionized biology in the 1990s. It earned its discoverer, the neuropsychiatrist Eric Kandel, a Nobel Prize. Kandel later found that if we don't use neural connections, they begin to shrink in just three weeks. In this way, we can reshape our brains via the signals we pass through our neural network.

In the same decade that Kandel and others measured neuroplasticity, other scientists discovered that few of our genes are static. The majority of genes (estimates range from 75 to 85 percent) are turned off and on by signals from our environment, including the environment of thoughts, beliefs, and emotions that we cultivate in our brains. One class of these genes, the *immediate early genes* (IEGs), takes only three seconds to reach peak expression. IEGs are often regulatory genes, controlling the expression of hundreds of other genes and thousands of other proteins at remote sites in our bodies. That kind of pervasive and rapid change is a plausible explanation for some of the radical healings you'll read about in these pages.

Joe is one of the few science writers to fully grasp the role of emotion in transformation. Negative emotion may literally be an addiction to high levels of our own stress hormones, like cortisol and adrenaline. Both these stress hormones and relaxation hormones like DHEA and oxytocin have set points, which explains why we feel uncomfortable in our skin when we think thoughts or countenance beliefs that drive our hormonal balance outside of that comfort zone. This idea is at the very frontier of the scientific understanding of addictions and cravings.

By changing your internal state, you can change your external reality. Joe masterfully explains the chain of events that starts with intentions originating in the frontal lobe of your brain and then translating into chemical messengers, called *neuropeptides,* that send signals throughout your body, turning genetic switches on or off. Some of these chemicals, like *oxytocin,* the "cuddle hormone" that's stimulated by touch, are associated with feelings of love and trust. With practice, you can learn to quickly adjust your set points for stress hormones and healing hormones.

The notion that you can heal yourself by simply translating thought into emotion might sound astounding at first. Not even Joe expected the results he began to observe in participants attending his workshops when they fully applied these ideas: spontaneous remission of tumors, wheelchair-bound patients walking, and migraines disappearing. With the openhearted delight and open-minded experimentation of a child at play, Joe began to push the envelope, wondering just how fast radical healing might occur if people applied the body's placebo effect with complete conviction. Hence, the title *You Are the Placebo* reflects the fact that it's your own thoughts, emotions, and beliefs that are generating chains of physiological events in your body.

At times, you will feel uncomfortable reading this book. But read on. That discomfort is just your old self, protesting the inevitability of transformative change, and your hormonal set points being disturbed. Joe reassures us that those feelings of discomfort may simply be the biological sensation of the dissolution of the old self.

Most of us won't have the time or inclination to understand these complex biological processes. Here's where this book provides a great service. Joe digs deep into the science behind these changes to present them in an understandable and digestible way. He does the heavy lifting behind the scenes in order to present elegant and simple explanations. Using analogies and case histories, he demonstrates exactly how we can apply these discoveries in our daily lives and illustrates the dramatic breakthroughs in health experienced by those who take them seriously.

A new generation of researchers has coined a term for the practice Joe outlines: *self-directed neuroplasticity* (or *SDN*). The idea behind the term is that we direct the formation of new neural pathways and the destruction of old ones through the quality of the experiences we cultivate. I believe that SDN will become one of the most potent concepts in personal transformation and neurobiology for the coming generation, and this book will be at the forefront of that movement.

In the meditation exercises in Part II of this book, metaphysics moves into concrete manifestation. You can do these meditations yourself easily, experiencing firsthand the expanded possibilities of being your own placebo. The goal here is to change your beliefs and perceptions about your life at a biological level so that you are, in essence, loving a new future into concrete material existence.

So embark on this enchanted journey that will expand your horizons of the possible and challenge you to embrace a radically higher level of healing and functioning. You have nothing to lose by throwing yourself enthusiastically into the process and dumping the thoughts, feelings, and biological set points that have limited your past. Believe in your ability to realize your highest potential and take inspired action, and you will become the placebo that creates a happy and healthy future for yourself and for our planet.

— **Dawson Church, Ph.D.**
Author of *The Genie in Your Genes*

PREFACE

Waking Up

I never planned on doing any of this. The work I'm currently involved in as a speaker, author, and researcher sort of found me. In order for some of us to wake up, we sometimes need a wake-up call. In 1986, I got the call. On a beautiful Southern California day in April, I had the privilege of being run over by an SUV in a Palm Springs triathlon. That moment changed my life and started me on this whole journey. I was 23 at the time, with a relatively new chiropractic practice in La Jolla, California, and I'd trained hard for this triathlon for months.

I had finished the swimming segment and was in the biking portion of the race when it happened. I was coming up to a tricky turn where I knew we'd be merging with traffic. A police officer, with his back to the oncoming cars, waved me on to turn right and follow the course. Since I was fully exerting myself and focused on the race, I never took my eyes off of him. As I passed two cyclists on that particular corner, a red four-wheel-drive Bronco going about 55 miles an hour slammed into my bike from behind. The next thing I knew, I was catapulted up into the air; then I landed squarely on my backside. Because of the speed of the vehicle and the slow reflexes of the elderly woman driving the Bronco, the SUV kept coming toward me, and I was soon reunited with its bumper. I quickly grabbed the bumper in order to avoid being run over and to stop my body from passing between metal and asphalt. So I was dragged down the road a bit before the driver realized what was happening. When she finally did abruptly stop, I tumbled out of control for about 20 yards.

I can still remember the sound of the bikes whizzing by and the horrified screams and profanities of the riders passing me—not knowing whether they should stop and help or continue the race. As I lay there, all I could do was surrender.

I would soon discover that I had broken six vertebrae: I had compression fractures in thoracic 8, 9, 10, 11, and 12 and lumbar 1 (ranging from my shoulder blades to my kidneys). The vertebrae are stacked like individual blocks in the spine, and when I hit the ground with that kind of force, they collapsed and compressed from the impact. The eighth thoracic vertebra, the top segment that I broke, was more than 60 percent collapsed, and the circular arch that contained and protected the spinal cord was broken and pushed together in a pretzel-like shape. When a vertebra compresses and fractures, the bone has to go somewhere. In my case, a large volume of shattered fragments went back toward my spinal cord. It was definitely not a good picture.

As if I were in a bad dream gone rogue, I woke up the next morning with a host of neurological symptoms, including several different types of pain; varying degrees of numbness, tingling, and some loss of feeling in my legs; and some sobering difficulties in controlling my movements.

So after I had all the blood tests, x-rays, CAT scans, and MRIs at the hospital, the orthopedic surgeon showed me the results and somberly delivered the news: In order to contain the bone fragments that were now on my spinal cord, I needed surgery to implant a Harrington rod. That would mean cutting out the back parts of the vertebrae from two to three segments above and below the fractures and then screwing and clamping two 12-inch stainless-steel rods along both sides of my spinal column. Then they'd scrape some fragments off my hip bone and paste them over the rods. It would be major surgery, but it would mean I'd at least have a chance to walk again. Even so, I knew I'd probably still be somewhat disabled, and I'd have to live with chronic pain for the rest of my life. Needless to say, I didn't like that option.

But if I chose not to have the surgery, paralysis seemed certain. The best neurologist in the Palm Springs area, who concurred with the first surgeon's opinion, told me that he knew of no other patient in the United States in my condition who had refused it. The impact of the accident had compressed my T-8 vertebra into a wedge shape that would prevent my spine from being able to bear the weight of my body if I were to stand up: My backbone would collapse, pushing those shattered bits of the vertebra deep into my spinal cord, causing instant paralysis from my chest down. That was hardly an attractive option either.

I was transferred to a hospital in La Jolla, closer to my home, where I received two additional opinions, including one from the leading orthopedic surgeon in Southern California. Not surprisingly, both doctors agreed that I should have the Harrington rod surgery. It was a pretty consistent prognosis: have the surgery or be paralyzed, never to walk again. If I had been the medical professional making the recommendation, I'd have said the same thing: It was the safest option. But it wasn't the option I chose for myself.

Maybe I was just young and bold at that time in my life, but I decided against the medical model and the expert recommendations. I believe that there's an intelligence, an invisible consciousness, within each of us that's the giver of life. It supports, maintains, protects, and heals us every moment. It creates almost 100 trillion specialized cells (starting from only 2), it keeps our hearts beating hundreds of thousands of times per day, and it can organize hundreds of thousands of chemical reactions in a single cell in every second—among many other amazing functions. I reasoned at the time that if this intelligence was real and if it willfully, mindfully, and lovingly demonstrated such amazing abilities, maybe I could take my attention off my external world and begin to go within and connect with it—developing a relationship with it.

But while I intellectually understood that the body often has the capacity to heal itself, now I had to apply every bit of philosophy that I knew in order to take that knowledge to the next level and beyond, to create a true experience with healing. And since I wasn't going anywhere and I wasn't doing anything except lying facedown, I decided on two things. First, every day I would put all of my conscious attention on this intelligence within me and give it a plan, a template, a vision, with very specific orders, and then I would surrender my healing to this greater mind that has unlimited power, allowing it to do the healing for me. And second, I wouldn't let any thought slip by my awareness that I didn't want to experience. Sounds easy, right?

A Radical Decision

Against the advice of my medical team, I left the hospital in an ambulance that brought me to the home of two close friends, where I stayed for the next three months to focus on my healing. I was on a mission. I decided that I would begin every day reconstructing my spine, vertebra by vertebra, and I would show this consciousness, if it was paying attention to my efforts, what I wanted. I knew that it would demand my absolute presence . . . that is, for me to be present in the moment—not thinking about or regretting my past, worrying about the future, obsessing about the conditions in my external life, or focusing on my pain or symptoms. Just as in any relationship we have with anybody, we all know when someone is present or not with us, right? Because consciousness is awareness, awareness is paying attention, and paying attention is being present and noticing, this consciousness would be aware of when I was present and when I wasn't. I would have to be totally present when I interacted with this mind; my presence would have to match its presence, my will would have to match its will, and my mind would have to match its mind.

So for two hours twice a day, I went within and began creating a picture of my intended result: a totally healed spine. Of course, I became aware of how unconscious and unfocused I was. It's ironic. I realized back then that when crisis or trauma occurs, we spend too much of our attention and energy thinking about what we *don't* want instead of what we *do* want. During those first several weeks, I was guilty of this tendency on what seemed like a moment-to-moment basis.

In the middle of my meditations on creating the life I wanted with a fully healed spine, I would all of a sudden become aware that I'd been unconsciously thinking about what the surgeons had told me a few weeks prior: that I would probably never walk again. I would be in the midst of inwardly reconstructing my spine, and the next thing I knew I was stressing over whether I should sell my chiropractic practice. While I was step-by-step mentally rehearsing walking again, I would catch myself imagining what it would be like to live the rest of my life sitting in a wheelchair—you get the idea.

So every time I lost my attention and my mind wandered to any extraneous thoughts, I would start from the beginning and do the whole scheme of imagery over again. It was tedious, frustrating, and, quite frankly, one of the most difficult things I'd ever done. But I reasoned that the final picture that I wanted the observer in me to notice had to be clear, unpolluted, and uninterrupted. In order for this intelligence to accomplish what I hoped—what I *knew*—it was capable of doing, from start to finish I had to stay conscious and not go unconscious.

Finally, after six weeks of battling with myself and making the effort to be present with this consciousness, I was able to make it through my inward reconstruction process without having to stop and start over from the beginning. I remember the day I did it for the first time: It was like hitting a tennis ball on the sweet spot. There was something *right* about it. It clicked. I clicked. And I felt complete, satisfied, and whole. For the first time, I was truly relaxed and present—in mind and body. There was no mental chatter, no analyzing, no thinking, no obsessing, no trying; something lifted, and a kind of peace and silence prevailed. It was as if I no longer cared about all of the things I should have been worried about in my past and future.

And that realization solidified the journey for me, because right around that time, as I was creating this vision of what I wanted, reconstructing my vertebrae, it started to get easier every day. Most important, I started to notice some pretty significant physiological changes. It was in that moment that I began to correlate what I was doing inside of me to create this change with what was taking place outside of me—in my body. The instant I made that correlation, I paid greater attention to what I was doing and did it with more conviction; and I did it again and again. As a result, I kept doing it with a level of joy and inspiration instead of such a dreadful, compromised effort. And all of a sudden, what had originally taken me two or three hours to accomplish in one session, I was able to do in a shorter period.

Now, I had quite a bit of time on my hands. So I started to think about what it would be like to see a sunset again from the water's edge or eat lunch with my friends at a table in a restaurant, and I thought about how I would never take any of that for granted. In detail, I imagined taking a shower and feeling the water on my face and body, or simply sitting up while using the toilet or taking a walk on the beach in San Diego, the wind blowing on my face. These were some things that I had never fully appreciated before the accident, but now they had meaning—and I took my time to emotionally embrace them until I felt as if I were already there.

I didn't know what I was doing at the time, but now I do: I was actually starting to think about all these future potentials that existed in the quantum field, and then I was emotionally embracing each of them. And as I selected that intentional future and married it with the elevated emotion of what it would be like to be there in that future, in the present moment my body began to believe it was actually *in* that future experience. As my ability to observe my desired destiny got sharper and sharper, my cells began to reorganize themselves. I began to signal new genes in new ways, and then my body *really* started getting better faster.

What I was learning is one of the main principles of quantum physics: that mind and matter are not separate elements, that our conscious and unconscious thoughts and feelings are the very blueprints that control our destiny. The persistence, conviction, and focus to manifest any potential future lies within the human mind and within the mind of the infinite potentials in the quantum field. Both of these minds must work together in order to bring about any future reality that potentially already exists. I realized that in that way, we are all divine creators, independent of race, gender, culture, social status, education, religious beliefs, or even past mistakes. I felt really blessed for the first time in my life.

I made other key decisions about my healing as well. I set up a whole regimen (described in detail in *Evolve Your Brain*) that included diet, visits from friends who practiced energy healing, and an elaborate rehabilitation program. But nothing was more important to me during that time than getting in touch with that intelligence within me and, through it, using my mind to heal my body.

At nine and a half weeks after the accident, I got up and walked back into my life—without having any body cast or any surgeries. I had reached full recovery. I started seeing patients again at 10 weeks and was back to training and lifting weights again, while continuing my rehabilitation, at 12 weeks. And now, almost 30 years after the accident, I can honestly say that I've hardly ever had back pain since.

Research Begins in Earnest

But that wasn't the end of this adventure. Not surprisingly, I couldn't go back into my life as my same self. I was changed in many ways. I'd been initiated into a reality that no one I knew could really understand. I couldn't relate with a lot of my friends, and I certainly couldn't return to the same life. The things that were once so important to me really no longer mattered. And I started asking big questions like "Who am I?"; "What is the meaning of this life?"; "What am I doing here?"; "What's my purpose?"; and "What or who is God?" I left San Diego within a short time and moved to the Pacific Northwest, eventually opening a chiropractic clinic near Olympia, Washington. But at first, I pretty much retreated from the world and studied spirituality.

In time, I also became very interested in spontaneous remissions: when people healed from a serious disease or condition deemed terminal or permanent, without traditional medical interventions like surgery or drugs. On those long, lonely nights during my recovery when I couldn't sleep, I had made a deal with that consciousness that if I were ever able to walk again, I'd spend the rest of my life investigating and researching the mind-body connection and the concept of mind over matter. And that's pretty much what I've been doing in the nearly three decades since then.

I traveled to several different countries, seeking out many people who had been diagnosed with illnesses and treated conventionally or nonconventionally, either staying the same or getting worse until, all of a sudden, they got better. I started interviewing these people to discover what their experiences had in common so I could understand and document what had made them improve, because I had a passion to marry science with spirituality. What I found was that each of these miraculous cases relied on a strong element of mind.

The scientist in me started getting very itchy, becoming even more inquisitive. I became re-involved in attending university classes and studying the latest research in neuroscience, and I advanced my postgraduate training in brain imaging, neuroplasticity, epigenetics, and psychoneuroimmunology. And I figured, now that I knew what these people had done to get better and now that I knew all about the science of changing your mind (or at least I *thought* I did), I should be able to reproduce it—in both sick people and people who are well who want to make changes to support not only their health, but also their relationships, careers, families, and lives in general.

I was then invited to be one of the 14 scientists and researchers featured in the 2004 documentary film *What the Bleep Do We Know!?* and that movie became an overnight sensation. *What the Bleep Do We Know!?* invited people to question the nature of reality and then try it out in their lives to see if their observation mattered or, perhaps more accurately put, if their observation *became* matter. People around the world were talking about the film and the concepts it espoused. In the wake of that, my first book, *Evolve Your Brain: The Science of Changing Your Mind,* was published in 2007. After *Evolve Your Brain* had been out for a while, people started to ask me, "How do you *do* it? How do you change, and how do you create the life you want?" It soon became the most common question people asked me.

So I assembled a team and started teaching workshops across the United States and internationally on how the brain is wired and how you can reprogram your thinking using neurophysiological principles. At first, these workshops were mostly just a sharing of information. But people wanted more, so I added meditations to synergize and complement the information, giving participants practical steps to making changes in their minds and bodies, and, as a result, changes in their lives as well. After I taught my introductory workshops in different parts of the world, people would then ask me, "What's next?" So I began teaching another level to the introductory workshop. After that was completed, more folks asked if I could teach another level, a more advanced workshop. This continued in most of the places where I presented.

I kept thinking that I was done, that I'd taught all I could teach, but people kept asking for more, so I'd learn more myself and then refine the presentations and meditations. A momentum developed, and I was getting good feedback; people were able to eliminate some of their self-destructive habits and lead happier lives. Even though up to this point, my associates and I had seen only small changes—nothing really significant—people loved the information and wanted to continue the practice. So I kept going where I was invited. I figured that when the time came that they stopped inviting me, I'd know I was done with this work.

About a year and a half after our first workshop, my team and I started receiving several e-mails from our participants commenting on positive changes they were experiencing from doing the meditations on a consistent basis. A flood of change began to manifest in people's lives, and they were overjoyed. The feedback we received over the next year caught my attention and that of my staff as well. Our participants began reporting not only subjective changes in their physical health, but also improvements in objective measurements from their medical tests. Sometimes the tests would even come back totally normal! These people were able to reproduce the exact physical, mental, and emotional changes that I studied, observed, and ultimately wrote about in *Evolve Your Brain*.

This was incredibly exciting for me to witness, because I knew that anything that is repeatable verges on becoming a scientific law. It seemed as though many folks were sending us e-mails starting with the same verbiage: "You're not going to believe this . . ." And those changes were now more than coincidence.

Then a little later that year, during each of two events in Seattle, some amazing things began to happen. At the first event, a woman with multiple sclerosis (MS), who was using a walker when she arrived, was walking unassisted by the time the workshop was over. At the second Seattle event that year, another woman, who had suffered with MS for ten years, started dancing around, declaring that the paralysis and numbness she'd experienced in her left foot were completely gone. (You'll read more about one of these women, and others like them, in the chapters to come.) By demand, in 2010 I taught a more progressive workshop in Colorado, where people started noticing that they were shifting their well-being right there, during the event. People stood up, took the microphone, and reported some pretty inspiring stories.

Around this time, I was also invited to speak to a lot of business leaders about the biology of change, the neuroscience of leadership, and the concept of how to transform individuals in order to transform a culture. After a keynote address to one group, several executives approached me about adapting the ideas for a corporate model of transformation. So I created an eight-hour course that could be tailored for companies and organizations, and the course was so successful that it spawned our "30 Days to Genius" corporate program. I found myself working with business clients such as Sony Entertainment Network, Gallo Family Vineyards, the telecommunications company WOW! (originally called Wide Open West), and many others. This led to offering private coaching for upper management.

The demand for our corporate programs became so great that I began training a coaching staff; I now have more than 30 active trainers, including ex-CEOs, corporate consultants, psychotherapists, attorneys, physicians, engineers, and Ph.D. professionals who travel all around, teaching this model of transformation to different companies. (We now have plans to begin certifying independent coaches in using the model of change with their own clients.) Never in my wildest dreams had I ever imagined this type of future for myself.

I wrote my second book, *Breaking the Habit of Being Yourself: How to Lose Your Mind and Create a New One*, published in 2012, to serve as a practical how-to companion to *Evolve Your Brain*. I not only explained more about the neuroscience of change and epigenetics, but also included a four-week program with step-by-step directions for implementing these changes, based on the workshops I was teaching at the time.

Then I did another, more advanced event in Colorado, where we had *seven* spontaneous remissions of various conditions. One woman who was living on lettuce because of severe food allergies was healed that weekend. Other people were healed of gluten intolerance, celiac disease, a thyroid condition, severe chronic pain, and other conditions. All of a sudden, I started seeing some really significant changes in people's health and in their lives, while they retreated from their then-current reality in order to create a new one. It was happening right before my eyes.

Information to Transformation

That event in Colorado in 2012 was the turning point in my career, because I could finally see that people not only were being helped to change their sense of well-being, but now also were signaling new genes in new ways *right there* during the meditations, in real time, in big ways. In order for someone who had been sick for years with a health condition like lupus to become well during a one-hour meditation, something significant *must* have occurred in the person's mind as well as her body. I wanted to figure out how to measure these changes while they were happening in the workshops so that we could see exactly what was going on.

So in early 2013, I offered a brand-new type of event that shot our workshops to a whole new level. For this event, which was in Arizona, I invited a team of researchers, including neuroscientists, technicians, and quantum physicists, with specialized instruments to join me for a four-day workshop attended by more than 200 participants. The experts used their equipment to measure the ambient electromagnetic field in the workshop room to see if the energy was changing as the workshop progressed. They also measured the field of energy around the participants' bodies and the energy centers of their bodies (also called *chakras*) to see if they were able to influence these centers.

To take these measurements, they used very sophisticated instrumentation, including electroencephalography (EEG) to gauge the brain's electrical activity, quantitative electroencephalography (QEEG) to make a computerized analysis of the EEG data, heart rate variability (HRV) to document the variation in time interval between heartbeats and heart coherence (a heart-rhythm measurement that reflects the communication between the heart and the brain), and gas discharge visualization (GDV) to measure changes in bioenergetic fields.

We did brain scans on many of the participants both before and after the event so that we could see what was going on in the inner world of people's brains, and we also randomly selected people to scan during the event to see if we could measure any changes in brain patterns in real time during the three meditations I led each day. It was a great event. A person with Parkinson's disease no longer had any tremors. Another person with a traumatic brain injury was healed. People with tumors in their brains and bodies found that these growths went away. Many individuals with arthritic pain experienced relief for the first time in years. All of these occurrences were among many other profound changes.

During this amazing event, we were finally able to capture objective changes in a scientific realm of measurement and document the subjective changes participants reported in their health. I don't think it's an exaggeration to say that what we observed and recorded made history. Later in the book, I'll show you what you're capable of doing, by sharing some of these stories—stories about ordinary people doing the extraordinary.

Here was my idea in developing that workshop: I wanted to give people scientific information and then provide them with the necessary instruction on how to apply that information so that they could achieve heightened degrees of personal transformation. Science is, after all, the contemporary language of mysticism. I learned that the moment you start talking in the language of religion or culture, the moment you start quoting tradition, you divide your audience members. But science unifies them and demystifies the mystical.

And I discovered that if I could teach people the scientific model of transformation (bringing in a little quantum physics to help them understand the science of possibility); combine it with the latest information in neuroscience, neuroendocrinology, epigenetics, and psychoneuroimmunology; give them the right kind of instruction; and provide the opportunity to apply that information, then they would experience a transformation. And if I could do this in a setting where I could measure the transformation as it was happening, then that measurement of transformation would become *more* information that I could use to teach the participants *about* the transformation they had just experienced. And with *that* information, they could have *another* transformation, and on it goes as people begin to close the gap between who they think they are and who they really are—divine creators—making it easier for them to keep doing it. I called this concept "information to transformation," and it has become my new passion.

Now, I offer a 7-hour introductory online intensive, and I also personally teach about nine or ten 3-day progressive workshops a year all around the world, plus one or two 5-day advanced workshops, where we have the aforementioned scientists come in with their equipment to measure brain changes, changes in heart function, changes in genetic expression, and energetic changes in real time. The results are nothing short of astounding, and they form the basis of this book.

INTRODUCTION

Making Minds Matter

The incredible results I've seen in the advanced workshops I offer and all the scientific data that has come out of that have led me to the idea of the *placebo:* how people can take a sugar pill or get a saline injection and then their belief in something outside of themselves makes them get better.

I began to ask myself, "What if people begin to believe in *themselves* instead of in something outside of themselves? What if they believe that they can change something inside of them and move themselves to the same state of being as someone who's taking a placebo? Isn't that what our workshop participants have been doing in order to get better? Do people really need a pill or injection to change their state of being? Can we teach people to accomplish the same thing by teaching them how the placebo really works?"

After all, the snake-handling preacher who drinks strychnine and has no biological effects certainly has changed his state of being, right? (You'll read more about this in the first chapter.) So if we can then begin to measure what's taking place in the brain and look at all this information, can we teach people how to do it themselves, without relying on something outside of them—without a placebo? Can we teach them that they *are* the placebo? In other words, can we convince them that instead of investing their belief in the known, like a sugar pill or a saline injection, they can place their belief in the unknown and make the unknown *known?*

And really that's what this book is about: empowering you to realize that you have all the biological and neurological machinery to do exactly that. My goal is to demystify these concepts with the new science of the way things really are so that it is within the reach of more people to change their internal states in order to create positive changes in their health and in their external world. If that sounds too amazing to be true, then as I've said, toward the end of the book you'll see some of the research compiled from our workshops to show you exactly how it's possible.

What This Book Is <u>Not</u> About

I want to take just a moment to talk about a few things that this book is *not* about, to clear up any potential misconceptions right from the start. For one, you won't read here about the ethics of using placebos in medical treatment. There's much debate about the moral correctness of treating a patient who isn't part of a medical trial with an inert substance. While a discussion about whether the end justifies such means may well be worthwhile in a broader conversation about placebos, that issue is completely separate from the message this book aims to deliver. *You Are the Placebo* is about putting you in the driver's seat of creating your own change, not about whether or not it's okay for other people to trick you into it.

This book is also not about denial. None of the methods you'll read about here involve denying whatever health condition you may presently have. Much to the contrary, this book is all about transforming illness and disease. My interest is in measuring the changes people make when they move from sickness to health. Instead of being about rejecting reality, *You Are the Placebo* is about projecting what's possible when you step into a *new* reality.

You'll discover that honest feedback, in the form of medical tests, will inform you if what you're doing is working. Once you see the effects you've created, you can pay attention to what you did to arrive at that end, and do it again. And if what you're doing isn't working, then it's time to change it until it is. That's combining science and spirituality. Denial, on the other hand, occurs when you're not looking at the reality of what's happening within and around you.

This book also won't question the efficacy of the various healing modalities. Many different modalities exist, and many of them work quite well. All of them have some type of measurable beneficial effect in at least some people, but a complete cataloging of these methods isn't what I want to focus on in this book. My purpose here is to introduce you to the particular modality that has most captured my attention: healing yourself through thought alone. I encourage you to continue using any and all healing modalities that work for you, be they prescription drugs, surgery, acupuncture, chiropractic, biofeedback, therapeutic massage, nutritional supplements, yoga, reflexology, energy medicine, sound therapy, and so on. *You Are the Placebo* is not about rejecting anything except your own self-imposed limitations.

What's Inside This Book?

You Are the Placebo is divided into two parts:

— Part I gives you all the detailed knowledge and background information you need to be able to understand what the placebo effect is and how it operates in your brain and body, as well as how to create the same kind of miraculous changes in your own brain and body *all by yourself, by thought alone.*

Chapter 1 starts off the book by sharing some incredible stories demonstrating the amazing power of the human mind. Some of these tales relate how people's thoughts have healed them, and others show how people's thoughts have actually made them sick (and sometimes even hastened their death). You'll read about a man who died after hearing he had cancer, even though his autopsy revealed that he'd been misdiagnosed; a woman plagued by depression for decades who improved dramatically during an antidepressant drug trial, despite the fact that she was in the group receiving a placebo; and a handful of veterans hobbled by osteo-arthritis who were miraculously cured by fake knee surgery. You'll even read some startling stories about voodoo curses and snake handling. My purpose in sharing these dramatic stories is to show the wide range of what the human mind is capable of doing all on its own, without any help from modern medicine. And hopefully, it will lead you to the question "How is that possible?"

Chapter 2 gives a brief history of the placebo, tracing accounts of related scientific discoveries from the 1770s (when a Viennese doctor used magnets to induce what he thought were therapeutic convulsions) all the way through the modern day, as neuroscientists solve exciting mysteries about the intricacies of how the mind works. You'll meet a doctor who developed techniques of hypnotism after arriving late for an appointment only to find his waiting patient mesmerized by a lamp flame, a World War II surgeon who successfully used saline injections as an analgesic on wounded soldiers when he ran out of morphine, and early psychoneuro-immunology researchers in Japan who switched poison-ivy leaves with harmless leaves and found that their test group reacted more to what they were told they were experiencing than to what they actually did experience.

You'll also read about how Norman Cousins laughed himself to health; how Harvard researcher Herbert Benson, M.D., was able to reduce cardiac patients' risk factors for heart disease by figuring out how Transcendental Meditation worked; and how Italian neuroscientist Fabrizio Benedetti, M.D., Ph.D., primed subjects who had been given a drug, and then switched the drug for a placebo—and watched the brain continue to signal the production of the same neurochemicals the drug produced without interruption. And you'll also read a striking new study that's a real game changer: It shows that irritable bowel syndrome (IBS) patients were able to dramatically improve their symptoms by taking placebos—even though they *knew full well* that the medication they were given was a placebo, not an active drug.

Chapter 3 will take you through the physiology of what happens in your brain when the placebo effect is operating. You'll read that, in one sense, the placebo works because you can embrace or entertain a new thought that you can be well, and then use it to replace the thought that you'll always be sick. That means you can change your thinking from unconsciously predicting that your future is your same familiar past to beginning to anticipate and expect a new potential outcome. If you agree with this idea, then it means that you'll have to examine how you think, what the mind is, and how these things affect the body.

I'll explain how as long as you're thinking the same thoughts, they'll lead to the same choices, which cause the same behaviors, which create the same experiences, which produce the same emotions, which in turn drive the same thoughts—so that neurochemically, you stay the same. In effect, you're reminding yourself of who you think you are. But hold on; you're not hardwired to be the same way for the rest of your life. I'll then explain the concept of neuroplasticity and how we now know that the brain is capable of changing throughout our lives, creating new neural pathways and new connections.

Chapter 4 moves into a discussion of the placebo effect in the body, explaining the next step of the physiology of the placebo response. It starts out telling the story of a group of elderly men who attend a weeklong retreat set up by Harvard researchers who asked the men to pretend they were 20 years younger. By the end of the week, the men had made numerous measurable physiological changes, all turning back the clock on their bodies, and you'll learn the secret behind how they did it.

To explain that, the chapter also discusses what genes are and how they are signaled in the body. You'll learn how the relatively new and exciting science of epigenetics has basically torched the old-school idea that your genes are your destiny, by teaching us that the mind truly can instruct new genes to behave in new ways. You'll discover how the body has elaborate mechanisms for turning some genes on and others off, which means that you're not doomed to express whatever genes you've inherited. This means you can learn how to change your neural wiring to select new genes and create real physical changes. You'll also read about how our bodies access stem cells—the physical matter that's behind many placebo-effect miracles—to make new, healthy cells in areas that have been damaged.

Chapter 5 ties the previous two chapters together, explaining how thoughts change your brain and your body. It begins by asking the question "If your environment changes and you then signal new genes in new ways, is it possible to signal the new gene *ahead* of the changing of the actual environment?" I'll then explain how you can use a technique called *mental rehearsal* to combine a clear intention with an elevated emotion (to give the body a sampling of the future experience) in order to experience the new future event in the present moment.

The key is making your inner thoughts more real than the outer environment, because then the brain won't know the difference between the two and will change to look as if the event has taken place. If you're able to do this successfully enough times, you'll transform your body and begin to activate new genes in new ways, producing epigenetic changes—just as though the imagined future event were real. And then you can walk right into that new reality and *become* the placebo. This chapter not only outlines the science behind how this happens, but also includes stories of many public figures from different walks of life who have used this technique (whether or not they were fully aware of what they were doing at the time) to make their wildest dreams come true.

Chapter 6, which concentrates on the concept of suggestibility, begins with a fascinating but chilling story of how a team of researchers set out to test whether a regular, law-abiding, mentally healthy person who was highly suggestible to hypnosis could be programmed to do something he or she would normally deem unthinkable: shoot a stranger with the intent to kill.

You'll see that people have differing degrees of suggestibility, and the more suggestible you are, the better able you are to gain access to your subconscious mind. This is key to understanding the placebo effect, because the conscious mind is only 5 percent of who we are. The remaining 95 percent is a set of subconscious programmed states in which the body has become the mind. You'll learn that you must get beyond the analytic mind and enter into the operating system of your subconscious programs if you want your new thoughts to result in new outcomes and change your genetic destiny, as well as learn how meditation is a powerful tool for doing just that. The chapter ends with a brief discussion of different brain-wave states and which are the most conducive to your becoming more suggestible.

Chapter 7 is all about how attitudes, beliefs, and perceptions change your state of being and create your personality—your personal reality—and how you can shift them to create a new reality. You'll read about the power that unconscious beliefs exert and have a chance to identify some of those beliefs you've been harboring without realizing it. You'll also read about how the environment and your associative memories can sabotage your ability to change your beliefs.

I'll explain more fully that in order for you to change your beliefs and perceptions, you must combine a clear intention with an elevated emotion that conditions your body to believe that the future potential that you selected from the quantum field has already happened. The elevated emotion is vital, because only when your choice carries an amplitude of energy that's greater than the hardwired programs in your brain and the emotional addiction in your body will you be able to change your brain's circuitry and your body's genetic expression, as well as recondition your body to a new mind (erasing any trace of the old neurocircuitry and conditioning).

In **Chapter 8**, I'll introduce you to the quantum universe, the unpredictable world of the matter and energy that make up the atoms and molecules of everything in the universe, which turn out to really be more energy (which looks like empty space) than solid matter. The quantum model, which states that all possibilities exist in this present moment, is your key to using the placebo effect for healing, because it gives you permission to choose a new future for yourself and actually *observe it into reality.* You'll then understand just how possible it really is to cross the river of change and make the unknown known.

Chapter 9 introduces you to three people from my workshops who have reported some truly remarkable results from using these same techniques to change their health for the better. First, you'll meet Laurie, who, at age 19, was diagnosed with a rare degenerative bone disease that her doctors told her was incurable. Although the bones in Laurie's left leg and hip suffered 12 major fractures over several decades, leaving her dependent on crutches for getting around, today she walks perfectly normally, without even needing a cane. Her x-rays show no evidence of any fractures in her bones.

Then I'll introduce you to Candace, who was diagnosed with Hashimoto's disease—a serious thyroid condition with a host of complications—during a time in her life when she was resentful and full of rage. Candace's doctor told her she'd have to take medication for the rest of her life, but she proved him wrong after she eventually was able to turn her condition around. Today, Candace is totally in love with a brand-new life and takes no medication for her thyroid, which blood tests show is completely normal.

Finally, you'll meet Joann (the woman mentioned in the Preface), a mother of five who was a successful businesswoman and entrepreneur whom many considered a superwoman—before she collapsed quite suddenly and was diagnosed with an advanced form of multiple sclerosis. Joann's condition went downhill quickly, and she was eventually unable to move her legs. When she first came to my workshops, she made only small changes—until one day when the woman who hadn't moved her legs in years walked around the room, completely unassisted, after just one hour-long meditation!

Chapter 10 shares more remarkable stories from workshop participants, along with the brain scans that go with them. You'll meet Michelle, who completely healed herself of Parkinson's disease, and John, a paraplegic who stood up from his wheelchair after a meditation. You'll read how Kathy (a CEO living on the fast track) learned to find the present moment and how Bonnie healed herself of fibroids and heavy menstrual bleeding. Finally, you'll meet Genevieve, who went into such states of bliss in meditation that tears of joy ran down her face, and Maria, whose experience can only be described as having an orgasm in her brain.

I'll show you the data my team of scientists collected from these people's brain scans so that you can see the changes we witnessed in real time during the workshops. The best part of all this data is that it proves you don't have to be a monk or nun, a scholar, a scientist, or a spiritual leader to accomplish similar feats. You don't need a Ph.D. or a medical degree. The folks in this book are ordinary people like you. After reading this chapter, you'll understand that what these people did is not magic or even all that miraculous; they simply learned and applied teachable skills. And if you practice the same skills, you'll be able to make similar changes.

— PART II of the book is all about meditation. It includes **Chapter 11**, which outlines some simple preparation steps for meditation and goes over specific techniques you'll find helpful, and **Chapter 12**, which gives you step-by-step instructions for using the meditation techniques I teach in my workshops—the very same techniques that participants used to produce the remarkable results you'll have read about earlier in the book.

I'm happy to say that although we don't have all the answers yet about harnessing the power of the placebo, all sorts of people are actually using these ideas *right now* to make extraordinary changes in their lives, the kinds of changes that many others consider practically impossible. The techniques I share in this book need not be limited to healing a physical condition; they can also be applied to improving any aspect of your life. My hope is that this book will inspire you to try these techniques, too, and to make possible in *your* life the same kind of seemingly impossible changes.

Author's note: While the stories of the individuals in my workshops who experienced healing are true, their names and certain identifying details have been changed in this book to protect their privacy.

Part I

INFORMATION

Chapter One

Is It Possible?

Sam Londe, a retired shoe salesman living outside of St. Louis in the early 1970s, began to have difficulty swallowing.[1] He eventually went to see a doctor, who discovered that Londe had metastatic esophageal cancer. In those days, metastatic esophageal cancer was considered incurable; no one had ever survived it. It was a death sentence, and Londe's doctor delivered the news in an appropriately somber tone.

To give Londe as much time as possible, the doctor recommended surgery to remove the cancerous tissue in the esophagus and in the stomach, where the cancer had spread. Trusting the doctor, Londe agreed and had the surgery. He came through as well as could be expected, but things soon went from bad to worse. A scan of Londe's liver revealed still more bad news: extensive cancer throughout the liver's entire left lobe. The doctor told Londe that sadly, at best, he had only months to live.

So Londe and his new wife, both in their 70s, arranged to move 300 miles to Nashville, where Londe's wife had family. Soon after the move to Tennessee, Londe was admitted to the hospital and assigned to internist Clifton Meador. The first time Dr. Meador walked into Londe's room, he found a small, unshaven man curled up underneath a mound of covers, looking nearly dead. Londe was gruff and uncommunicative, and the nurses explained that he'd been like that since his admission a few days before.

While Londe had high blood-glucose levels due to diabetes, the rest of his blood chemistry was fairly normal except for slightly higher levels of liver enzymes, which was to be expected of someone with liver cancer. Further medical examination showed nothing more amiss, a blessing considering the patient's desperate condition. Under his new doctor's orders, Londe begrudgingly received physical therapy, a fortified liquid diet, and lots of nursing care and attention. After a few days, he grew a little stronger, and his grumpiness started to subside. He began talking to Dr. Meador about his life.

Londe had been married before, and he and his first wife had been true soul mates. They had never been able to have children but otherwise had had a good life. Because they loved boating, when they retired they had bought a house by a large man-made lake. Then late one night, the nearby earthen dam burst, and a wall of water crushed their house and swept it away. Londe miraculously survived by hanging on to some wreckage, but his wife's body was never found.

"I lost everything I ever cared for," he told Dr. Meador. "My heart and soul were lost in the flood that night."

Within six months of his first wife's death, while still grieving and in the depths of depression, Londe had been diagnosed with esophageal cancer and had had the surgery. It was then that he had met and married his second wife, a kind woman who knew about his terminal illness and agreed to care for him in the time he had left. A few months after they married, they made the move to Nashville, and Dr. Meador already knew the rest of the story.

Once Londe finished the story, the doctor, amazed by what he'd just heard, asked with compassion, "What do you want me to do for you?" The dying man thought for a while.

"I'd like to live through Christmas so I can be with my wife and her family. They've been good to me," he finally answered. "Just help me make it through Christmas. That's all I want." Dr. Meador told Londe he would do his best.

By the time Londe was discharged in late October, he was actually in much better shape than when he had arrived. Dr. Meador was surprised but pleased by how well Londe was doing. The doctor saw his patient about once a month after that, and each time, Londe looked good. But exactly one week after Christmas (on New Year's Day), Londe's wife brought him back to the hospital.

Dr. Meador was surprised to find that Londe again looked near death. All he could find was a mild fever and a small patch of pneumonia on Londe's chest x-ray, although the man didn't seem to be in any respiratory distress. All of Londe's blood tests looked good, and the cultures the doctor ordered for him came back negative for any other disease. Dr. Meador prescribed antibiotics and put his patient on oxygen, hoping for the best, but within 24 hours, Sam Londe was dead.

As you might assume, this story is about a typical cancer diagnosis followed by an unfortunate death from a fatal disease, right?

Not so fast.

A funny thing happened when the hospital performed Londe's autopsy. The man's liver was, in fact, *not* filled with cancer; he had only a very tiny nodule of cancer in its left lobe and another very small spot on his lung. The truth is, neither cancer was big enough to kill him. And in fact, the area around his esophagus was totally free of disease as well. The abnormal liver scan taken at the St. Louis hospital had apparently yielded a false positive result.

Sam Londe didn't die of esophageal cancer, nor did he die of liver cancer. He also didn't die of the mild case of pneumonia he had when he was readmitted to the hospital. He died, quite simply, because everybody in his immediate environment thought he was dying. His doctor in St. Louis thought Londe was dying, and then Dr. Meador, in Nashville, thought Londe was dying. Londe's wife and family thought he was dying, too. And, most important, Londe himself thought he was dying. Is it possible that Sam Londe died *from thought alone?* Is it possible that thought is that powerful? And if so, is this case unique?

Can You Overdose on a Placebo?

Twenty-six-year-old graduate student Fred Mason (not his real name) became depressed when his girlfriend broke up with him.[2] He saw an ad for a clinical trial of a new antidepressant medication and decided to enroll. He'd had a bout of depression four years previously, at which time his doctor prescribed the antidepressant amitriptyline (Elavil), but Mason had been forced to stop the medication when he became excessively drowsy and developed numbness. He had felt the drug was too strong for him and now hoped the new drug would have fewer side effects.

After he'd been in the study for about a month, he decided to call his ex-girlfriend. The two of them argued on the phone, and after Mason hung up, he impulsively grabbed his bottle of pills from the trial and swallowed all 29 that were left in the container, attempting suicide. He immediately repented. Running into the hallway of his apartment building, Mason desperately called out for help and then collapsed on the floor. A neighbor heard his cry and found him on the ground.

Writhing, he told his neighbor he'd made a terrible mistake, that he had taken all his pills but didn't really want to die. When he asked the neighbor to take him to the hospital, she agreed. When Mason got to the emergency room, he was pale and sweating, and his blood pressure was 80/40 with a pulse rate of 140. Breathing rapidly, he kept repeating, "I don't want to die."

When the doctors examined him, they found nothing wrong other than his low blood pressure, rapid pulse, and rapid breathing. Even so, he seemed lethargic, and his speech was slurred. The medical team inserted an IV and hooked it up to a saline drip, took samples of Mason's blood and urine, and asked what drug he'd taken. Mason couldn't remember the name.

He told the doctors it was an experimental antidepressant drug that was part of a trial. He then handed them the empty bottle, which indeed had information about the clinical trial printed on the label, although not the name of the drug. There was nothing to do but wait for the lab results, monitor his vital signs to make sure he didn't take a turn for the worse, and hope that the hospital staff could contact the researchers who were conducting the trial.

Four hours later, after the results of the lab tests came back totally normal, a physician who had been part of the clinical drug trial arrived. Checking the code on the label of Mason's empty pill bottle, the researcher looked into the records for the trial. He announced that Mason had actually been taking a placebo and that the pills he'd swallowed contained no drugs at all. Miraculously, Mason's blood pressure and pulse returned to normal within a few minutes. And as if by magic, he was no longer excessively drowsy either. Mason had fallen victim to the *nocebo:* a harmless substance that, thanks to strong expectations, causes harmful effects.

Is it really possible that Mason's symptoms had been brought on solely because that's what he'd expected to happen from swallowing a huge handful of antidepressants? Could Mason's mind, as in the case of Sam Londe, have taken control of his body, driven by expectations of what seemed to be the most probable future scenario, to the extent that he *made* that scenario real? Could that happen *even if* that meant his mind would have to take control of functions not normally under conscious control? And if that *were* possible, could it also be true that if our thoughts can make us sick, we also have the ability to use our thoughts to make us well?

Chronic Depression Magically Lifts

Janis Schonfeld, a 46-year-old interior designer living in California, had suffered with depression since she was a teenager. She'd never sought help with the condition until she saw a newspaper ad in 1997. The UCLA Neuropsychiatric Institute was looking for volunteer subjects for a drug trial to test a new antidepressant called venlafaxine (Effexor). Schonfeld, whose depression had escalated to the point where the wife and mother had actually entertained thoughts of suicide, jumped at the chance to be part of the trial.

When Schonfeld arrived at the institute for the first time, a technician hooked her up to an electroencephalograph (EEG) to monitor and record her brain-wave activity for about 45 minutes, and not long after that, Schonfeld left with a bottle of pills from the hospital pharmacy. She knew that roughly half the group of 51 subjects would be getting the drug, and half would receive a placebo, although neither she nor the doctors conducting the study had any idea which group she had been randomly assigned to. In fact, no one would know until the study was over. But at the time, that hardly mattered to Schonfeld. She was excited and hopeful that after decades of battling clinical depression, a condition that would cause her to sometimes suddenly burst into tears for no apparent reason, she might finally be getting help.

Schonfeld agreed to return every week for the entire eight weeks of the study. On each occasion, she'd answer questions about how she was feeling, and several times, she sat through yet another EEG. Not long after she started taking her pills, Schonfeld began feeling dramatically better for the first time in her life. Ironically, she also felt nauseated, but that was *good* news because she knew that nausea was one of the common side effects of the drug being tested. She thought that she surely must have gotten the active drug if her depression was lifting and she was also experiencing side effects. Even the nurse she spoke to when she returned every week was convinced Schonfeld must be getting the real thing because of the changes she was experiencing.

Finally, at the end of the eight-week study, one of the researchers revealed the shocking truth: Schonfeld, who was no longer suicidal and felt like a new person after taking the pills, had actually been in the placebo group. Schonfeld was floored. She was sure the doctor had made a mistake. She simply didn't believe that she could have felt so much better after so many years of suffocating depression simply from taking a bottle of sugar pills. And she'd even gotten the side effects! There *must* have been a mix-up. She asked the doctor to check the records again. He laughed good-naturedly as he assured her that the bottle she had taken home with her, the bottle that had given Schonfeld her life back, indeed contained nothing but placebo pills.

As she sat there in shock, the doctor insisted that just because she hadn't been getting any real medication, it didn't mean that she had been imagining her depression or her improvement; it only meant that whatever had made her feel better wasn't due to Effexor.

And she wasn't the only one: The study results would soon show that 38 percent of the placebo group felt better, compared to 52 percent of the group who received Effexor. But when the rest of the data came out, it was the researchers' turn to be surprised:

The patients like Schonfeld, who had improved on the placebos, hadn't just imagined feeling better; they had actually *changed their brain-wave patterns*. The EEG recordings taken so faithfully over the course of the study showed a significant increase in activity in the prefrontal cortex, which in depressed patients typically has very low activity.[3]

Thus the placebo effect was not only altering Schonfeld's mind, but also bringing about real physical changes in her biology. In other words, it wasn't just in her *mind;* it was in her *brain*. She wasn't just *feeling* well—she *was* well. Schonfeld literally had a different brain by the end of the study, without taking any drug or doing anything differently. It was her mind that had changed her body. More than a dozen years later, Schonfeld still felt much improved.

How is it possible that a sugar pill could not only lift the symptoms of deep-seated depression, but also cause bona fide side effects like nausea? And what does it mean that the same inert substance actually has the power to change how brain waves fire, increasing activity in the very part of the brain most affected by depression? Can the subjective mind really create those kinds of measurable objective physiological changes? What's going on in the mind and in the body that would allow a placebo to so perfectly mimic a real drug in this way? Could the same phenomenal healing effect occur not only with chronic mental illness, but also with a life-threatening condition such as cancer?

A "Miracle" Cure: Now You See It, Now You Don't

In 1957, UCLA psychologist Bruno Klopfer published an article in a peer-reviewed journal telling the story of a man he referred to as "Mr. Wright," who had advanced lymphoma, a cancer of the lymph glands.[4] The man had huge tumors, some as big as an orange, in his neck, groin, and armpits, and his cancer was not responding at all to conventional treatments. He lay in his bed for weeks, "febrile, gasping for air, completely bedridden." His doctor, Philip West, had given up hope—although Wright himself had not. When Wright found out that the hospital where he was being treated (in Long Beach, California) just happened to be one of ten hospitals and research centers in the country that were evaluating an experimental drug extracted from horse blood called Krebiozen, he got very excited. Wright unrelentingly badgered Dr. West for days until the physician agreed to give him some of the new remedy (even though Wright couldn't officially be part of the trial, which required patients to have at least a three-month life expectancy).

Wright received his injection of Krebiozen on a Friday, and by Monday, he was walking around, laughing, and joking with his nurses, acting pretty much like a new man. Dr. West reported that the tumors "had melted like snowballs on a hot stove." Within three days, the tumors were half their original size. In ten more days, Wright was sent home—he'd been cured. It seemed like a miracle.

But two months later, the media reported that the ten trials showed that Krebiozen turned out to be a dud. Once Wright read the news, became fully conscious of the results, and embraced the thought that the drug was useless, he relapsed immediately, with his tumors soon returning. Dr. West suspected that Wright's initial positive response was due to the placebo effect, and knowing that his patient was terminal, he figured he had little to lose—and Wright had everything to gain—by testing out his theory. So the doctor told Wright not to believe the newspaper reports and that he'd suffered a relapse because the Krebiozen they'd given Wright was found to be part of a bad batch. What Dr. West called "a new, super-refined, double-strength" version of the drug was on its way to the hospital, and Wright could have it as soon as it arrived.

In anticipation of being cured, Wright was elated, and a few days later, he received the injection. But this time, the syringe Dr. West used contained no drug, experimental or not. The syringe was filled only with distilled water.

Again, Wright's tumors magically vanished. He happily returned home and did well for another two months, free of tumors in his body. But then the American Medical Association made the announcement that Krebiozen was indeed worthless. The medical establishment had been duped. The "miracle drug" turned out to be a hoax: nothing more than mineral oil containing a simple amino acid. The manufacturers were eventually indicted. Upon hearing the news, Wright relapsed a final time—*no longer believing in the possibility of health*. He returned to the hospital hopeless and two days later was dead.

Is it possible that Wright somehow changed his *state of being*, not once but twice, to that of a man who simply didn't have cancer—in a matter of days? Did his body then automatically respond to a new mind? And could he have changed his state back to that of a man with cancer once he heard the drug was purported to be worthless, with his body creating exactly the same chemistry and returning to the familiar sickened condition? Is it possible to achieve such a new biochemical state not only when taking a pill or getting a shot, but also when undergoing something as invasive as surgery?

The Knee Surgery That Never Happened

In 1996, orthopedic surgeon Bruce Moseley, then of the Baylor College of Medicine and one of Houston's leading experts in orthopedic sports medicine, published a trial study based on his experience with ten volunteers—all men who had served in the military and suffered from osteoarthritis of the knee.[5] Due to the severity of their conditions, many of these men had a noticeable limp, walked with a cane, or needed some type of assistance to get around.

The study was designed to look at arthroscopic surgery, a popular surgery that involved anesthetizing the patient before making a small incision to insert a fiber-optic instrument called an arthroscope, which the surgeon would use to get a good look at the patient's joint. In the surgery, the doctor would then scrape and rinse the joint to remove any fragments of degenerated cartilage that were thought to be the cause of the inflammation and pain. At that time, about three-quarters of a million patients received this surgery every year.

In Dr. Moseley's study, two of the ten men were to be given the standard surgery, called a *debridement* (where the surgeon scrapes strands of cartilage from the knee joint); three of them were to receive a procedure called a *lavage* (where high-pressured water is injected through the knee joint, rinsing and flushing out the decayed arthritic material); and five of them would receive *sham surgery,* in which Dr. Moseley would deftly slice through their skin with a scalpel and then just sew them back up again without performing any medical procedure at all. For those five men, there would be no arthroscope, no scraping of the joint, no removal of bone fragments, and no washing—just an incision and then stitches.

The start of each of the ten procedures was exactly the same: The patient was wheeled into the operating room and given general anesthesia while Dr. Moseley scrubbed up. Once the surgeon entered the operating theater, he would find a sealed envelope waiting for him that would tell him which of the three groups the patient on the table had been randomly assigned to. Dr. Moseley would have no idea what the envelope contained until he actually ripped it open.

After the surgery, all ten of the patients in the study reported greater mobility and less pain. In fact, the men who received "pretend" surgery did just as well as those who'd received debridement or lavage surgery. There was no difference in the results—even six months later. And six years later, when two of the men who'd received the placebo surgery were interviewed, they reported that they were still walking normally, without pain, and had greater range of motion.[6] They said that they could now perform all the everyday activities that they hadn't been able to do before the surgery, six years earlier. The men felt as though they'd regained their lives.

Fascinated by the results, Dr. Moseley published another study in 2002 involving 180 patients who were followed for two years after their surgeries.[7] Again, all three groups improved, with patients beginning to walk without pain or limping immediately after the surgery. But again, neither of the two groups who actually had the surgery improved any more than the patients who received the placebo surgery—and this held true even after two years.

Could it be possible that these patients got better simply because they had faith and belief in the healing power of the surgeon, the hospital, and even in the gleaming, modern operating room itself? Did they somehow envision a life with a fully healed knee, simply surrender to that possible outcome, and then literally walk right into it? Was Dr. Moseley, in effect, nothing more than a modern-day witch doctor in a white lab coat? And is it possible to attain the same degree of healing when facing something more threatening, maybe something as serious as heart surgery?

The Heart Surgery That Wasn't

In the late 1950s, two groups of researchers conducted studies comparing the then-standard surgery for angina to a placebo.[8] This was well before the *coronary-artery bypass graft,* the surgery most often used today. Back then, most heart patients received a procedure known as *internal mammary ligation,* which involved exposing the damaged arteries and intentionally tying them off. The thinking was that if surgeons blocked the blood flow in this way, it would force the body to sprout new vascular channels, increasing blood flow to the heart. The surgery was extremely successful for the huge majority of patients who had it, although doctors had no solid proof that any new blood vessels were ever actually created—hence the motivation for the two studies.

These groups of researchers, one in Kansas City and one in Seattle, each followed the same procedure, dividing their study subjects into two groups. One received the standard internal mammary ligation, and the other received a sham surgery; the surgeons made the same small incisions into the patients' chests that they made for the real surgery, exposing the arteries, but then they just sewed the patients back up, doing nothing more.

The results of both studies were strikingly similar: 67 percent of the patients who had received the actual surgery felt less pain and needed less medication, while 83 percent of those who had received the sham surgery enjoyed the same level of improvement. The placebo surgery had actually worked better than the real surgery!

Could it be that somehow the patients who had received the sham surgery so believed that they'd get better that they actually *did* get better—through nothing more than holding that expectation for the best? And if that is possible, what does that say about the effects our everyday thoughts, whether positive or negative, have on our bodies and our health?

Attitude Is Everything

A wealth of research now exists to show that our attitude does indeed affect our health, including how long we live. For example, the Mayo Clinic published a study in 2002 that followed 447 people for more than 30 years, showing that optimists were healthier physically and mentally.[9] *Optimist* literally means "best," suggesting that those folks focused their attention on the best future scenario. Specifically, the optimists had fewer problems with daily activities as a result of their physical health or their emotional state; experienced less pain; felt more energetic; had an easier time with social activities; and felt happier, calmer, and more peaceful most of the time. This came right on the heels of another Mayo Clinic study that followed more than 800 people for 30 years, showing that optimists live longer than pessimists.[10]

Researchers at Yale followed 660 people, aged 50 and older, for up to 23 years, discovering that those with a positive attitude about aging lived more than seven years longer than those who had a more negative outlook about growing older.[11] Attitude had more of an influence on longevity than blood pressure, cholesterol levels, smoking, body weight, or level of exercise.

Additional studies have looked more specifically at heart health and attitude. Around the same time, a Duke University study of 866 heart patients reported that those who routinely felt more positive emotions had a 20 percent greater chance of being alive 11 years later than those who habitually experienced more negative emotions.[12] Even more striking are the results of a study of 255 medical students at the Medical College of Georgia who were followed for 25 years: Those who were the most hostile had five times greater incidence of coronary heart disease.[13] And a Johns Hopkins study presented at the American Heart Association's 2001 Scientific Sessions even showed that a positive outlook may offer the strongest known protection against heart disease in adults at risk due to family history.[14] This study suggests that having the right attitude can work as well as or better than eating the proper diet, getting the right amount of exercise, and maintaining the ideal body weight.

How is it that our everyday mind-set—whether we're generally more joyful and loving or more hostile and negative—can help determine how long we live? Is it possible for us to change our current mind-set? If so, could having a new mind-set override the way our minds have been conditioned by past experiences? Or could expecting something negative to recur actually help to bring that about?

Nauseated Before the Needle

According to the National Cancer Institute, a condition called *anticipatory nausea* occurs in about 29 percent of patients receiving chemotherapy when they are exposed to the smells and sights that remind them of their chemo treatments.[15] About 11 percent feel so sick before their treatments that they actually vomit. Some cancer patients start feeling nauseated in the car on the way to get chemo, before they even set foot inside the hospital, while others throw up while still in the waiting room.

A 2001 study from the University of Rochester Cancer Center published in the *Journal of Pain and Symptom Management* concluded that expecting nausea was the strongest predictor that patients would actually experience it.[16] The researchers' data reported that

40 percent of chemo patients who thought they would get sick—because their doctors told them that they probably would be sick *after* the treatment—went on to develop nausea *before* the treatment was even administered. An additional 13 percent who said they were unsure of what to expect also got sick. Yet *none* of the patients who didn't expect to get nauseated got sick.

How can it be that some people become so convinced that they will get sick from chemotherapy drugs that they get ill before any of the drugs are even administered? Is it possible that the power of their thoughts could be what's making them sick? And if that's true of 40 percent of chemo patients, could it also be true that 40 percent of folks could just as easily *get well* by simply changing their thoughts about what to expect about their health or from their day? Could a single thought that a person accepts also make that person *better?*

Digestive Difficulties Disappear

Not long ago, as I was about to get off an airplane in Austin, I met a woman who was reading a book that caught my eye. We were standing and waiting to deplane, and I saw the book sticking out of her bag; the title mentioned the word *belief*. We smiled at each other, and I asked her what the book was about.

"Christianity and faith," she answered. "Why do you ask?" I told her that I was writing a new book on the placebo effect and that my book was all about belief.

"I want to tell you this story," she said. She went on to tell me that years ago, she had been diagnosed with gluten intolerance, celiac disease, colitis, and a host of other ills, and experienced chronic pain. She'd read up on the diseases and gone to see several different health professionals for advice. They had advised her to avoid certain foods and to take certain prescription drugs, which she had done, but she'd still felt pain throughout her entire body. She also hadn't been able to sleep, had skin rashes and severe digestive disturbances, and suffered from a whole list of other unpleasant symptoms. Then, years later, the woman went to see a new doctor, who decided to do some blood tests. When the blood tests came back, all of the results were negative.

"The day I found out I was really normal and there was nothing wrong with me, I thought, *I'm fine,* and all my symptoms went away. I immediately felt great and could eat whatever I wanted," she told me with a flourish. Smiling, she added, "What do you believe about *that?*"

If it's true that learning new information that leads to a 180-degree turnaround in what we believe about ourselves can actually make our symptoms disappear, what's going on in our bodies that's supporting that and making it happen? What's the exact relationship between the mind and the body? Could it be possible that those new beliefs could actually change our brains and body chemistries, physically rewire our neurological circuitry of who we think we are, and alter our genetic expression? Could we in fact become different people?

Parkinson's vs. the Placebo

Parkinson's disease is a neurological disorder marked by the gradual degeneration of nerve cells in the portion of the midbrain called the *basal ganglia,* which controls body movements. The brains of those who have this heartbreaking disease don't produce enough of the neurotransmitter dopamine, which the basal ganglia needs for proper functioning. Early symptoms of Parkinson's, which is currently considered incurable, include motor issues such as muscle rigidity, tremors, and changes in gait and speech patterns that override voluntary control.

In one study, a group of researchers at the University of British Columbia in Vancouver informed a group of Parkinson's patients that they were going to receive a drug that would significantly improve their symptoms.[17] In reality, the patients received a placebo—nothing more than a saline injection. Even so, half of them who had no drug intervention, in fact, had much better motor control after receiving the injection.

The researchers then scanned the patients' brains to get a better idea of what had happened and found that the people who responded positively to the placebo were actually manufacturing dopamine in their brains—as much as 200 percent more than before. To get an equivalent effect with a drug, you'd have to administer roughly a full dose of amphetamine—a mood-elevating drug that also increases dopamine.

It seemed that merely expecting to get better unleashed some previously untapped power within the Parkinson's patients that triggered the production of the dopamine—exactly what their bodies needed to get better. And if this is true, then what is the process by which thought alone can manufacture dopamine in the brain? Might such a new internal state, brought on by the combination of clear intention and heightened emotional state, actually make us invincible in certain situations, by activating our own inner storehouse of pharmaceuticals and overriding the genetic circumstances of disease that we once considered outside our conscious control?

Of Deadly Snakes and Strychnine

In parts of Appalachia exist pockets of a 100-year-old religious ritual known as snake handling, or "taking up serpents."[18] While West Virginia is the only state where it's still legal, that doesn't stop the faithful, and local police in other states are known to turn a blind eye to the practice. In these small and modest churches, as congregations gather for the worship service, the preacher enters carrying one or more briefcase-shaped locked wooden boxes with hinged, clear-plastic doors perforated with air holes, and places the boxes carefully on the platform at the front of the sanctuary or meeting room, near the pulpit. Before long, the music starts, a high-energy blend of country-and-western and bluegrass melodies with deeply religious lyrics about salvation and the love of Jesus. Live musicians wail away on keyboards, electric guitars, and even drum sets that any teenage band would envy, while the parishioners shake tambourines as the spirit moves them. As the energy builds, the preacher might light a flame in a container on top of the pulpit and hold his hand in the fire, allowing the flames to lick his outstretched palm before he picks up the container to sweep the fire slowly over his bare forearms. He's just getting "warmed up."

The congregants soon begin swaying and laying hands on one another, speaking in tongues and jumping up and down, dancing to the music in praise of their savior. They are overcome with the spirit, what they call "being anointed." Then it's time for the preacher to flip open one of the locked boxes, reach a hand in, and pull out a deadly snake—usually a rattlesnake, cottonmouth, or copperhead. He, too, is dancing and working up quite a sweat as he holds the live serpent around its middle so that the snake's head is frighteningly close to the preacher's own head and throat.

He might hold the snake high in the air before bringing it back down closer to his body, dancing all the while, as the snake winds its lower half around his arm and gyrates its upper half in the air in whatever manner it pleases. The preacher might then get a second or even a third snake from additional wooden cases, and the congregants, men and women alike, might join him in handling the serpents as they feel the anointing coming over them. In some services, the preacher might even ingest a poison, like strychnine, from a simple drinking glass, without suffering any ill effects.

Although the snake handlers do sometimes get bitten, considering the thousands of services where feverish believers have reached into those hinged wooden boxes without a trace of doubt or fear, it doesn't happen often. And even when it does, they don't always die—even though they don't rush to the hospital, preferring instead to have the congregation gather around them in prayer. Why are these people not bitten more often? And why aren't there more deaths when they do get bitten? How can they get into a state of mind where they are not afraid of such venomous creatures, whose bite is known to be deadly, and how can that state of mind protect them?

Then there are the displays of extreme strength in emergency situations, known as "hysterical strength." In April 2013, for example, 16-year-old Hannah Smith and her 14-year-old sister, Haylee, of Lebanon, Oregon, lifted a 3,000-pound tractor to free their father, Jeff Smith, who was trapped underneath.[19] And what about firewalkers—indigenous tribes practicing sacred rituals, and Westerners taking workshops—who stroll across burning coals? Or even the carnival showmen or Javanese trance dancers who feel compelled to chew and swallow glass (a disorder known as *hyalophagia*)?

How are such seemingly superhuman feats possible, and do they have something vital in common? Could it be that at the height of their uncompromising belief, these people are somehow changing their bodies such that they become immune to their environments? And can the same rock-solid belief that empowers snake handlers and firewalkers also go the other way, causing us to harm ourselves—and even die—without our having any awareness of what we're doing?

Victory Over Voodoo

In 1938, a 60-year-old man in rural Tennessee spent four months getting sicker and sicker, before his wife brought him to a 15-bed hospital at the edge of town.[20] By this time, Vance Vanders (not his real name) had lost more than 50 pounds and appeared to be near death. The doctor, Drayton Doherty, suspected that Vanders was suffering from tuberculosis or possibly cancer, but repeated tests and x-rays came up negative. Dr. Doherty's physical examination showed nothing that could be causing Vanders's distress. Vanders refused to eat, so he was given a feeding tube, but he stubbornly vomited whatever was put down the tube. He continued to get worse, repeating the conviction that he was going to die, and eventually he was barely able to talk. The end seemed near, although Dr. Doherty still had no idea what the man's affliction was.

Vanders's distraught wife asked to speak to Dr. Doherty privately and, swearing him to secrecy, told him that her husband's problem was that he'd been "voodoo'd." It seems that Vanders, who lived in a community where voodoo was a common practice, had had an argument with a local voodoo priest. The priest had summoned Vanders to the cemetery late one night, where he put a hex on the man by waving a bottle of malodorous liquid in front of Vanders's face. The priest told Vanders that he would soon die and that no one could save him. That was it. Vanders was convinced that his days were numbered and thus believed in a new, dismal future reality. The defeated man returned home and refused to eat. Eventually, his wife brought him to the hospital.

After Dr. Doherty had heard the whole story, he came up with a rather unorthodox plan for treating his patient. In the morning, he summoned Vanders's family to his bedside and told them that he was now certain that he knew how to cure the sick man. The family listened intently as Dr. Doherty spun the following fabricated tale. He said that on the previous night, he had gone to the cemetery, where he'd tricked the voodoo priest into meeting with him and divulging how he had voodoo'd Vanders. It hadn't been easy, Dr. Doherty said. The priest had understandably not wanted to cooperate, although he finally relented once Dr. Doherty had pinned him against a tree and choked him.

Dr. Doherty said that the priest had told him that he'd rubbed some lizard eggs onto Vanders's skin and that the eggs had found their way to Vanders's stomach, where they'd hatched. Most of the lizards had died, but a large one had survived and was now eating Vanders's body from the inside out. The doctor announced that all he had to do was remove the lizard from Vanders's body and the man would be cured.

He then called for the nurse, who dutifully brought a large syringe filled with what Dr. Doherty claimed was a powerful medicine. In truth, the syringe was filled with a drug that induced vomiting. Dr. Doherty carefully inspected the syringe to make sure it was working right and then ceremoniously injected his frightened patient with the fluid. In a grand gesture, he left the room, not saying another word to the stunned family.

It wasn't long before the patient began to vomit. The nurse provided a basin and Vanders heaved, wailed, and retched for a time. At a point that Dr. Doherty judged to be near the end of the vomiting, he confidently strode back into the room. Nearing the bedside, he reached into his black doctor's bag and scooped up a green lizard, hiding it in his palm beyond anyone's notice. Then just as Vanders vomited again, Dr. Doherty slipped the reptile into the basin.

"Look, Vance!" he immediately cried out with all the drama he could muster. "Look what has come out of you. You are now cured. The voodoo curse is lifted!"

The room was buzzing. Some family members fell to the floor, moaning. Vanders himself jumped back away from the basin, in a wide-eyed daze. Within a few minutes, he'd fallen into a deep sleep that lasted more than 12 hours.

When Vanders finally awoke, he was very hungry and eagerly consumed so much food that the doctor feared his stomach would burst. Within a week, the patient had regained all his weight and strength. He left the hospital a well man and lived at least another ten years.

Is it possible that a man could just curl up and die simply because he thought he'd been hexed? Does the contemporary witch doctor, adorned with a stethoscope and holding a prescription pad, speak with the same conviction for us as the voodoo priest did for Vanders—and is our belief the same? And if it's indeed true that a person could, on one level, just decide to die, then could it also be true that a person with a terminal disease could make the decision to *live?* Can someone permanently change his or her internal state—dropping his or her identity as a cancer or arthritis victim or a heart patient or a person with Parkinson's—and simply walk into a healthy body just as easily as shedding one set of clothes and donning another? In the upcoming chapters, we'll explore what's really possible and how that applies to you.

Chapter Two

A Brief History
of the Placebo

As the saying goes, desperate times call for desperate measures. When Harvard-educated American surgeon Henry Beecher was serving in World War II, he ran out of morphine. Near the end of the war, morphine was in short supply in military field hospitals, so this situation wasn't uncommon. At the time, Beecher was about to operate on a badly wounded soldier. He was afraid that without a painkiller, the soldier might go into fatal cardiovascular shock. What happened next astounded him.

Without skipping a beat, one of the nurses filled a syringe with saline and gave the soldier a shot, just as if she were injecting him with morphine. The soldier calmed down right away. He reacted as though he'd actually received the drug, even though all he'd received was a squirt of saltwater. Beecher went ahead with the operation, cutting into the soldier's flesh, making what repairs were necessary, and sewing him back up, all without anesthesia. The soldier felt little pain and did not go into shock. How could it be, Beecher wondered, that saltwater could stand in for morphine?

After that stunning success, whenever the field hospital ran out of morphine, Beecher did the same thing again: injected saline, just as if he were injecting morphine. The experience convinced him of the power of placebos, and when he returned to the United States after the war, he began to study the phenomenon.

In 1955, Beecher made history when he authored a clinical review of 15 studies published by the *Journal of the American Medical*

Association that not only discussed the huge significance of placebos, but also called for a new model of medical research that would randomly assign subjects to receive active medications or placebos—what we now refer to as randomized, controlled trials— so that this powerful placebo effect wouldn't distort results.[1]

The idea that we can alter physical reality through thought, belief, and expectation alone (whether we are fully aware of what we're doing or not) certainly didn't start in that World War II field hospital. The Bible is filled with stories of miraculous healings, and even in modern times, people regularly flock to places such as Lourdes in southern France (where a 14-year-old peasant girl named Bernadette had a vision of the Virgin Mary in 1858), leaving behind their crutches, braces, and wheelchairs as proof that they've been healed. Similar miracles also have been reported in Fátima, Portugal (where three shepherd children saw an apparition of the Virgin Mary in 1917), and in connection with a traveling statue of Mary carved for the 30th anniversary of the apparition. The statue was based on the description given by the oldest of the three children, who by then had become a nun, and it was blessed by Pope Pius XII before it was sent traveling around the world.

Faith healing is certainly not confined to the Christian tradition. The late Indian guru Sathya Sai Baba, widely considered by his followers to be an *avatar*—a manifestation of a deity—was known to manifest holy ash called *vibhuti* from the palms of his hands. This fine gray ash has been said to have the power to heal many physical, mental, and spiritual ills when either eaten or applied to the skin as a paste. Tibetan lamas are also said to have healing powers, using their breath to heal by blowing on the sick.

Even French and English kings reigning between the 4th and 9th centuries used the laying on of hands to cure their subjects. King Charles II of England was known to be particularly adept at this, performing the practice about 100,000 times.

What is it that causes such so-called miraculous events, whether the instrument of healing is faith in a deity alone or belief in the extraordinary powers of a person, an object, or even a place deemed sacred or holy? What is the process by which faith and belief can bring about such profound effects? Might how we assign meaning to a ritual—whether that ritual is saying the rosary, rubbing a pinch of holy ash onto our skin, or taking a new miracle drug prescribed by a trusted physician—play a role in the placebo phenomenon? What if the internal state of mind of the people who received these cures was influenced or altered by the conditions in their external environment (a person, place, or thing at the proper time) to such a degree that their new state of mind could actually effect real physical changes?

From Magnetism to Hypnotism

In the 1770s, Viennese physician Franz Anton Mesmer made quite a name for himself by developing and demonstrating what was considered at that time a medical model of miraculous healing. Expanding on an idea of Sir Isaac Newton's about the effect of planetary gravitation on the human body, Mesmer came to believe that the body contained an invisible fluid that could be manipulated to heal people using a force he called "animal magnetism."

His technique involved asking his patients to look deeply into his eyes before moving magnets over their bodies to direct and balance this magnetic fluid. Later, he found that he could wave his hands (without the magnets) to produce the same effect. Soon after each session began, his patients would start trembling and twitching before going into convulsions that Mesmer considered therapeutic. Mesmer would continue the fluid balancing until they were calm again. He used this technique to heal a variety of maladies, from serious conditions like paralysis and convulsive disorders to more minor difficulties, such as menstrual problems and hemorrhoids.

In what became his most famous case, Mesmer partially cured teenage concert pianist Maria-Theresia von Paradis of "hysterical blindness," a psychosomatic condition she'd had since about the age of three. She stayed in Mesmer's home for weeks as he worked with her and finally helped her to be able to perceive motion and even distinguish color. But her parents were less than overjoyed by her progress, because they stood to lose a royal pension if their daughter was cured. In addition, as her sight returned, her piano playing deteriorated because she now was able to watch her fingers on the keyboard. Rumors, never substantiated, began circulating that Mesmer's relationship to the pianist was improper. Her parents forcibly removed her from Mesmer's house, her blindness returned, and Mesmer's reputation diminished considerably.

Armand-Marie-Jacques de Chastenet, a French aristocrat known as the Marquis de Puységur, observed Mesmer and took his ideas to the next level. Puységur would induce a deep state that he called "magnetic somnambulism" (similar to sleepwalking), in which his subjects had access to deep thoughts and even intuitions about their health and that of others. In this state, they were extremely suggestible and would follow instructions, although they had no memory of what happened once they came out of it. Whereas Mesmer thought that the power was in the practitioner over the subject, Puységur believed that the power was in the thought of the subject (directed by the practitioner) over his or her own body; this was perhaps one of the first therapeutic attempts to explore the mind-body relationship.

In the 1800s, Scottish surgeon James Braid took the idea of mesmerism still further, developing a concept he called "neurypnotism" (what we now know as hypnotism). Braid became intrigued by the idea when one day he arrived late for an appointment only to find his waiting patient calmly staring in intense fascination at the flickering flame of an oil lamp. Braid found the patient to be in an extremely suggestible state as long as his attention remained so locked, thereby "fatiguing" certain parts of his brain.

After many experiments, Braid learned to get his subjects to concentrate on a single idea while staring at an object, which put them into a similar trance that he felt he could use to cure their disorders, including chronic rheumatoid arthritis, sensory impairment, and the various complications of spinal injuries and stroke. Braid's book *Neurypnology* details many of his successes, including the story of how he cured both a 33-year-old woman whose legs were paralyzed and a 54-year-old woman with a skin disorder and severe headaches.

Then esteemed French neurologist Jean-Martin Charcot weighed in on Braid's work, claiming that the ability to go into such a trance was possible only in those suffering from the condition of hysteria, which he considered an inherited neurological disorder that was irreversible. He used hypnosis not to cure patients, but to study their symptoms. Finally, a rival of Charcot's, a doctor named Hippolyte Bernheim at the University of Nancy, insisted that the suggestibility so central to hypnotism was not confined to hysterics but was a natural condition for all humans. He implanted ideas in subjects, telling them that when they awoke from their trance, they would feel better and their symptoms would disappear; thus he used the power of suggestion as a therapeutic tool. Bernheim's work continued into the early 1900s.

Although each of these early explorers of suggestibility had a slightly different focus and technique, they were all able to help hundreds and hundreds of people heal a wide variety of physical and mental problems by changing their minds about their maladies and about how those illnesses were expressed in their bodies.

During the first two world wars, military doctors, most notably Army psychiatrist Benjamin Simon, used the concept of hypnotic suggestibility (which I'll discuss further later) to help returning soldiers who suffered from the trauma that was first labeled "shell shock" but is now known as *post-traumatic stress disorder* (PTSD). These veterans had suffered through such horrible war experiences that many of them numbed themselves to their emotions as a form of self-preservation, developed amnesia surrounding the horrific events, or, worse, kept reliving their experiences in flashbacks—all of which can cause stress-induced physical illness. Simon and his colleagues found hypnosis extremely useful for helping the veterans face their traumas and cope with them so that they wouldn't have to resurface as anxiety and physical

ailments (including nausea, high blood pressure and other cardiovascular disorders, and even suppressed immunity). Like those
practitioners in the century before them, Army doctors employing
hypnosis helped their patients alter their patterns of thinking in
order to get well and reclaim their mental and physical health.

These hypnosis techniques were so successful that civilian
doctors also became interested in using suggestibility, although
many did so not by putting their patients into a trance but by oc-
casionally giving them sugar pills and other placebos and telling
them that these "drugs" would make them better. The patients
often *did* get better, responding to suggestibility in the same way
that Beecher's wounded soldiers responded to the belief that they
were receiving shots of morphine. This was, in fact, Beecher's era,
and after he wrote his groundbreaking 1955 review calling for
the use of randomized, controlled trials with placebos for testing
drugs, the placebo became a serious part of medical research.

Beecher's point was well taken. Initially, researchers expected
that a study's control group (the group taking the placebo) would
remain neutral so that comparisons between the control group
and the group taking the active treatment would show how well
the active treatment worked. But in so many studies, the control
group was indeed getting better—not just on their own but because of their *expectation and belief* that they might be taking a
drug or receiving a treatment that would help them. The placebo
itself might have been inert, but its effect was certainly not, and
these beliefs and expectations were proving to be extremely powerful! So somehow, that effect had to be teased out from the data
if that data was to have any real meaning.

To that end, and heeding Beecher's petition, researchers began
making the randomized, double-blind trial the norm, randomly
assigning subjects to either the active or the placebo group and
making sure none of the subjects or any of the researchers themselves knew who was taking the real drug and who was taking the
placebo. This way, the placebo effect would be equally active in
each group, and any possibility that the researchers might treat
subjects differently according to what group they were in would

be eliminated. (These days, studies are sometimes even *triple blind,* meaning that not only are the participants and the researchers who are conducting the trial in the dark about who's taking what until the end of the study, but the statisticians analyzing the data also don't know until their job is done.)

Exploring the Nocebo Effect

Of course, there's always a flip side. While suggestibility was garnering more attention because of its ability to heal, it also became apparent that the same phenomenon could be used to harm. Such practices as hexes and voodoo curses illustrated the negative side of suggestibility.

In the 1940s, Harvard physiologist Walter Bradford Cannon (who had in 1932 coined the term *fight or flight*) studied the ultimate nocebo response—a phenomenon that he called "voodoo death."[2] Cannon examined a number of anecdotal reports of people with strong cultural beliefs in the power of witch doctors or voodoo priests suddenly falling ill and dying—despite no apparent injury or evidence of poison or infection—after ending up on the receiving end of a hex or curse. His research laid the groundwork for much of what we know today about how physiological response systems enable emotions (fear in particular) to create illness. The victim's belief in the power of the curse itself to kill him was only part of the psychological soup that brought about his ultimate demise, Cannon said. Another factor was the effect of being socially ostracized and rejected, even by the victim's own family. Such people quickly became the walking dead.

Harmful effects from harmless sources aren't restricted to voodoo, of course. Scientists in the 1960s coined the term *nocebo* (Latin for "I shall harm," as opposed to "I shall please," the Latin translation of *placebo*), referring to an inert substance that causes a harmful effect—simply because someone believes or expects it will harm her.[3] The nocebo effect commonly pops up in drug studies when subjects who are taking placebos either just expect that there will be side effects to the drug being tested, or when the subjects are specifically warned of potential side effects—and then they experience those same side effects by associating the thought of the drug with all of the potential causations, even though they've not taken the drug.

For obvious ethical reasons, few studies are designed specifically to look at this phenomenon, although some do exist. A famous example is a 1962 study done in Japan with a group of children who were all extremely allergic to poison ivy.[4] Researchers rubbed one forearm of each child with a poison-ivy leaf but told them the leaf was harmless. As a control, they rubbed the child's other forearm with a harmless leaf that they claimed was poison ivy. All the children developed a rash on the arm rubbed with the harmless leaf that was thought to be poison ivy. And 11 of the 13 children developed no rash at all where the poison had actually touched them.

This was an astounding finding; how could children who were highly allergic to poison ivy *not* get a rash when exposed to it? *And how could they develop a rash from a totally benign leaf?* The new thought that the leaf wouldn't hurt them *overrode* their memory and belief that they were allergic to it, rendering real poison ivy harmless. And the reverse was true in the second part of the experiment: A harmless leaf was made toxic by thought alone. In both cases, it seemed as if the children's *bodies* instantaneously responded to a new *mind*.

In this instance, we could say that the children were somehow freed from the future expectation of a physical reaction to the toxic leaf, based on their past experiences of being allergic. In effect, they somehow transcended a predictable line of time. This also suggests that by some means, they became greater than the conditions in their environment (the poison-ivy leaf). Finally, the children were able to alter and control their physiology by simply changing a thought. This astonishing evidence that thought (in the form of expectation) could have a greater effect on the body than the "real" physical environment helped to usher in a new era of scientific study called *psychoneuroimmunology*—the effect of thoughts and emotions on the immune system—an important segment of the mind-body connection.

Another notable nocebo study from the '60s looked at people with asthma.[5] Researchers gave 40 asthma patients inhalers containing nothing but water vapor, although they told the subjects that the inhalers contained an allergen or irritant; 19 of them (48 percent) experienced asthmatic symptoms, such as restriction of their airways, with 12 (30 percent) of the group suffering full-blown asthmatic attacks. Researchers then gave the subjects inhalers said to contain medicine that would relieve their symptoms, and in each case, their airways did indeed open back up—although again, the inhalers contained only water vapor.

In both situations—bringing on the asthma symptoms and then dramatically reversing them—the patients were responding to suggestion alone, the thought planted in their minds by the researchers, which played out exactly as they expected. They were harmed when they thought they'd inhaled something harmful, and they got better when they thought they were receiving medicine—and these thoughts were greater than their environment, greater than reality. We could say that their thoughts created a *brand-new* reality.

What does this say about the beliefs we hold and the thoughts we think every day? Are we more susceptible to catching the flu because all winter long, everywhere we look, we see articles about flu season and signs about flu-shot availability—all of which reminds us that if we don't get a flu shot, we'll get sick? Could it be that when we simply see someone with flu-like symptoms, we become ill from thinking in the same ways as the children in the poison-ivy study who got a rash from the inert leaf or from thinking like the asthmatics who experienced a significant bronchial reaction after inhaling simple water vapor?

Are we more likely to suffer from arthritis, stiff joints, poor memory, flagging energy, and decreased sex drive as we age, simply because that's the version of the truth that ads, commercials, television shows, and media reports bombard us with? What other self-fulfilling prophecies are we creating in our minds without being aware of what we're doing? And what "inevitable truths" can we successfully reverse simply through thinking new thoughts and choosing new beliefs?

The First Big Breakthroughs

A groundbreaking study in the late '70s showed for the first time that a placebo could trigger the release of endorphins (the body's natural painkillers), just as certain active drugs do. In the study, Jon Levine, M.D., Ph.D., of the University of California, San Francisco, gave placebos, instead of pain medication, to 40 dental patients who had just had their wisdom teeth removed.[6] Not surprisingly, because the patients thought they were getting medicine that would indeed relieve their pain, most reported relief. But then the researchers gave the patients an antidote to morphine called naloxone, which chemically blocks the receptor sites for both morphine and endorphins (endogenous morphine) in the brain. When the researchers administered it, the patients' pain returned! This proved that by taking the placebos, the patients had been creating their own endorphins—their own natural pain relievers. It was a milestone in placebo research, because it meant that the relief the study subjects experienced wasn't all in their minds; it was in their minds *and* their bodies—in their *state of being.*

If the human body can act like its own pharmacy, producing its own pain drugs, then might it not *also* be true that it's fully capable of dispensing other natural drugs when they're needed from the infinite blend of chemicals and healing compounds it houses—drugs that act just like the ones doctors prescribe or maybe even *better* than the drugs doctors prescribe?

Another study in the '70s, this one by psychologist Robert Ader, Ph.D., at the University of Rochester, added a fascinating new dimension to the placebo discussion: the element of conditioning. *Conditioning,* an idea made famous by Russian physiologist Ivan Pavlov, depends on associating one thing with another—like Pavlov's dogs associating the sound of the bell with food after Pavlov started ringing it every day before he fed them. In time, the dogs were conditioned to automatically salivate in anticipation of a meal whenever they heard a bell. As a result of this type of conditioning, their bodies became trained to physiologically respond to a new stimulus in the environment (in this case, the bell), even without the original stimulus that elicited the response (the food) being present.

Therefore, in a conditioned response, we could say that a subconscious program, which is housed in the body (I'll talk more about this in the coming chapters), seemingly overrides the conscious mind and takes charge. In this way, the body is actually conditioned to *become* the mind because conscious thought is no longer totally in control.

In the case of Pavlov, the dogs were repeatedly exposed to the smell, sight, and taste of the food, and then Pavlov rang a bell. Over time, just the sound of the bell caused the dogs to automatically change their physiological and chemical state without thinking about it consciously. Their *autonomic nervous system*—the body's subconscious system that operates below conscious awareness—took over. So conditioning creates subconscious internal changes in the body by associating past memories with the expectation of internal effects (what we call *associative memory*) until those expected or anticipated end results automatically occur. The stronger the conditioning, the less conscious control we have over these processes and the more automatic the subconscious programming becomes.

Ader started out attempting to study how long such conditioned responses could be expected to last. He fed lab rats saccharine-sweetened water that he'd spiked with a drug called cyclophosphamide, which causes stomach pain. After conditioning the rats to associate the sweet taste of the water with the ache in their gut, he expected they'd soon refuse to drink the spiked water. His intention was to see how long they'd continue to refuse the water so that he could measure the amount of time their conditioned response to the sweet water would last.

But what Ader didn't know initially was that the cyclophosphamide also suppresses the immune system, so he was surprised when his rats started unexpectedly dying from bacterial and viral infections. Changing gears in his research, he continued to give the rats saccharine water (force-feeding them with an eyedropper) but without the cyclophosphamide. Although they were no longer receiving the immune-suppressing drug, the rats continued to die of infections (while the control group that had received only the sweetened water all along continued to be fine). Teaming up with University of Rochester immunologist Nicholas Cohen, Ph.D., Ader further discovered that when the rats had been conditioned to associate the taste of the sweetened water with the effect of the immune-suppressing drug, the association was so strong that just drinking the sweetened water alone produced the same physiological effect as the drug—signaling the nervous system to suppress the immune system.[7]

Like Sam Londe, whose story was in Chapter 1, Ader's rats died by thought alone. Researchers were beginning to see that the mind was clearly able to subconsciously activate the body in several powerful ways they'd never imagined.

West Meets East

By this time, the Eastern practice of *Transcendental Meditation* (TM), taught by Indian guru Maharishi Mahesh Yogi, had caught on in the United States, fueled by the enthusiastic participation of several celebrities (starting with the Beatles in the 1960s). The goal of this technique, which involves quieting the mind and repeating a mantra during a 20-minute meditation session performed twice a day, is spiritual enlightenment. But the practice caught the attention of Harvard cardiologist Herbert Benson, who became interested in how it might help reduce stress and lessen the risk factors for heart disease. Demystifying the process, Benson developed a similar technique, which he called the "relaxation response," described in his 1975 book by the same title.[8] Benson found that just by changing their thought patterns, people could switch off the stress response, thereby lowering blood pressure, normalizing heart rate, and attaining deep states of relaxation.

While meditation involves maintaining a neutral attitude, attention was also being paid to the beneficial effects of cultivating a more positive attitude and pumping up positive emotions. The way had been paved in 1952, when former minister Norman Vincent Peale published the book *The Power of Positive Thinking*, which popularized the idea that our thoughts can have a real effect, both positive and negative, on our lives.[9] That idea grabbed the attention of the medical community in 1976, when political analyst and magazine editor Norman Cousins published an account in the *New England Journal of Medicine* of how he had used laughter to reverse a potentially fatal disease.[10] Cousins also told his story in his best-selling book *Anatomy of an Illness*, published a few years later.[11]

Cousins's doctor had diagnosed him with a degenerative disorder called *ankylosing spondylitis*—a form of arthritis that causes the breakdown of collagen, the fibrous proteins that hold our bodies' cells together—and had given him only a 1-in-500 chance of recovery. Cousins suffered from tremendous pain and had such difficulty moving his limbs that he could barely turn over in bed. Grainy nodules appeared under his skin, and at his lowest point, his jaw nearly locked shut.

Convinced that a persistent negative emotional state had contributed to his illness, he decided it was equally possible that a more positive emotional state could reverse the damage. While continuing to consult with his doctor, Cousins started a regimen of massive doses of vitamin C and Marx Brothers movies (as well as other humorous films and comedy shows). He found that ten minutes of hearty laughter gave him two hours of pain-free sleep. Eventually, he made a complete recovery. Cousins, quite simply, laughed himself to health.

How? Although scientists at the time didn't have a way to understand or explain such a miraculous recovery, research now tells us it's likely that epigenetic processes were at work. Cousins's shift of attitude changed his body chemistry, which altered his internal state, enabling him to program new genes in new ways; he simply *downregulated* (or turned off) the genes that were causing his illness and *upregulated* (or turned on) the genes responsible for his recovery. (I'll go into more detail about turning genes on and off in the coming chapters.)

Many years later, research by Keiko Hayashi, Ph.D., of the University of Tsukuba in Japan showed the same thing.[12] In Hayashi's study, diabetic patients watching an hour-long comedy program upregulated a total of 39 genes, 14 of which were related to natural killer cell activity. While none of these genes were directly involved in blood-glucose regulation, the patients' blood-glucose levels were better controlled than after they listened to a diabetes health lecture on a different day. Researchers surmised that laughter influences many genes involved with immune response, which in turn contributed to the improved glucose control. The elevated emotion, triggered by the patients' brains, turned on the genetic variations, which activated the natural killer cells and also somehow improved their glucose response—probably in addition to many other beneficial effects.

As Cousins said of placebos back in 1979, "The process works not because of any magic in the tablet, but because the human body is its own best apothecary and because the most successful prescriptions are filled by the body itself."[13]

Inspired by Cousins's experience, and with alternative and mind-body medicine now in full swing, Yale University surgeon Bernie Siegel started to look at why some of his cancer patients with poor odds survived while others with better odds died. Siegel's work defined cancer survivors largely as those who had a feisty, fighting spirit, and he concluded that there were no incurable diseases, only incurable patients. Siegel also began writing about hope as a powerful force for healing and about unconditional love, with the natural pharmacy of elixirs it provides, as the most powerful stimulant of the immune system.[14]

Placebos Outperform Antidepressants

The profusion of new antidepressants that appeared around the late 1980s and into the '90s would next ignite a controversy that would ultimately (although not immediately) increase respect for the power of placebos. In researching a 1998 meta-analysis of published studies on antidepressant drugs, psychologist Irving Kirsch, Ph.D., then at the University of Connecticut, was shocked to find that in 19 randomized, double-blind clinical trials involving more than 2,300 patients, most of the improvement was due not to the antidepressant medications, but to the placebo.[15]

Kirsch then used the Freedom of Information Act to gain access to the data from the drug manufacturers' unpublished clinical trials, which by law had to be reported to the Food and Drug Administration. Kirsch and his colleagues did a second meta-analysis, this time on the 35 clinical trials conducted for four of the six most widely prescribed antidepressants approved between 1987 and 1999.[16] Now looking at data from more than 5,000 patients, the researchers found again that placebos worked just as well as the popular antidepressant drugs Prozac, Effexor, Serzone, and Paxil a whopping 81 percent of the time. In most of the remaining cases where the drug *did* perform better, the benefit was so small that it wasn't statistically significant. Only with severely depressed patients were the prescription drugs clearly better than placebo.

Not surprisingly, Kirsch's study caused quite an uproar, although many researchers seemed quite willing to throw the placebo baby out with the bathwater. While most of the fracas focused on the fact that these drugs weren't any better than the placebo, the patients in the trials *did*, in fact, get better on antidepressants. The drugs did work. But the patients taking placebos got better, too. Instead of seeing Kirsch's work as proof that antidepressants failed, some researchers chose to see the glass as half-full and pointed to the data as proof that placebos succeeded.

After all, the trials provided stunning proof that thinking that you can get better from depression can actually heal depression just as well as taking a drug. The people in the study who got better on placebos were actually making their *own natural antidepressants*, just as Levine's patients in the '70s who had their wisdom teeth out made their own natural painkillers. What Kirsch had brought to light was more evidence that our bodies do have an innate intelligence that enables them to serve us with a chemical array of natural healing compounds. Interestingly enough, the percentage of people who improve while taking placebos in depression trials has gotten greater over time, as has the response to active medication; some researchers have suggested that this is because the public has greater expectations for the antidepressant drugs, which in turn makes the placebos more effective in these blind trials.[17]

The Neurobiology of the Placebo

It was only a matter of time before neuroscientists would start using sophisticated brain scans to take an intricate look at what happens neurochemically when a placebo is administered. An example is the 2001 study on Parkinson's patients who regained motor skills after receiving only an injection of saline that they thought was medication (described in Chapter 1).[18] Italian researcher Fabrizio Benedetti, M.D., Ph.D., a pioneer in placebo research, did a similar Parkinson's study a few years later and, for the first time, was able to show a placebo's effect on individual neurons.[19]

His studies explored not only the neurobiology of expectation, as with the Parkinson's patients, but also the neurobiology at work with classical conditioning—what Ader had been able to glimpse years previously with his nauseated lab rats. In one experiment, Benedetti gave study subjects the drug sumatriptan to stimulate growth hormone and inhibit cortisol secretion, and then without the patients' knowledge, he replaced the drug with a placebo. He found that the patients' brain scans continued to light up in the same places as when they were getting the sumatriptan; this was proof that the brain was indeed producing the same substance—in this case, growth hormone—on its own.[20]

The same was seen to be true for other drug-placebo combinations as well; the chemicals made in the brain closely tracked those that the subjects initially received via drugs that were given to treat immune system disorders, motor disorders, and depression.[21] In fact, Benedetti even showed that placebos caused the same side effects as the drugs. For example, in one placebo study using narcotics, the subjects suffered the same side effects of slow and shallow breathing when taking the placebo, because the placebo effect so closely mimicked the physiological effects of the drug.[22]

If the truth be told, our bodies are indeed capable of creating a host of biological chemicals that can heal, protect us from pain, help us sleep deeply, enhance our immune systems, make us feel pleasure, and even encourage us to fall in love. Reason this for a moment: If a particular gene was already expressed so that we made those specific chemicals at one point in our lives, but then we stopped making them because of some type of stress or illness that turned off that gene, maybe it's possible for us to turn the gene back on again, because our bodies *already know* how to do that from previous experience. (Stay tuned for research to prove this.)

So let's begin to look at how this happens. The neurological research shows something truly remarkable: If a person keeps taking the same substance, his or her brain keeps firing the same circuits in the same way—in effect, memorizing what the substance does. The person can easily become conditioned to the effect of a particular pill or injection from associating it with a familiar internal change from past experience. Because of this kind of conditioning, when the person then takes a placebo, the same hardwired circuits will fire as when he or she took the drug. An associative memory elicits a subconscious program that makes a connection between the pill or injection and the hormonal change in the body, and then the program automatically signals the body to make the related chemicals found in the drug. . . . Isn't that amazing?

Benedetti's research also makes another point very clear: Different types of placebo treatments work best with different goals. For example, in the sumatriptan study, initial verbal suggestions that the placebo would work had no effect on the production of growth hormone. To use placebos to effect unconscious physiological responses by associative memory (such as to secrete hormones or alter the functioning of the immune system), conditioning gets results, whereas to use placebos to change more conscious responses (such as to relieve pain or lessen depression), a simple suggestion or an expectation works. So there isn't just *one* placebo response, Benedetti insisted, but *several.*

Taking Mind Over Matter into Your Own Hands

An astonishing new twist to placebo research came in a 2010 pilot study led by Harvard's Ted Kaptchuk, D.O.M., that showed that placebos worked *even when people knew they were taking a placebo.*[23] In the study, Kaptchuk and his colleagues gave 40 patients with irritable bowel syndrome (IBS) a placebo. Each patient received a bottle clearly labeled "placebo pills" and was told it contained "placebo pills made of an inert substance, like sugar pills, that have been shown in clinical studies to produce significant improvement in IBS symptoms through mind-body, self-healing processes." A second group of 40 IBS patients, given no pills, served as a control group.

After three weeks, the group taking the placebos reported *twice as much symptom relief* as the no-treatment group—a difference that Kaptchuk noted is comparable to the performance of the best *real* IBS drugs. These patients hadn't been tricked into healing themselves. They *knew full well* that they weren't getting any medication—and yet after hearing the suggestion that the placebos could relieve their symptoms and believing in an outcome independent of the cause, their bodies were influenced to make it happen.

Meanwhile, a parallel track of studies that examines the effect of attitude, perceptions, and beliefs is leading the way in current mind-body research, showing that even something as seemingly concrete as the physical benefit of exercise can be affected by belief. A 2007 study at Harvard by psychologists Alia Crum, Ph.D., and Ellen Langer, Ph.D., involving 84 hotel maids is a perfect example.[24]

At the start of the study, none of the maids knew that the routine work they performed in their jobs exceeded the Surgeon General's recommendation for a healthy amount of daily exercise (30 minutes). In fact, 67 percent of the women told the researchers that they didn't exercise regularly, and 37 percent said they didn't get any exercise. After this initial assessment, Crum and Langer divided the maids into two groups. They explained to the first group how their activity related to the number of calories they burned and told the maids that just by doing their jobs, they got more than enough exercise. They didn't give any such information to the second group (who worked in different hotels from the first group and so wouldn't benefit from conversations with the other maids).

One month later, the researchers found that the first group lost an average of two pounds, lowered their percentage of body fat, and lowered their systolic blood pressure by an average of 10 points—even though they hadn't performed any additional exercise outside of work or changed their eating habits in any way. The other group, doing the same job as the first, remained virtually unchanged.

This echoed similar research done earlier in Quebec, where a group of 48 young adults participated in a ten-week aerobic exercise program, attending three 90-minute exercise sessions per week.[25] The group was divided into two. The instructors told the first half, the test subjects, that the study was specifically designed to improve both their aerobic capacity and their psychological well-being. They mentioned only the physical benefits of aerobics to the second half, who served as the control group. At the end of the ten weeks, the researchers found that both groups increased their aerobic capacity, but it was only the test subjects, not the controls, who also received a significant boost in self-esteem (a measure of well-being).

As these studies show, our awareness alone can have an important physical effect on our bodies and our health. What we learn, the language that's used to define what we'll experience, and how we assign meaning to the explanations that are offered all affect our intention—and when we put greater intention behind what we're doing, we naturally get better results.

In short, the more you learn about the "what" and the "why," the easier and more effective the "how" becomes. (My hope is that this book will do the same for you; the more you know what you're doing and why you're doing it, the better results you're bound to get.)

We also assign meaning to subtler factors, such as the color of the medicine we take and the quantity of pills we ingest, as shown in an older but classic study from the University of Cincinnati. In this study, researchers gave 57 medical students either one or two pink or blue capsules—all of them inert, although the students were told that the pink capsules were stimulants and the blue ones were sedatives.[26] The researchers reported, "Two capsules produced more noticeable changes than one, and blue capsules were associated with more sedative effects than pink capsules." Indeed, the students rated the blue pills as being two and a half times more effective as sedatives than the pink pills—even though *all* the pills were placebos.

More recent research shows that beliefs and perceptions can also affect scores in mental performance on standardized tests. In a 2006 study from Canada, 220 female students read fake research reports claiming that men had a 5 percent advantage over women in math performance.[27] The group was divided into two, with one group reading that the advantage was due to recently discovered genetic factors, while the other group read that the advantage resulted from the way teachers stereotype girls and boys in elementary school. Then the subjects were given a math test. The women who'd read that men had a genetic advantage scored lower than those who'd read that men had an advantage due to stereotyping. In other words, when they were primed to *think* that their disadvantage was inevitable, the women performed as if they truly had a disadvantage.

A similar effect has been documented with African-American students, who have historically scored lower than whites on vocabulary, reading, and math tests, including the Scholastic

Aptitude Test (SAT), even when socioeconomic class is not a factor. In fact, the average black student scores below 70 to 80 percent of the white students of the same age on most standardized tests.[28] Stanford University social psychologist Claude Steele, Ph.D., explains that an effect called "stereotype threat" is to blame. His research shows that students who belong to groups that have been negatively stereotyped perform less well when they think their scores will be evaluated in light of that stereotype than they do when they feel no such pressure.[29]

In Steele's landmark study, conducted with Joshua Aronson, Ph.D., researchers gave a series of verbal reasoning tests to Stanford sophomores. Some of the students were given instructions that primed the stereotype that blacks score lower than whites by saying that the quiz they were about to take was designed to measure their cognitive ability, while the others were told that the test was merely an unimportant research tool. In the group where the stereotype was primed, blacks scored lower than whites who had similar SAT scores. When the stereotype was *not* primed, performance of blacks and whites whose SAT scores were similar was the same—proving that the priming made a critical difference.

Priming is, basically, when some*one,* some*place,* or some*thing* in our environment (for example, taking a test) triggers all sorts of associations that are hardwired into our brains (that people grading this test think black students score lower than whites), causing us to act in certain ways (not scoring as highly) without being conscious of what we're doing. It's called "priming," because it works just as priming a pump does. You have to have water already in the pumping system in order to pump more water out of it. So in this example, the idea or belief that others expect black students to score lower than whites is like the water that's already in the system—it's just there all the time. When you do something to stimulate the system (grabbing the pump handle or taking the test), you're stirring up all those related thoughts, behaviors, or emotions, and you produce exactly what was waiting to emerge from the system all along—be that water, in the case of a pump, or lower test scores, if it's a test.

Think about this for a moment. Most automatic behaviors that priming elicits are produced by unconscious or subconscious programming, which, for the most part, is happening behind the scenes of our awareness. Are we, then, primed to behave unconsciously all day long—without our even knowing it?

Steele replicated this effect with other stereotyped groups as well. When Steele gave a math test to a group of white and Asian men who were strong in math, the white men in the group who were told that Asians do slightly better than whites on the test indeed didn't do as well as the white men in the control group who weren't told that. Steele's experiments with strong female math students showed similar results. Again, when the students' unconscious expectation was that they would score lower, they, in fact, did.

The greater meaning behind Steele's research, then, is quite profound: What we're conditioned to believe about ourselves, and what we're programmed to think other people think about us, affects our performance, including how successful we are. It's the same with placebos: What we're conditioned to believe will happen when we take a pill, and what we think that everyone around us (including our doctors) expects will happen when we do, affects how our bodies respond to the pill. Could it be that many drugs or even surgeries actually work better because we're repeatedly primed, educated, and conditioned to believe in their effects—when if it weren't for the placebo effect, those drugs might not work as well or at all?

Can You Be Your Own Placebo?

Two recent studies from the University of Toledo perhaps shed the best light on how the mind alone can determine what someone perceives and experiences.[30] For each study, researchers divided a group of healthy volunteers into two categories—optimists and pessimists—according to how the volunteers answered questions on a diagnostic questionnaire. In the first study, they gave the subjects a placebo but told them it was a drug that would make them feel unwell. The pessimists had a stronger negative reaction to the pill than the optimists. In the second study, the researchers gave the subjects a placebo as well, but told them it would help them sleep better. The optimists reported much better sleep than the pessimists.

So the optimists were more likely to respond positively to a suggestion that something would make them feel better, because they were primed to hope for the best future scenario. And the pessimists were more likely to respond negatively to a suggestion that something would make them feel worse, because they consciously or unconsciously expected the worst potential outcome. It's as if the optimists were unconsciously making the specific chemicals to help them sleep, while the pessimists were unconsciously making a pharmacy of substances that made them feel unwell.

In other words, in exactly the same environment, those with a positive mind-set tend to create positive situations, while those with a negative mind-set tend to create negative situations. This is the miracle of our own free-willed, individual, biological engineering.

While we may not know *exactly* how many medical healings are due to the placebo effect (Beecher's 1955 paper, mentioned earlier in this chapter, claimed the number was 35 percent, but modern-day research shows it can range anywhere from 10 to 100 percent[31]), the overall number is certainly extremely significant. Given that, we have to ask ourselves, *What percentage of diseases and illnesses are due to the effects of negative thoughts in the nocebo?* Considering that the latest scientific research in psychology estimates that about 70 percent of our thoughts are negative and redundant, the number of unconsciously created nocebo-like illnesses might be impressive indeed—certainly much higher than we realize.[32] This idea makes a lot of sense, given that so many mental, physical, and emotional health conditions seem to arise from nowhere.

Although it may seem incredible that your mind could actually be that powerful, the research of the past several decades clearly points to a few empowering truths: What you think is what you experience, and when it comes to your health, that's made possible by the amazing pharmacopeia that you have within your body that automatically and exquisitely aligns with your thoughts. This miraculous dispensary activates naturally occurring healing molecules that already exist within your body—delivering different compounds designed to elicit different effects in any number of different circumstances. Of course, this raises the question: *How do we do it?*

The chapters that follow will explain how this all unfolds on a biological level and thus how you can apply this innate ability to consciously and intentionally create the health—and the life—that you want to experience.

Chapter Three

The Placebo Effect in the Brain

If you've read my previous book, *Breaking the Habit of Being Yourself,* you'll find that this chapter reviews much of that material. If you feel that you already have a good command of that information, you may choose to either skip this chapter completely or skim it to brush up on those concepts as needed. If in doubt, I recommend that you read this chapter, because a thorough understanding of what is presented here will be necessary to fully understand the chapters that follow.

As the stories in the last two chapters illustrate, when we truly change our state of being, our bodies can respond to a new mind. And changing our state of being begins with changing our thoughts. Because of the size of our enormous forebrain, the privilege of being a human being is that we can make thought more real than anything else—and that's how the placebo works. To see how the process unfolds, it's vital to examine and review three key elements: *conditioning, expectation,* and *meaning.* As you'll see, these three concepts all seem to work together in orchestrating the placebo response.

I explained *conditioning,* the first element, in the discussion about Pavlov in the previous chapter. To recap, conditioning happens when we associate a past memory (for example, taking an aspirin) with a physiological change (getting rid of a headache) because we've experienced it so many times. Think about it like this: If you notice that you have a headache, essentially you become aware of a physiological change in your inner environment (you're feeling pain). The next thing you automatically do is look for something in your outer world (in this case, an aspirin) to create a change in your inner world. We could say it was your internal state (being in pain) that prompted you to think about some past choice you made, action you took, or experience you had in your external reality that changed how you were feeling (taking an aspirin and getting relief).

Thus, the stimulus, or cue, from the outer environment, called the aspirin, creates a specific experience. When that experience produces a physiological response or reward, it changes your internal environment. The moment you notice a change in your inner environment, you pay attention to what it was in your outer environment that caused the change. That event—where something outside of you changes something inside of you—is called an *associative memory.*

If we keep repeating the process over and over again, by association the outer stimulus can become so strong or reinforced that we can replace the aspirin for a sugar pill that looks like an aspirin, and it will produce an automatic inner response (lessening the pain of the headache). That's one way the placebo works. Figure 3.1A, Figure 3.1B, and Figure 3.1C illustrate the conditioning process.

Expectation, the second element, comes into play when we have reason to anticipate a different outcome. So, for example, if we have chronic pain from arthritis and get a new medication from the doctor, who enthusiastically explains to us that it's supposed to alleviate our pain, we accept his suggestion and expect that when we take this new medication, something different will happen (we won't be in pain anymore). Then, in effect, our doctor has influenced our level of suggestibility.

Once we become more suggestible, we're naturally associating something outside of ourselves (the new medication) with the selection of a different possibility (being pain-free). In our minds, we are picking a different future potential and hoping, anticipating, and expecting that we'll get that different result. If we emotionally accept and then embrace that new outcome we've selected, and

FIGURE 3.1A

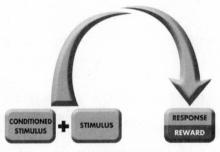

FIGURE 3.1B

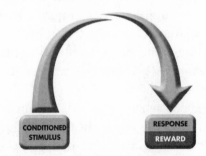

FIGURE 3.1C

In Figure 3.1A, a stimulus produces a physiological change called a response or a reward. Figure 3.1B demonstrates that if you pair a stimulus with a conditioned stimulus enough times, it will still produce a response. Figure 3.1C shows if you remove the stimulus and substitute a conditioned stimulus—like a placebo—it can produce the same physiological response.

the intensity of our emotion is great enough, our brains and our bodies won't know the difference between imagining that we've changed our state of being to being pain-free and the actual event that caused the change to a new state of being. To the brain and the body, they are the same.

Consequently, the brain fires the same neural circuits as it would if our state had changed (if the drug worked to relieve the pain) while it releases similar chemicals into the body. What we're expecting (to be pain-free) then actually happens, because the brain and the body create the perfect pharmacy to alter our internal condition. We are now in a new state of being—that is, the mind and body are working as one. We're that powerful.

Assigning *meaning,* the third element, to a placebo helps it work, because when we give an action a new meaning, then we have added intention behind it. In other words, when we learn and understand something new, we put more of our conscious, purposeful energy into it. So, for example, in the study about the hotel maids from the previous chapter, once the maids understood how much physical exercise they were doing every day just by performing their jobs, as well as the benefits of that exercise, they assigned more meaning to those actions. They weren't just vacuuming, scrubbing, and mopping; they realized they were working their muscles, increasing their strength, and burning calories. Because the vacuuming, scrubbing, and mopping had more meaning after the researchers educated them about the physical advantages of exercise, the maids' intention or aim as they worked wasn't just to complete their tasks—it was also to get physical exercise and become healthier.

And that's exactly what happened. The members of the control group didn't assign the same meaning to their tasks, because they didn't *know* that what they were doing was beneficial to their health, so they also didn't receive the same benefits—even though they were performing exactly the same actions.

The placebo works the same way. The more you believe that a particular substance, procedure, or surgery will work because you've been educated about its benefits, the better your chances of responding to the thought of improving your health and getting better. In other words, if you place more meaning behind a possible experience with a person, place, or thing in your external environment in order to change your internal environment, then you're more likely to be successful at intentionally changing your inner state by *thought alone*. In addition, the more you can accept a new outcome related to your health—because you've been educated about the possible rewards of what you're doing—the clearer the model you're creating in your own mind, and so the better you'll be at priming your brain and your body to replicate exactly that. Simply said, the more you *believe* in the cause, the better the effect.

The Placebo: Anatomy of a Thought

If the placebo effect is a function of how a thought can change physiology—we could call it mind over matter—then perhaps we should examine our thoughts and how they interact with our brains and our bodies. Let's begin with our own personal daily thoughts.

We are creatures of habit. We think somewhere between 60,000 to 70,000 thoughts in one day,[1] and 90 percent of those thoughts are exactly the same ones we had the day before. We get up on the same side of the bed, go through the same routine in the bathroom, comb our hair in the same way, sit in the same chair as we eat the same breakfast and hold our mug in the same hand, drive the same route to the same job, and do the same things we know how to do so well with the same people (who push the same emotional buttons) every day. And then we hurry up and go home so that we can hurry up and check our e-mail so that we can hurry up and eat dinner so that we can hurry up and watch our favorite TV shows so that we can hurry up and brush our teeth in the same bedtime routine so that we can hurry up and go to bed at the same time so that we can hurry up and do it all over again the next day.

If it sounds as though I'm saying that we live a huge part of our lives on autopilot, that's exactly right. Thinking the same *thoughts* leads us to make the same *choices*. Making the same *choices* leads to demonstrating the same *behaviors*. Demonstrating the same *behaviors* leads us to create the same *experiences*. Creating the same *experiences* leads us to produce the same *emotions*. And those same *emotions* then drive the same *thoughts*. Take a look at Figure 3.2 and follow the sequence of how our same thoughts create the same reality as usual.

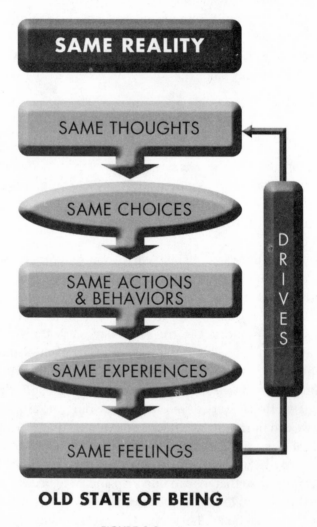

FIGURE 3.2

How we create the same reality by thought alone.

As a result of this conscious or unconscious process, your biology stays the same. Neither your brain nor your body changes at all, because you're thinking the same thoughts, performing the same actions, and living by the same emotions—even though you may be secretly hoping your life will change. You create the same brain activity, which activates the same brain circuits and reproduces the same brain chemistry, which affects your body chemistry in the same way. And that same chemistry signals the same genes in the same ways. And the same gene expression creates the same proteins, the building blocks of cells, which keep the body the same (I'll go into more on proteins later). And since the expression of proteins is the expression of life or health, your life and your health stay the same.

Now take a look at your life for a moment. What does this mean for *you?* If you're thinking the same thoughts as yesterday, more than likely, you're making the same choices today. Those same choices today are leading to the same behaviors tomorrow. The same habitual behaviors tomorrow are producing the same experiences in your future. The same events in your future reality are creating the same predictable emotions for you all the time. And as a result, you're feeling the same every day. Your yesterday becomes your tomorrow—so in truth, your past is your future.

If you agree with me up to this point, then we could say that the familiar feeling I just described is "you"—your identity or your personality. It's your state of being. And it's comfortable, effortless, and automatic. It's the known you who, quite frankly, is living in the past. When you keep this redundant process going on a daily basis (because you wake up in the morning and anticipate and re-member the feeling of "you" every day), in time that known state of being can drive only the same thoughts that will influence you to crave the same automatic cycle of choices, behaviors, and experiences in order to arrive back at that familiar feeling that you think of as "you." So everything stays the same about your personality.

If this is your personality, then *your personality creates your personal reality.* It's that simple. And your personality is made up of how you *think,* how you *act,* and how you *feel.* So the present personality who is reading this page has created the present personal reality called your life; and that also means that if you want to create a new personal reality—a new life—then you have to begin to examine or think about the thoughts you've been thinking and change them. You must become conscious of the unconscious behaviors you've been choosing to demonstrate that have led to the same experiences, and then you must make new choices, take new actions, and create new experiences. Figure 3.3 shows how your personality influences your personal reality.

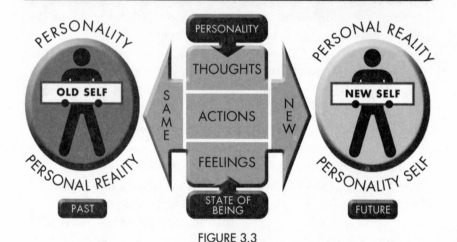

FIGURE 3.3

Your personality is made up of how you think, act, and feel.
It is your state of being. Therefore, your same thoughts, actions, and feelings
will keep you enslaved to the same past personal reality. However, when you
as a personality embrace new thoughts, actions, and feelings, you will
inevitably create a new personal reality in your future.

You must observe and pay attention to those emotions that you've memorized and that you live by on a daily basis, and decide if living by those emotions over and over again is loving to you. You see, most people try to create a new personal reality as the same old personality, and it doesn't work. In order to change your life, you have to literally become someone else. Stay tuned for some sound science to support this process. Take a glance at Figure 3.4 and follow the sequence again.

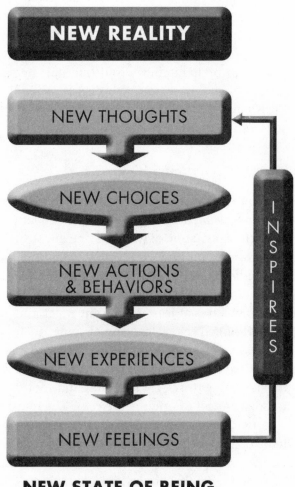

NEW STATE OF BEING

FIGURE 3.4

How we create a *new* reality by thought alone.

So if you understand this model, then you should agree with me that your new thoughts should lead to new choices. New choices should lead to new behaviors. New behaviors should lead to new experiences. New experiences should create new emotions, and new emotions and feelings should inspire you to think in new ways. That's called "evolution." And your personal reality and your biology—your brain circuitry, your internal chemistry, your genetic expression, and ultimately your health—should change as a result of this new personality, this new state of being. And it all seems to start with a thought.

A Quick Look at How the Brain Works

Up to this point, I've briefly mentioned terms like *brain circuitry, neural networks, brain chemistry,* and *genetic expression* without giving you much explanation of what they mean. So for the rest of the chapter, I want to outline some simple scientific understandings of how the brain and body work together in order to build a complete model of how you really can become your own placebo.

Your brain, which is at least 75 percent water and is the consistency of a soft-boiled egg, is made up of some 100 billion nerve cells, called *neurons,* that are seamlessly arranged and suspended in this aqueous environment. Each nerve cell resembles a leafless but elastic oak tree, with wiggly branches and root systems that connect and disconnect to other nerve cells. The number of connections a particular nerve cell might make can range from 1,000 to more than 100,000, depending on where in the brain the nerve cell resides. For example, your *neocortex*—your thinking brain—has about 10,000 to 40,000 connections per neuron.

We used to think of the brain as a computer, and while there are certainly some similarities, we now know there's much more to the story. Each neuron is its own unique biocomputer, with more than 60 megabytes of RAM. It's capable of processing enormous amounts of data—up to hundreds of thousands of functions per second. As we learn new things and have new experiences in our lives, our neurons make new connections, exchanging electrochemical information with each other. Those connections are called *synaptic connections,* because the place where the cells exchange information—the gap between the branch of one neuron and the root of another—is called a *synapse.*

If learning is making new synaptic connections, then remembering is keeping those connections wired together. So in effect, a memory is a long-term relationship or connection between the nerve cells. And the creation of these connections, and the ways they change over time, alters the physical structure of the brain.

As the brain makes these changes, our thoughts produce a blend of various chemicals called *neurotransmitters* (serotonin, dopamine, and acetylcholine are a few examples you may recognize). When we think thoughts, neurotransmitters at one branch of one neuron tree cross the synaptic gap to reach the root of another neuron tree. Once they cross that gap, the neuron fires with an electrical bolt of information. When we continue thinking the same thoughts, the neuron keeps firing in the same ways, strengthening the relationship between the two cells so that they can more readily convey a signal the next time those neurons fire. As a result, the brain shows physical evidence that something was not only learned, but also remembered. This process of selective strengthening is called *synaptic potentiation.*

When jungles of neurons fire in unison to support a new thought, an additional chemical (a protein) is created within the nerve cell and makes its way to the cell's center, or *nucleus,* where it lands in the DNA. The protein then switches on several genes. Since the job of the genes is to make proteins that maintain both the structure and function of the body, the nerve cell then quickly makes a new protein to create new branches between nerve cells. So when we repeat a thought or an experience enough times, our brain cells make not only stronger connections between each other (which affects our physiological functions), but also a greater number of total connections (which affects the physical structure of the body). The brain becomes more enriched microscopically.

So as soon as you think a new thought, you become changed— neurologically, chemically, and genetically. In fact, you can gain thousands of new connections in a matter of seconds from novel learning, new ways of thinking, and fresh experiences. This means that by thought alone, you can personally activate new genes right away. It happens just by changing your mind; it's mind over matter.

Nobel laureate Eric Kandel, M.D., showed that when new memories are formed, the number of synaptic connections in the sensory neurons that are stimulated doubles, to 2,600. However, unless the original learning experience is repeated over and over again, the number of new connections falls back to the original 1,300 in a matter of only three weeks.

Therefore, if we repeat what we learn enough times, we strengthen communities of neurons to support us in remembering it the next time. If we don't, then the synaptic connections soon disappear and the memory is erased. This is why it's important for us to continually update, review, and remember our new thoughts, choices, behaviors, habits, beliefs, and experiences if we want them to solidify in our brains.[2] Figure 3.5 will help you become familiar with neurons and neural networks.

To get an idea of how vast this system really is, imagine a nerve cell connecting to 40,000 other nerve cells. Let's say it's processing 100,000 bits of information per second and sharing that information with other neurons that are also processing 100,000 functions per second. This network, formed from clusters of neurons working together, is called a *neural network* (or a *neural net* for short). Neural nets form communities of synaptic connections. We can also call them your *neurocircuitry*.

So as there are physical changes in the nerve cells that make up your brain's gray matter, and as neurons are selected and instructed to organize themselves into these vast networks capable of processing hundreds of millions of bits of information, the physical hardware of the brain also changes, adapting to the information it receives from the environment. In time, as the networks—converging and diverging propagations of electrical activity like a

FIGURE 3.5

This is a simple graphic representation of neurons in a neural network. The minute space between the branches of individual neurons that facilitates communication between them is called the synaptic gap. About 100,000 neurons can fit into the same space as a grain of sand and will have more than a billion connections among them.

crazy lightning storm in thick clouds—are repeatedly turned on, the brain will keep using the same hardware systems (the physical neural networks) but will also create a software program (an automatic neural network). That's how the programs are installed in the brain. The hardware creates the software, and the software system is embedded into the hardware—and every time the software is used, it reinforces the hardware.

So when you're thinking the same thoughts and having the same feelings all the time because you're not learning or doing anything new, your brain is firing its neurons and activating the neural networks in exactly the same sequences, patterns, and combinations. They become the automatic programs that you unconsciously use every day. You have an automatic neural network to speak a language, to shave your face or put on makeup, to type on the computer, to judge your co-worker, and so on, because you've performed those actions so many times that they've become practically unconscious. You no longer have to consciously think about it. It's effortless.

You've reinforced those circuits so often that they've become hardwired. The connections between neurons become more glued together, additional circuits are formed, and the branches actually expand and become physically thicker—just as we might strengthen and reinforce a bridge, build a few new roads, or widen a freeway to accommodate more traffic.

One of the most basic principles in neuroscience states, "Nerve cells that fire together wire together."[3] As your brain fires repeatedly in the same manner, you're reproducing the same level of mind. According to neuroscience, *mind* is the brain in action or at work. Thus, we can say that if you're reminding yourself of who you think you are on a daily basis by reproducing the same mind, you're making your brain fire in the same ways and you'll activate the same neural networks for years on end. By the time you reach your mid-30s, your brain has organized itself into a very finite signature of automatic programs—and that fixed pattern is called your *identity*.

Think of it as a box inside your brain. There's no literal box inside your head, of course. But it's safe to say that thinking inside the box means you've physically hardwired your brain into a limited pattern, as illustrated in Figure 3.6. By reproducing the same level of mind over and over again, the most commonly fired, neurologically wired set of circuits has predetermined who you are as a result of your own volition.

NEURORIGIDITY

THINKING IN THE BOX

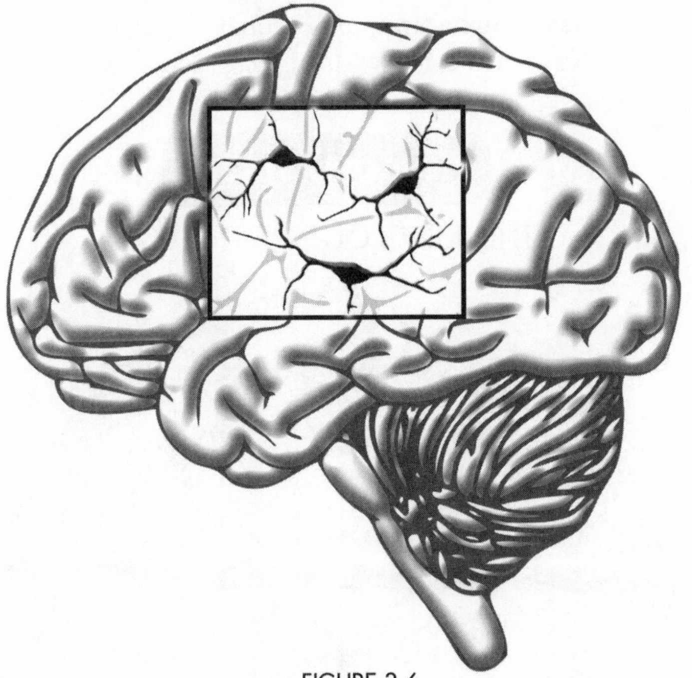

FIGURE 3.6

If your thoughts, choices, behaviors, experiences, and emotional states remain the same for years on end—and the same thoughts are always equal to the same feelings, reinforcing the same endless cycle—then your brain becomes hardwired into a finite signature. That's because you are re-creating the same mind every day by making your brain fire in the same patterns. Over time, this biologically reinforces a specific limited set of neural networks, making your brain physically more prone to creating the same level of mind—you're now thinking in the box. The totality of those hardwired circuits is called your identity.

Neuroplasticity

So our goal, then, needs to be thinking *outside* the box to make the brain fire in new ways, as Figure 3.7 illustrates. That's what having an open mind means, because whenever you make your brain work differently, you're literally changing your mind.

Research shows that as we use our brains, they grow and change, thanks to *neuroplasticity*—the brain's ability to adapt and change when we learn new information. For example, the longer mathematicians study math, the more neural branches sprout in the area of the brain used for math.[4] And after years of performing in symphonies and orchestras, professional musicians expand the part of their brains associated with language and musical abilities.[5]

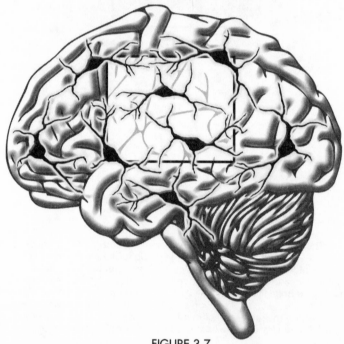

NEUROPLASTICITY

THINKING OUT OF THE BOX

FIGURE 3.7

When you learn new things and begin to think in new ways, you are making your brain fire in different sequences, patterns, and combinations. That is, you are activating many diverse networks of neurons in different ways. And whenever you make your brain work differently, you're changing your mind. As you begin to think outside the box, new thoughts should lead to new choices, new behaviors, new experiences, and new emotions. Now your identity is also changing.

The official scientific terms for how neuroplasticity works are *pruning* and *sprouting,* which mean exactly what they sound like: getting rid of some neural connections, patterns, and circuits and creating new ones. In a well-functioning brain, this process can happen in a matter of seconds. Researchers at the University of California at Berkeley demonstrated this in a study on laboratory rats. They found that rats living in an enriched environment (sharing a cage with siblings and offspring and having access to many different toys) had larger brains with more neurons and more connections between those neurons than did the rats in less-enriched environments.[6] Again, when we learn new things and have new experiences, we're literally changing our brains.

To break free from the chains of hardwired programming and the conditioning that keeps you the same takes considerable effort. It also requires knowledge, because when you learn vital information about yourself or your life, you stitch a whole new pattern into the three-dimensional embroidery of your own gray matter. Now you have more raw materials to make the brain work in new and different ways. You begin to think about and perceive reality differently, because you begin to see your life through the lens of a new mind.

Crossing the River of Change

At this point, you can see that in order to change, you have to become conscious of your unconscious self (which you now know is just a set of hardwired programs).

The hardest part about change is *not making the same choices we made the day before.* The reason it's so difficult is that the moment we no longer are thinking the same thoughts that lead to the same choices—which cause us to automatically act in habitual ways so that we can experience the same events in order to reaffirm the same emotions of our identity—we immediately feel uncomfortable. This new state of being is unfamiliar; it's unknown. It doesn't feel "normal." We don't feel like ourselves anymore—because we're not ourselves. And because everything feels uncertain, we no longer can predict the feeling of the familiar self and how it's mirrored back to us in our lives.

As uncomfortable as that may be at first, that's the moment we know we've stepped into the river of change. We've entered the unknown. The instant that we no longer are being our old selves, we have to cross a gap between the old self and the new self, which Figure 3.8 clearly shows. In other words, we don't all just waltz into a new personality in a matter of moments. It takes time.

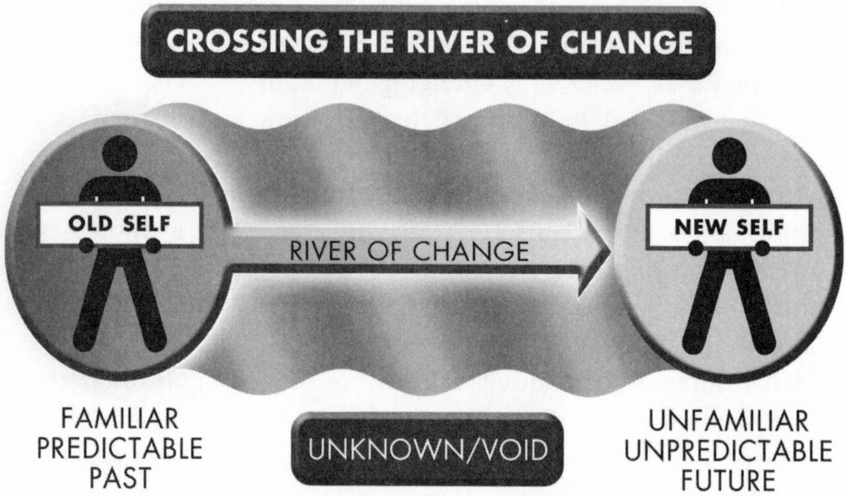

CROSSING THE RIVER OF CHANGE

OLD SELF — RIVER OF CHANGE → NEW SELF

FAMILIAR PREDICTABLE PAST — UNKNOWN/VOID — UNFAMILIAR UNPREDICTABLE FUTURE

FIGURE 3.8

Crossing the river of change requires that you leave the same familiar predictable self—connected to the same thoughts, same choices, same behaviors, and same feelings—and step into a void or the unknown. The gap between the old self and the new self is the biological death of your old personality. If the old self must die, then you have to create a new self with new thoughts, new choices, new behaviors, and new emotions. Entering this river is stepping toward a new unpredictable, unfamiliar self. The unknown is the only place where you can create—you cannot create anything new from the known.

Usually when people step into the river of change, that void between the old self and the new self is so uncomfortable that they immediately slip back into being their old selves again. They unconsciously think, *This doesn't feel right, I'm uncomfortable,* or *I don't feel so good.* The moment they accept that *thought,* or autosuggestion (and become suggestible to their own thoughts), they will unconsciously make the same old *choices* again that will lead to the progression of the same habitual *behaviors* to create the same *experiences* that automatically endorse the same *emotions* and *feelings*. And then they say to themselves, *This feels right.* But what they really mean is that it feels *familiar.*

Once we understand that crossing the river of change and feeling that discomfort is actually the biological, neurological, chemical, and even genetic death of the old self, we have power over change and we can set our sights on the other side of the river. If we embrace the fact that change is the denaturing of the hardwired circuitry from years of unconsciously thinking the same way, we can cope. If we understand that the discomfort we feel is the dismantling of old attitudes, beliefs, and perceptions that have been repeatedly etched into our cerebral architecture, we can endure. If we can reason that the cravings we battle in the midst of change are real withdrawals from the chemical-emotional addictions of the body, we can ride it out. If we can comprehend that real biological variations are occurring from subconscious habits and behaviors in which our bodies are changing on a cellular level, we can forge on. And if we can remember that we are modifying our very genes from this life and from untold previous generations, we can stay focused and inspired to an end.

Some people call this experience the dark night of the soul. It's the phoenix igniting itself and burning to ashes. The old self has to die for a new one to be reborn. Of *course* that feels uncomfortable!

But that's okay, because that unknown is the perfect place to create from—it's the place where possibilities exist. What could be better than that? Most of us have been conditioned to run from the unknown, so now we have to learn to become comfortable in the void or the unknown, instead of fearing it.

If you told me that you didn't like being in that void because it's so disorienting and that you can't see what lies ahead because you can't predict your future, I'd say that's actually great, because the best way to predict the future is to *create* it—not from the known, but *from the unknown.*

As the new self is born, we must be biologically different, too. New neuronal connections must be sprouted and sealed by the conscious choice to think and act in new ways every day. Those connections must be reinforced by our repeatedly creating the same experiences until they become a habit. New chemical states must become familiar to us from the emotions of enough new experiences. And new genes must be signaled to make new proteins to alter our state of being in new ways. And if, as we've seen, the expression of proteins is the expression of life and the expression of life is equal to the health of the body, then a new level of structural and functional health and life will follow. A renewed mind and a renewed body must emerge.

Now, when a new day dawns for us after the long night of darkness and the phoenix rises regenerated from its ashes, we have invented a new self. And the physical, biological expression of the new self is literally becoming someone else. That's true metamorphosis.

Overcoming Your Environment

Another way to look at the brain is to say that it's organized to reflect everything you know and have experienced in your life. Now you can understand that each time you've interacted with your external world, those events have shaped and molded who you are today. The complex networks of neurons that have fired and wired together throughout your days on Earth formed trillions and trillions of connections, because you learned and formed memories. And since every place where one neuron connects with another neuron is called a "memory," then your brain is a living record of the past. The vast experiences with every person and thing at different times and places in your external environment have been stamped into the recesses of your gray matter.

So by nature, most of us are thinking in the past, because we're using the same hardware and software programs from our past memories. And if we're living the same life every day by doing the same things at the same time, seeing the same people at the same place, and creating the same experiences from yesterday, then we're enslaved to having our outer worlds influence our inner worlds. It's our environment that is controlling how we think, act, and feel. We're victims of our personal realities, because our personal realities are creating our personalities—and it's become an unconscious process. Then that, of course, reaffirms the same thinking and feeling, and now there's a tango or a match between our outer worlds and our inner worlds, and they merge and become the same—and so do we.

If our environment is regulating how we're thinking and feeling every day, then in order to change, something about ourselves or our lives would have to be greater than the present circumstances in our environment.

Thinking and Feeling, and Feeling and Thinking

Just as thoughts are the language of the brain, feelings are the language of the body. And how you think and how you feel create a state of being. A *state of being* is when your mind and body are working together. So your present state of being is your genuine mind-body connection.

Every time you have a thought, in addition to making neurotransmitters, your brain also makes another chemical—a small protein called a *neuropeptide* that sends a message to your body. Your body then reacts by having a feeling. The brain notices that the body is having a feeling, so the brain generates another thought matched exactly to that feeling that will produce more of the same chemical messages that allow you to think the way you were just feeling.

So thinking creates feeling, and then feeling creates thinking that's equal to those feelings. It's a loop (one that, for most people, can go on for years). And because the brain acts on the body's feelings by generating the same thoughts that will produce the same emotions, it becomes clear that redundant thoughts hardwire your brain into a fixed pattern of neurocircuitry.

But what happens in the body? Because feelings are the modus operandi of the body, the emotions you continually feel based on your automatic thinking will condition the body to memorize those emotions that are equal to the unconscious hardwired mind and brain. That means that the conscious mind isn't really in charge. The body has subconsciously been programmed and conditioned, in a very real way, to become its own mind.

Eventually, when this loop of thinking and feeling and then feeling and thinking has been operating long enough, our bodies memorize the emotions that our brains have signaled our bodies to feel. The cycle becomes so established and ingrained that it creates a familiar state of being—one based on old information that keeps recycling. Those emotions, which are nothing more than the chemical records of past experiences, are driving our thoughts and are being played out over and over again. As long as this continues, we're living in the past. No wonder it's so hard for us to change our future!

If the neurons are firing the same way, they're triggering the release of the same chemical neurotransmitters and neuropeptides in the brain and body, and then these same chemicals begin to train the body to further remember those emotions by altering it physically once again. The cells and tissues receive these very specific chemical signals at specific receptor sites. Receptor sites are akin to docking stations for chemical messengers. The messengers fit perfectly in place, like a child's puzzle in which certain shapes, like a circle, a triangle, or a square, fit into specific openings.

Think of those chemical messengers, which are really molecules of emotion, as carrying bar codes that enable the cell receptors to read the messengers' electromagnetic energy. When the exact match is made, the receptor site prepares itself. The messenger docks, the cell receives the chemical messages, and then the cell creates or alters a protein. The new protein activates the cell's DNA within the nucleus. The DNA opens up and unwinds, the gene is read for that corresponding message from outside the cell, and the cell makes a new protein from its DNA (for example, a particular hormone) and releases it into the body.

Now the body is being trained by the mind. If this process continues for years and years because the same signals outside of the cell are coming from the same level of mind in the brain (because the person is thinking, acting, and feeling the same every day), then it makes sense that the same genes will be activated in the same ways, because the body is receiving the same data from the environment. There are no new thoughts ignited, no new choices made, no new behaviors demonstrated, no new experiences embraced, and no new feelings created. When the same genes are repeatedly activated by the same information from the brain, then the genes keep getting selected over and over again, and just like gears in a car, they start to wear out. The body makes proteins with weaker structures and lesser functions. We get sick and we age.

In time, one of two scenarios can occur. The intelligence of the cell membrane, which is consistently receiving the same information, can adapt to the body's needs and demands by modifying its receptor sites so that it can accommodate more of those chemicals. Basically, it creates more docking stations to satisfy the demand—just as supermarkets open up additional checkout lanes when the lines get too long. If business stays good (if those same chemicals keep coming), then you'll have to hire more employees and keep more lanes open. Now the body is equal to and has become the mind.

In the other scenario, the cell becomes too overwhelmed with the continual bombardment of feelings and emotions on a moment-to-moment basis to allow all the chemical messengers to dock. Because the same chemicals are more or less hanging around outside the cell's docking-station doors day in and day out, the cell gets used to those chemicals being there. So only when the brain produces a lot more heightened emotions does the cell become willing to open its doors. Once you increase the intensity of the emotion, the cell is stimulated enough so that the docking-station doors open and the cell turns on. (You'll hear more about the importance of emotion later—this is a key part of the placebo equation.)

In the first scenario, when the cell makes new receptor sites, the body will crave those specific chemicals when the brain doesn't make enough, and consequently, our feelings will determine our thinking—our bodies will control our minds. That's what I mean when I say *the body memorizes the emotion.* It has become biologically conditioned and altered to be a reflection of the mind.

In the second scenario, once the cell is overwhelmed by the bombardment and the receptors become desensitized, then just as a drug addict does, the body will require a greater chemical thrill to turn on the cell. In other words, in order for the body to become stimulated and get its fix, you'll need to get angrier, more worried, guiltier, or more confused than last time. So you might feel the need to start a bit of drama by yelling at your dog for no reason, just to give the body its drug of choice. Or maybe you can't help talking about how much you despise your mother-in-law just so the body has even more chemicals available with enough strength to arouse the cell. Or you start obsessing about some horrible imagined outcome just so the body can get a rush of adrenal hormones. When the body isn't getting its emotional chemical needs met, it will signal the brain to make more of those chemicals—the body is controlling the mind. That sounds very much like an addiction. So now when I use the term *emotional addiction,* you'll understand what I mean.

When feelings have become the means of thinking in this manner—or we can't think greater than how we feel—then we're *in the program.* Our thinking is how we feel, and our feelings are how we think. What we experience is like a merger of thoughts and feelings—we're *finking* or *theeling.* Since we're caught in this loop, then our bodies, as the unconscious mind, actually believe they're living in the same past experience 24 hours a day, 7 days a week, 365 days a year. Our minds and bodies are one, aligned to a destiny predetermined by our unconscious programs. So to change requires being greater than the body and all its emotional memories, addictions, and unconscious habituations—that is, to no longer be defined by the body as the mind.

The repetition of the cycle of thinking and feeling and then feeling and thinking is the conditioning process of the body that the conscious mind delivers. Once the body becomes the mind, that's called a "habit"—a habit is when your body *is* the mind. Ninety-five percent of who you are by the time you're 35 years old is a set of memorized behaviors, skills, emotional reactions, beliefs, perceptions, and attitudes that functions like a subconscious automatic computer program.

So 95 percent of who you are is a subconscious or even an unconscious state of being. And that means your conscious mind's 5 percent is working against the 95 percent of what you've memorized subconsciously. You can think positively all you want, but that 5 percent of your mind that's conscious will feel as if it's swimming upstream against the current of the other 95 percent of your mind—your unconscious body chemistry that has been remembering and memorizing whatever negativity you've been harboring for the past 35 years; that's mind and body working in opposition. No wonder you don't get very far when you try to fight that current!

That's why I called my last book *Breaking the Habit of Being Yourself,* because that's the greatest habit we have to break—thinking, feeling, and behaving in the same way that reinforces the unconscious programs that reflect our personalities and our personal realities. We can't create a new future while we're living in our past. It's simply impossible.

What It Takes to Be Your Own Placebo

Here's an example that will pull all of this together. I'm intentionally choosing a negative event, because these types of events tend to keep us limited, whereas more successful, empowering, and uplifting events usually help us create a better future. (That process will become clear soon.)

So let's say that you had a horrific past experience with public speaking that scarred you emotionally. (Feel free to substitute any emotionally scarring experience of your choice here.) Because of that experience, you now fear standing up to talk in front of a group of people. It makes you feel insecure, anxious, and anything but confident. Just thinking about looking out over a meeting room of even 20 people causes your throat to close up, your hands to go cold and clammy, your heart to race, your face and neck to flush, your stomach to twist, and your brain to freeze.

All of these reactions come under the jurisdiction of your autonomic nervous system, the nervous system that functions *subconsciously*—below your conscious control. Think of autonomic as *automatic*—it's the part of the nervous system that regulates digestion, hormones, circulation, body temperature, and so on without your having any conscious control over them. You can't decide to change your heart rate, alter blood flow to your extremities to cool them off, heat up your face and neck, change the metabolic secretions of your digestive enzymes, or shut off millions of nerve cells from firing on command. Try as you might to consciously change any one of these functions, you'll probably find that you won't be able to do it.

So when your body makes these autonomic physiological changes, it's because you have associated the *future thought* of standing in front of an audience delivering a presentation with the *past emotional memory* of your flawed public-speaking experience. And when that future thought, idea, or possibility is consistently associated with the past feelings of anxiety, failure, or embarrassment, in time the mind will condition the body to respond automatically to that feeling. This is how we continuously move into familiar states of being—our thoughts and feelings become one with the past because we can't think greater than how we feel.

Now let's take a closer look at how that works inside your brain. The particular event that was embossed and patterned neurologically as a past memory (remember, experience enriches brain circuitry) becomes physically wired in your brain just like a footprint. As a consequence, you can retrace your steps and recall the negative public-speaking experience as a thought. In order for you to remember it on command, the experience must have had a significant enough emotional charge as well. So you can also emotionally bring to mind all of the feelings related to your foiled attempt to be a successful orator, because it seems as though you were chemically altered from the experience.

I want to point out that feelings and emotions are the end products of past experiences. When you're caught up in an experience, your senses capture the event and then relay all of that vital information back to your brain through five different sensory pathways. Once all of that new data reaches the brain, mobs of nerve cells organize into fresh networks to reflect the novel external event. The moment those circuits jell, the brain makes a chemical to signal the body and alter its physiology. That chemical is called a feeling or an emotion. Thus, we can remember past events, because we can remind ourselves of how they felt.

So when your lecture went amiss, all of the information that your five senses were picking up in your external environment changed how you were feeling in your inner environment. The information that your senses were processing—the sight of the faces in the audience, the expansiveness of the room, and the bright lights above your head; the echoing sound of the microphone and the deafening silence after your first attempted joke; the immediate rise in the room's temperature the moment you started talking; the smell of your old cologne evaporating from your own perspiration—changed your inner state of being. And the moment you correlated this unique event in your outer world of the senses (the cause) with the changes going on in your inner world of thoughts and feelings (the effect), you created a memory. You associated a cause with an effect—and your own conditioning process began.

So after the self-inflicted torture of that day, which fortunately ended with no rotten fruits or vegetables being thrown in your direction, you drove home. On the ride, you kept recalling the event over and over again. And to varying degrees, every time you reminded yourself (which is exactly that: *re*producing the same level of *mind*) of your experience, you produced the same chemical changes in your brain and body. In a sense, you repeatedly reaffirmed the past and continued the conditioning process further.

Because your body acts as your unconscious mind, it didn't know the difference between the actual event in your life that created the emotional state and the emotions you created by thought alone when you remembered the event. Your body believed that it was living in the same experience over and over again, even though you were actually alone in the comfort of your car, and the body responded physiologically as though you were indeed reliving that experience in the present time. As you fired and wired the circuits in your brain that were derived from the thoughts related to that experience, you were physically maintaining the synaptic connections, and you were now creating even more lasting connections within those networks—you were creating a long-term memory.

Once you arrived home, you told your partner, your friends, and maybe even your mother about the events of that day. As you described the trauma in grievous detail, you were working yourself into an emotional froth. As you also relived the emotions of the incident, you chemically conditioned your body to the day's past event. You physiologically trained your body to become your personal history—subconsciously, unconsciously, and automatically.

In the days that followed, you were moody. People couldn't help noticing this, and every time someone asked you, "What's wrong?" you just couldn't resist. You opportunistically took them up on the invitation to become more addicted to the rush of chemistry from your past. The mood created from that experience was just one long emotional reaction lasting for days. When weeks of feeling the same way every time you remembered the event turned into months, even years, it became a prolonged emotional reaction. It's now not only a part of your temperament, character, and nature, but also your personality. It's who you are.

If someone else asks you to talk in front of a group again, you automatically cringe, shrink, and become anxious. Your external environment is controlling your internal environment, and you're unable to be greater than it. As you expect the thought that your future (a public-speaking opening) will be more like the feeling of your past (unlivable torment), just like magic, your body, as the mind, automatically and subconsciously responds. Try as you might, it seems as if your conscious mind can gain no control over it. In a matter of seconds, a host of conditioned responses from your brain and body's own pharmacy manifest—profuse sweating, dry mouth, weak knees, nausea, dizziness, shortness of breath, and uncontrollable fatigue—all from a single thought that changes your physiology. Sounds like the placebo to me.

If you could, you'd turn down the opportunity to do the talk, saying something like, "I am not a public speaker," "I am insecure in front of people," "I am a bad presenter," or "I am too afraid to talk in front of large audiences." Whenever you say, "I am . . ." (insert your own words here), what you are declaring is that your mind and body are aligned to a future or that your thoughts and feelings are one with your destiny. You're reinforcing a memorized state of being.

If, by chance, you were then asked why you chose to be defined by your past, as well as your own limitation, I'm certain that you'd tell a story equal to your past memories and emotions—reaffirming yourself to be that way. You'd probably even embellish it a little. From a biological level, what you'd really be proclaiming is that you were altered physically, chemically, and emotionally from that event several years ago and haven't changed much since then. You've chosen to be defined by your own limitation.

In this example, one could say that you're enslaved by your *body* (because it has now become the mind), you're trapped by the conditions in your *environment* (because the experience of people and things at a certain place and time are influencing how you think, act, and feel), and you're lost in *time* (because by living in the past and anticipating the same future, your mind and body are never in the present moment). So in order to change your current state of being, you'd have to be greater than these three elements: your body, your environment, and time.

So, then, thinking back to the beginning of this chapter, where you read that the placebo is created from three elements—conditioning, expectation, and meaning—you can now see that you are your own placebo. Why? Because all three elements come into play in the previous example.

First, like a talented animal trainer, you've *conditioned* your body into a subconscious *state of being* where mind and body are one—your thoughts and feelings have merged—and your body has now been programmed to automatically, biologically, and physiologically be the mind by *thought alone*. And anytime a stimulus from your external environment is presented to you—like an opportunity to teach—you've conditioned your body, just as Pavlov conditioned his dogs, to subconsciously and automatically respond to the mind of the past experience.

Since most of the placebo studies show that a single thought could activate the body's autonomic nervous system and produce significant physiological changes, then you're regulating your internal world by simply associating a thought with an emotion. All of your subconscious, autonomic systems are being reinforced neurochemically by the familiar feelings and bodily sensations related to your fear—and your biology perfectly reflects it.

Second, if your *expectation* is that your future will be like your past, then you are not only thinking in the past, but also selecting a known future based only *on* your past and emotionally embracing that event until your body (as the unconscious mind) believes that it's living in that future in the present moment. All of your attention is on a known, predictable reality, which causes you to limit any new choices, behaviors, experiences, and emotions. You're unconsciously forecasting your future by physiologically clinging to the past.

Third, if you assign *meaning* or conscious intention to an action, the result is amplified. What you're telling yourself on a daily basis (in this case, that you're not a good speaker and that public speaking elicits a panic reaction) is what has meaning to you. You've become susceptible to your own autosuggestions. And if your present knowledge is based on your own conclusions from past experiences, then without any new knowledge, you'll always keep creating the outcome that's equal to your mind. Change your meaning and change your intention, and just as the hotel maids in the study from the last chapter did, you change the results.

So whether you've been trying to effect positive change to create a new state of being or you've been running on autopilot and staying stuck in the same old state of being, the truth is that you've *always* been your own placebo.

Chapter Four

The Placebo Effect in the Body

On a crisp September day in 1981, a group of eight men in their 70s and 80s climbed into a few vans headed two hours north of Boston to a monastery in Peterborough, New Hampshire. The men were about to take part in a five-day retreat where they were asked to pretend that they were young again—or at least 22 years younger than they were at the time. The retreat was organized by a team of researchers, headed by Harvard psychologist Ellen Langer, Ph.D., who would take another group of eight elderly men to the same place the following week. The men in the second group, the control group, were asked to actively reminisce about being 22 years younger but not to pretend that they weren't their current age.

When the first group of men arrived at the monastery, they found themselves surrounded by all sorts of environmental cues to help them re-create an earlier age. They flipped through old issues of *Life* and the *Saturday Evening Post,* they watched movies and television shows popular in 1959, and they listened to recordings of Perry Como and Nat King Cole on the radio. They also talked about "current" events, such as Fidel Castro's rise to power in Cuba, Russian premier Nikita Khrushchev's visit to the United States, and even the feats of baseball star Mickey Mantle and boxing great Floyd Patterson. All of these elements were cleverly designed to help the men imagine that they were really 22 years younger.

After each five-day retreat, the researchers took several measurements and compared them to those they'd taken before the start of the study. The bodies of the men from both groups were physiologically younger, structurally as well as functionally, although those in the first study group (who pretended they were younger) improved significantly more than the control group, who'd merely reminisced.[1]

The researchers discovered improvements in height, weight, and gait. The men grew taller as their posture straightened, and their joints became more flexible and their fingers lengthened as their arthritis diminished. Their eyesight and hearing got better. Their grip strength improved. Their memory sharpened, and they scored better on tests of mental cognition (with the first group improving their score by 63 percent compared to 44 percent for the control group). The men literally *became younger* in those five days, right in front of the researchers' eyes.

Langer reported, "At the end of the study, I was playing football—touch, but still football—with these men, some of whom gave up their canes."[2]

How did that happen? Clearly, the men were able to turn on the circuits in their brains that reminded them of who they had been 22 years ago, and then their body chemistry somehow magically responded. They didn't just *feel* younger; they physically *became* younger, as evidenced by measurement after measurement. The change wasn't just *in their minds;* it was *in their bodies.*

But what happened in their bodies to produce such striking physical transformations? What could be responsible for all of these measurable changes in physical structure and function? The answer is their *genes*—which aren't as immutable as you might think. So let's take some time to look at what exactly genes are and how they operate.

Demystifying DNA

Imagine a ladder or a zipper twisted into a spiral, and you'll have a pretty good picture of what *deoxyribonucleic acid* (better known as *DNA*) looks like. Stored in the nucleus of every living cell in our bodies, DNA contains the raw information, or instructions, that makes us who and what we are (although as we'll soon see, those instructions are not an unchangeable blueprint that our cells must follow for our entire lives). Each half of that DNA zipper contains corresponding nucleic acids that, together, are called *base pairs,* numbering about three billion per cell. Groups of long sequences of these nucleic acids are called *genes.*

Genes are unique little structures. If you were to take the DNA out of the nucleus of just one cell in your body and stretch it out from end to end, it would be six feet long. If you took all the DNA out of your entire body and stretched it out from end to end, it would go to the sun and back 150 times.[3] But if you took all the DNA out of the almost seven billion people on the planet and scrunched it together, it would fit in a space as small as a grain of rice.

Our DNA uses the instructions imprinted within its individual sequences to produce proteins. The word *protein* is derived from the Greek *protas,* meaning "of primary importance." Proteins are the raw materials our bodies use to construct not only coherent three-dimensional structures (our physical anatomy), but also the intricate functions and complex interactions that make up our physiology. Our bodies are, in fact, protein-producing machines. Muscle cells make actin and myosin; skin cells make collagen and elastin; immune cells make antibodies; thyroid cells make thyroxine; certain eye cells make keratin; bone-marrow cells make hemoglobin; and pancreatic cells make enzymes like protease, lipase, and amylase.

All of the elements that these cells manufacture are proteins. Proteins control our immune system, digest our food, heal our wounds, catalyze chemical reactions, support the structural integrity of our bodies, provide elegant molecules to communicate between cells, and much more. In short, proteins are the expression of life (and the health of our bodies). Take a look at Figure 4.1 and review a simplistic understanding of genes.

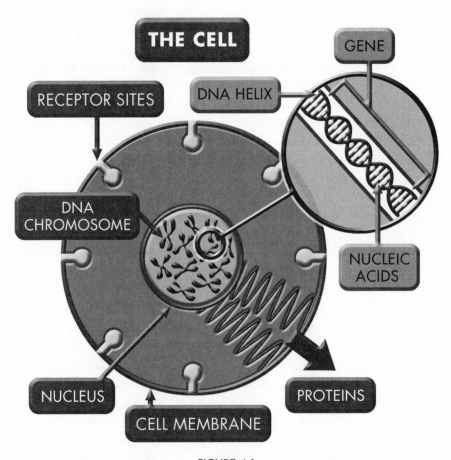

FIGURE 4.1

This is a very simplistic representation of a cell with DNA
housed within the cell nucleus. The genetic material once stretched out into
individual strands looks like a twisted zipper or ladder called a DNA helix. The rungs
of the ladder are the nucleic acids that are paired together, which act as codes to
make proteins. A different length and sequence of the DNA strand is called a gene.
A gene is expressed when it makes a protein. Various cells of the body
make different proteins for both structure and function.

For the 60 years since James Watson, Ph.D., and Francis Crick,
Ph.D., discovered the double helix of DNA, what Watson proclaimed in a 1970 issue of *Nature*[4] as the "central dogma," that

one's genes determine all, has held fast. As contradictory evidence popped up here and there, researchers tended to dismiss it as a mere anomaly within a complex system.[5]

Some 40-odd years later, the genetic-determinism concept still reigns in the general public's mind. Most people believe the common misconception that our genetic destiny is predetermined and that if we have inherited the genes for certain cancers, heart disease, diabetes, or any number of other conditions, we have no more control over that than we do our eye color or the shapes of our noses (notwithstanding contact lenses and plastic surgery).

The news media reinforce this by repeatedly suggesting that specific genes cause this condition or that disease. They've programmed us into believing that we're victims of our biology and that our genes have the ultimate power over our health, our well-being, and our personalities—and even that our genes dictate our human affairs, determine our interpersonal relationships, and forecast our future. But are we who we are, and do we do what we do, because we're born that way? This concept implies that genetic determinism is deeply entrenched in our culture and that there are genes for schizophrenia, genes for homosexuality, genes for leadership, and so on.

These are all dated beliefs built on yesterday's news. First of all, there's no gene for dyslexia or ADD or alcoholism, for example, so not every health condition or physical variation is associated with a gene. And fewer than 5 percent of people on the planet are born with some genetic condition—like type 1 diabetes, Down syndrome, or sickle-cell anemia. The other 95 percent of us who develop such a condition acquire it through lifestyle and behaviors.[6] The flip side is also true: Not everyone born with the genes associated with a condition (say, Alzheimer's or breast cancer) ends up getting that. It's not as though our genes are eggs that will ultimately hatch someday. That's just not the way it works. The real questions are whether or not any gene we might be carrying has been expressed yet and what we're doing that might signal that gene to turn either on or off.

A huge shift in the way we look at genes came when scientists finally mapped the human genome. In 1990, at the beginning of the project, the researchers expected they'd eventually discover that we have 140,000 different genes. They came up with that number because genes manufacture (and supervise the production of) proteins—and the human body manufactures 100,000 different proteins, plus 40,000 regulatory proteins needed to make other proteins. So the scientists mapping the human genome were anticipating that they'd find one gene per protein, but by the end of the project, in 2003, they were shocked to discover that, in fact, humans have only 23,688 genes.

From the perspective of Watson's central dogma, that's not only not enough genes to create our complex bodies and keep them running, but also not even enough genes to keep the brain functioning. So if it's not contained in the genes, where does all of the information come from that's required to create so many proteins and sustain life?

The Genius of Your Genes

The answer to that question led to a new idea: Genes must work together in systemic cooperation with one another so that many are expressed (turned on) or suppressed (turned off) at the same time within the cell; it's the combination of the genes that are turned on at any one time that produces all the different proteins we depend on for life. Picture a string of blinking Christmas-tree lights, with some flashing on together while others flash off. Or imagine a city skyline at night—with the lights in the individual rooms in each building flipping on or off as the night progresses.

This doesn't happen randomly, of course. The entire genome or DNA strand knows what every other part is doing in an interconnected fashion that's intimately choreographed. Every atom, molecule, cell, tissue, and system of the body functions at a level of energetic coherence equal to the intentional or unintentional (conscious or unconscious) state of being of the individual personality.[7] So it makes sense that genes can be activated (turned on) or deactivated (turned off) by the environment outside the cell, which sometimes means the environment *inside* the body (the emotional, biological, neurological, mental, energetic, and even spiritual states of being) and at other times means the environment *outside* the body (trauma, temperature, altitude, toxins, bacteria, viruses, food, alcohol, and so on).

Genes are, in fact, classified by the type of stimulus that turns them on and off. For example, experience-dependent or activity-dependent genes are activated when we're having novel experiences, learning new information, and healing. These genes generate protein synthesis and chemical messengers to instruct stem cells to morph into whatever types of cells are needed at the time for healing (more about stem cells and their role in healing will be coming up soon).

Behavioral-state-dependent genes are activated during periods of high emotional arousal, stress, or different levels of awareness (including dreaming). They provide a link between our thoughts and our bodies—that is, they're the mind-body connection. These genes offer an understanding of how we can influence our health in states of mind and body that promote well-being, physical resilience, and healing.

Scientists now believe it's even possible that our genetic expression fluctuates on a moment-to-moment basis. The research is revealing that our thoughts and feelings, as well as our activities— that is, our choices, behaviors, and experiences—have profound healing and regenerative effects on our bodies, as the men in the monastery study discovered. Thus your genes are being affected by your interactions with your family, friends, co-workers, and spiritual practices, as well as your sexual habits, your exercise levels, and the types of detergents you use. The latest research shows that approximately 90 percent of genes are engaged in cooperation with signals from the environment.[8] And if our *experience* is what activates a good number of our genes, then our nature is influenced by nurturing. So why not harness the power of these ideas so that we can do everything possible to maximize our health and minimize our dependence on the prescription pad?

As Ernest Rossi, Ph.D., writes in *The Psychobiology of Gene Expression,* "Our subjective states of mind, consciously motivated behavior, and our perception of free will can modulate gene expression to optimize health."[9] Individuals can alter their genes during a single generation, according to the latest scientific thinking. While the process of genetic evolution can take thousands of years, a gene can successfully alter its expression through a behavior change or a novel experience within minutes, and then it may be passed on to the next generation.

It helps to think of our genes less like stone tablets onto which our fate has been ceremoniously carved and more like storehouses of an enormous amount of coded information or even massive libraries of possibilities for the expression of proteins. But we can't just call the stored information up to make use of it the way a company might order something from its warehouse. It's as if we don't know what's in storage or how to access it, so we end up using just a small portion of what's truly available. In fact, we actually express only about 1.5 percent of our DNA, while the other 98.5 percent lies dormant in the body. (Scientists called it "junk DNA," but it's not really junk—they just don't know how all of that material is used yet, although they do know that at least some of it is responsible for making regulatory proteins.)

"In reality, genes contribute to our characteristics but do not determine them," writes Dawson Church, Ph.D., in his book *The Genie in Your Genes.* "The tools of our consciousness—including our beliefs, prayers, thoughts, intentions, and faith—often correlate much more strongly with our health, longevity, and happiness than our genes do."[10] The fact is, just as there's more to our bodies than a sack of bones and flesh, there's more to our genes than just stored information.

The Biology of Gene Expression

Now let's take a closer look at how genes are switched on. (Several different factors can be responsible, actually, but for the sake of our discussion here about the mind-body connection, we'll keep it simple.)

Once a chemical messenger (for example, a neuropeptide) from outside of the cell (from the environment) locks into the cell's docking station and passes through the cell membrane, it travels to the nucleus, where it encounters the DNA. The chemical messenger modifies or creates a new protein, and then the signal it was carrying is translated to information now inside the cell. Then it enters the nucleus of the cell through a small window, and depending on the content of the protein message, it looks for a specific chromosome (a single piece of coiled DNA that contains many genes) within the nucleus—just as you might look for a specific book on the shelf in the library.

Each of these strands is covered in a protein sleeve that acts as a filter between the information contained in the DNA strand and the rest of the intracellular environment of the nucleus. In order for the DNA code to be selected, the sleeve must be removed or unwrapped so that the DNA can be exposed (just as a book chosen from a library shelf then has to be opened before anyone can read it). The genetic code of DNA contains information waiting to be read and activated to create a particular protein. Until that information is exposed in the gene by unwrapping that protein sleeve, the DNA is latent. It's a potential storehouse of encoded information just waiting to be unlocked or opened. You could think of the DNA as a parts list of potentials that are awaiting instructions to construct proteins, which regulate and maintain every aspect of life.

Once the protein selects the chromosome, it opens it up by removing the outer covering around the DNA. Another protein then regulates and readies an entire gene sequence within the chromosome (think of it as a chapter within a book) to be read, all the way from the start of the sequence to its end. Once the gene is exposed and the protein sleeve is removed and read, another nucleic acid, called *ribonucleic acid* (RNA), is produced from the regulatory protein reading the gene.

Now the gene is expressed or activated. The RNA exits the nucleus of the cell to be assembled into a new protein from the code the RNA carries. It has gone from being a blueprint of latent potential to being an active expression. The protein the gene creates can now construct, assemble, interact with, restore, maintain, and influence many different aspects of life both within the cell and outside of it. Figure 4.2 gives an overview of the process.

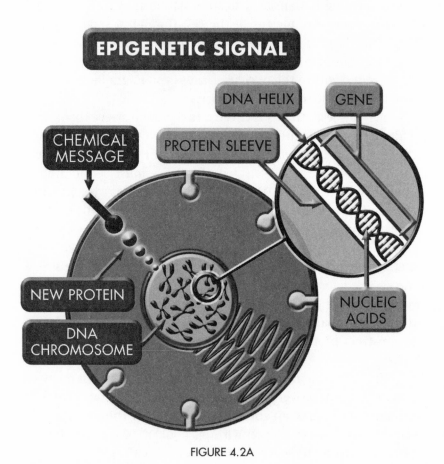

FIGURE 4.2A

Figure 4.2A shows the epigenetic signal entering the cell receptor site. Once the chemical messenger interacts at the level of the cell membrane, another signal in the form of a new protein is sent to the nucleus of the cell to select a gene sequence. The gene still has a protein covering protecting it from its outer environment, and that covering has to be removed in order for it to be read.

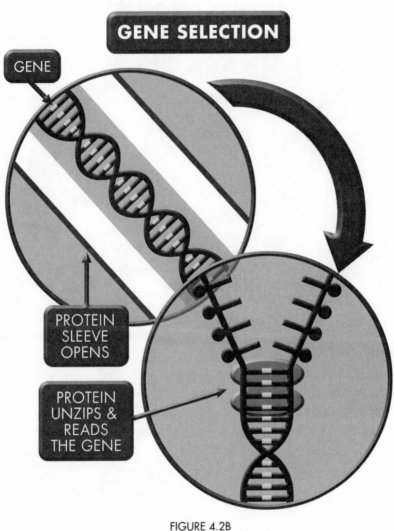

FIGURE 4.2B

Figure 4.2B illustrates how the protein sleeve around the gene sequence of the DNA is opened so that another protein, called a regulatory protein, can unzip and read the gene at a precise location.

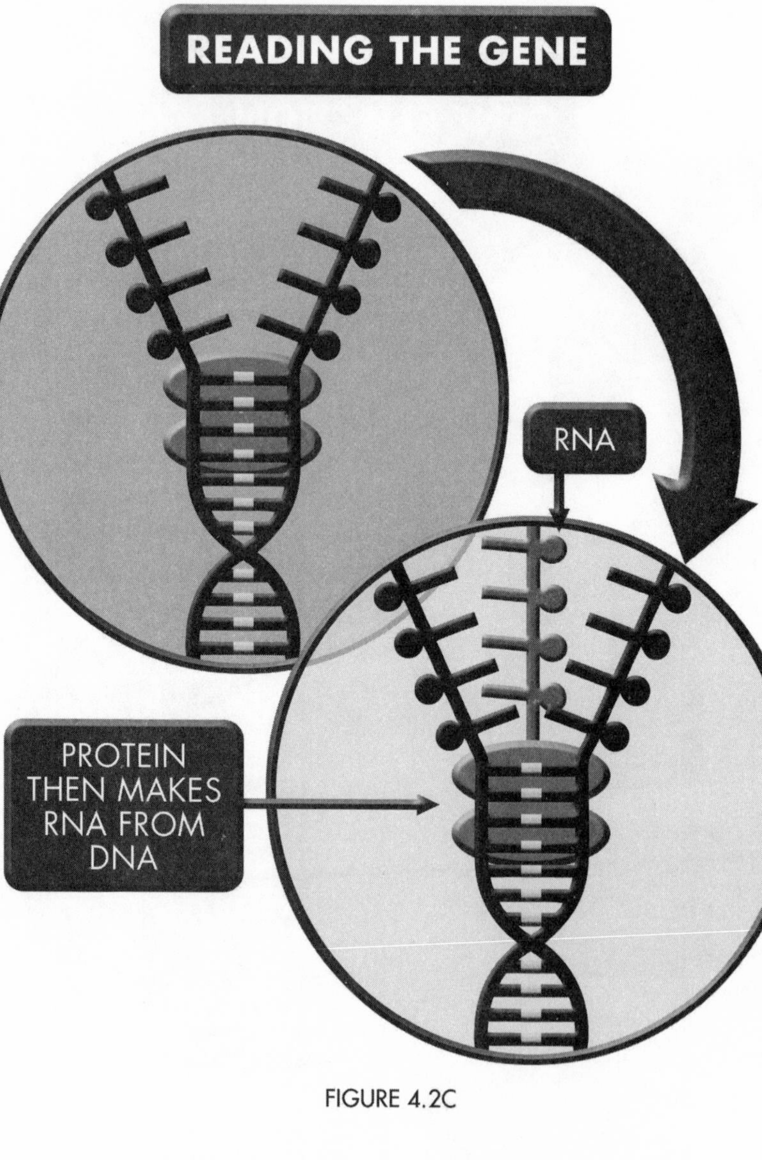

FIGURE 4.2C

Figure 4.2C demonstrates how the regulatory protein creates another molecule, called RNA, which organizes the translation and the transcription of the genetically coded material into a protein.

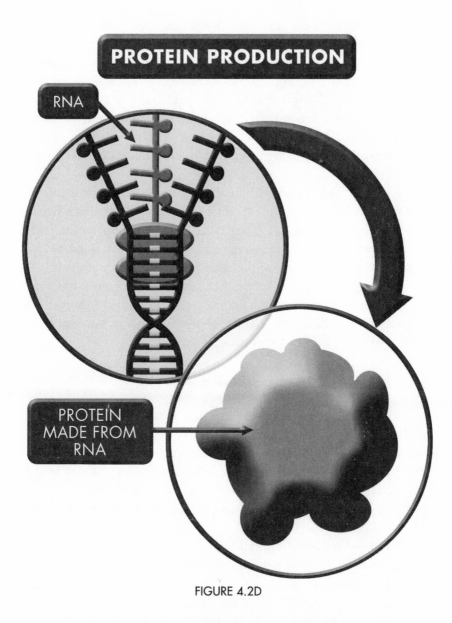

FIGURE 4.2D

Figure 4.2D shows protein production. RNA assembles a new
protein from the individual building blocks of proteins called amino acids.

Just as an architect gets all of the information that's necessary to build a structure from a blueprint, the body gets all the instructions it needs to create complex molecules that keep us alive and operating from the chromosomes of our DNA. But before the architect reads the blueprint, it has to be pulled out of its cardboard tube and unrolled. Until then, it's just latent information waiting to be read. The cell is the same way: The gene is inert until its protein sheathing is removed and the cell chooses to read the gene sequence.

Scientists used to believe all the body needed was the information itself (the blueprint) to start construction, so that's what most of them focused on. They paid little attention to the fact that the whole cascade of events starts with *the signal outside of the cell,* which is, in fact, responsible for what genes within its library the cell chooses to read. That signal, as we now know, includes thoughts, choices, behaviors, experiences, and feelings. So it makes sense that if you can change these elements, you can also determine your genetic expression.

Epigenetics: How We Mere Mortals Get to Play God

If our genes don't seal our fate and if they actually contain an enormous library of possibilities just waiting to be taken off the shelf and read, then what gives us access to those potentials— potentials that could have a huge effect on our health and well-being? The men in the monastery study surely gained such access, but how did they do it? The answer lies in a relatively new field of study called epigenetics.

The word *epigenetics* literally means "above the gene." It refers to the control of genes not from within the DNA itself but from messages coming from outside the cell—in other words, from the environment. These signals cause a methyl group (one carbon atom attached to three hydrogen atoms) to attach to a specific spot on a gene, and this process (called *DNA methylation*) is one of the main processes that turns the gene off or on. (Two other processes, *covalent histone modification* and *noncoding RNA,* also turn genes on and off, but the details of those processes are more than we need for this discussion.)

Epigenetics teaches that we, indeed, are *not* doomed by our genes and that a change in human consciousness can produce physical changes, both in structure and function, in the human body. We can modify our genetic destiny by turning on the genes we want and turning off the ones we don't want through working with the various factors in the environment that program our genes. Some of those signals come from within the body, such as feelings and thoughts, while others come from the body's response to the external environment, such as pollution or sunlight.

Epigenetics studies all of these external signals that tell the cell what to do and when to do it, looking at both the sources that activate, or turn on, gene expression (upregulating) and those that suppress, or turn off, gene expression (downregulating)—as well as the dynamics of energy that adjust the process of cellular function on a moment-to-moment basis. Epigenetics suggests that even though our DNA code never changes, thousands of combinations, sequences, and patterned variations in a single gene are possible (just as thousands of combinations, sequences, and patterns of neural networks are possible in the brain).

Looking at the entire human genome, so many millions of possible epigenetic variations exist that scientists find their heads spinning just thinking about it. The Human Epigenome Project, begun in 2003 as the Human Genome Project drew to a close, is under way in Europe,[11] and some researchers have said that when it's completed, it "will make the Human Genome Project look like homework that 15th century kids did with an abacus."[12] Going back to the blueprint model, we can change the color of what we build, the type of materials we use, the scale of the construction, and even the positioning of the structure—making an almost infinite number of variations—all without ever changing the actual blueprint.

A great example of epigenetics at work involves identical twins, who share exactly the same DNA. If we embrace the idea of genetic predeterminism—the idea that all diseases are genetic—then identical twins should have exactly the same gene expression. However, they don't always manifest the same illnesses in the same way, and sometimes one will manifest a genetic disease that the other doesn't manifest at all. Twins can have the same genes, but different outcomes.

A Spanish study illustrates this perfectly. Researchers at the Cancer Epigenetics Laboratory at the Spanish National Cancer Center in Madrid studied 40 pairs of identical twins, ranging in age from 3 to 74. They found that younger twins who had similar lifestyles and spent more years together had similar epigenetic patterns, while older twins, in particular those with dissimilar lifestyles who spent fewer years together, had very different epigenetic patterns.[13] For example, researchers found *four times as many* differentially expressed genes between one pair of 50-year-old twins as they did between a pair of 3-year-old twins.

The twins were born with exactly the same DNA, but those with different lifestyles (and different lives) ended up expressing their genes very differently—especially as time went on. To use another analogy, the older twin pairs were like exact copies of the same model of a computer. The computers came loaded with some similar starter software, but as time went on, each downloaded very different additional software programs. The computer (the DNA) stays the same, but depending on what software a person has downloaded (the epigenetic variations), what the computer does and the way it operates can be quite different. So when we think our thoughts and feel our feelings, our bodies respond in a complex formula of biological shifts and alterations, and each experience pushes the buttons of real genetic changes within our cells.

The speed of these changes can be truly remarkable. In *just three months,* a group of 31 men with low-risk prostate cancer were able to upregulate 48 genes (mostly dealing with tumor suppression) and downregulate 453 genes (mostly dealing with tumor promotion) by following an intensive nutrition and lifestyle regimen.[14] The men, enrolled in a study by Dean Ornish, M.D., at the University of California at San Francisco, lost weight and reduced their abdominal obesity, blood pressure, and lipid profile over the course of the study. Ornish noted, "It is not really so much about risk-factor reduction or preventing something bad from happening. These changes can occur so quickly you don't have to wait years to see the benefits."[15]

Even more impressive are the number of epigenetic changes made over a six-month period in a Swedish study of 23 slightly overweight, healthy men who went from being relatively sedentary to attending spinning and aerobics classes an average of just under twice per week. Researchers at Lund University discovered that the men had epigenetically altered 7,000 genes—almost 30 percent of all the genes in the entire human genome![16]

These epigenetic variations may even be inherited by our children and then passed on to our grandchildren.[17] The first researcher to show this was Michael Skinner, Ph.D., who was director of the Center for Reproductive Biology at Washington State University. In 2005, Skinner led a study that exposed pregnant rats to pesticides.[18] The male pups of the exposed mother rats had higher rates of infertility and decreased sperm production, with epigenetic changes in two genes. These changes were also present in about 90 percent of the males in each of the four generations that followed, even though none of these other rats were exposed to any pesticides.

Our experiences from our external environment are only part of the story, however. As we've been learning, how we assign meaning to those experiences includes a barrage of physical, mental, emotional, and chemical responses that also activate genes. How we perceive and interpret the data we receive from our senses as factual information—whether that information is actually true or not—and the meaning we give it produce significant biological changes on a genetic level. Thus, our genes interact with our conscious awareness in complex relationships. We could say that *meaning* is continually affecting the neural structures that influence who we are on the microscopic level, which then influences who we are on the macroscopic level.

The study of epigenetics also raises the question: What if nothing is changing in your external environment? What if you do the same things with the same people at exactly the same time every day—things leading to the same experiences that produce the same emotions that signal the same genes in the same way?

We could say that as long as you perceive your life through the lens of the past and react to the conditions with the same neural architecture and from the same level of mind, you're headed toward a very specific, predetermined genetic destiny. In addition, what you believe about yourself, your life, and the choices you make as a result of those beliefs also keeps sending the same messages to the same genes.

Only when the cell is ignited in a new way, by new information, can it create thousands of variations of the same gene to rewrite a new expression of proteins—which changes your body. You may not be able to control all the elements in your outer world, but you can manage many aspects of your inner world. Your beliefs, your perceptions, and how you interact with your external environment have an influence on your internal environment, which is still the external environment of the cell. This means that *you*—not your preprogrammed biology—hold the keys to your genetic destiny. It's just a matter of finding the right key that fits into the right lock to unleash your potential. So why not see your genes for what they really are? Providers of possibility, resources of unlimited potential, a code system of personal commands—in truth, they're nothing short of tools for *transformation,* which literally means "changing form."

Stress Keeps Us Living in Survival Mode

Stress is one of the biggest causes of epigenetic change, because it knocks your body out of balance. It comes in three forms: physical stress (trauma), chemical stress (toxins), and emotional stress (fear, worry, being overwhelmed, and so on). Each type can set off more than 1,400 chemical reactions and produce more than 30 hormones and neurotransmitters. When that chemical cascade of stress hormones is triggered, your mind influences your body through the autonomic nervous system and you experience the ultimate mind-body connection.

Ironically, feeling stressed was designed to be adaptive. All organisms in nature, including humans, are programmed to deal with short-term stress so that they'll have the resources they need for emergency situations. When you sense a threat in your external environment, the fight-or-flight response in your sympathetic nervous system (a subsystem of your autonomic nervous system) is activated, and your heart rate and blood pressure increase, your muscles tense, and hormones like adrenaline and cortisol shoot through your body to prepare you to either flee or face your foe in battle.

If you're being chased by a pack of wild, hungry wolves or a party of violent warriors, and you outrun them, your body will return to homeostasis (its normal, balanced state) soon after you reach safety. That's the way our bodies were designed to operate when we're living in survival mode. The body is out of balance—but only for a short period of time, until the danger passes. At least, that's how it was meant to be.

The same thing happens in our modern world, although the setting is usually a little different. If someone cuts you off when you're driving on the highway, you might be momentarily frightened, but once you realize that you're okay and you let go of the fear of having an accident, your body returns to normal—unless that was only one of countless stressful situations you stumbled into that day.

If you're like most people, a string of nerve-racking incidents keeps you in fight-or-flight response—and out of homeostasis—a large part of the time. Maybe the car cutting you off is the only actual life-threatening situation you encounter all day, but the traffic on the way to work, the pressure of preparing for a big presentation, the argument you had with your spouse, the credit-card bill that came in the mail, the crashing of your computer hard drive, and the new gray hair you noticed in the mirror keep the stress hormones circulating in your body on a near-constant basis.

Between remembering stressful experiences from the past and anticipating stressful situations coming up in your future, all these repetitive short-term stresses blur together into long-term stress. Welcome to the 21st-century version of living in survival mode.

In fight-or-flight mode, life-sustaining energy is mobilized so that the body can either run or fight. But when there isn't a return to homeostasis (because you keep perceiving a threat), vital energy is lost in the system. You have less energy in your internal environment for cell growth and repair, long-term building projects on a cellular level, and healing when that energy is being channeled elsewhere. The cells shut down, they no longer communicate with one another, and they become "selfish." It's not time for routine maintenance (let alone for making improvements); it's time for defense. It's every cell for itself, so the collective community of cells working together becomes fractured. The immune and endocrine systems (among others) become weakened as genes in those related cells are compromised when informational signals from outside the cells are turned off.

It's like living in a country where 98 percent of the resources go toward defense, and nothing is left for schools, libraries, road building and repair, communication systems, growing of food, and so on. Roads develop potholes that aren't fixed. Schools suffer budget cuts, so students wind up learning less. Social welfare programs that took care of the poor and the elderly have to close down. And there's not enough food to feed the masses.

Not surprisingly, then, long-term stress has been linked to anxiety, depression, digestive problems, memory loss, insomnia, hypertension, heart disease, strokes, cancer, ulcers, rheumatoid arthritis, colds, flu, aging acceleration, allergies, body pain, chronic fatigue, infertility, impotence, asthma, hormonal issues, skin rashes, hair loss, muscle spasms, and diabetes, to name just a few conditions (all of which, by the way, are the result of epigenetic changes). No organism in nature is designed to withstand the effects of long-term stress.

Several studies give strong evidence to show how epigenetic instructions for healing shut down during emergencies. For example, researchers at the Ohio State University Medical Center found that more than 170 genes were affected by stress, with 100 of them shutting off completely (including many that directly make proteins to facilitate the proper type of wound healing). The researchers reported that wounds of stressed patients took 40 percent longer to heal and that "stress tilted the genomic balance towards genes [that were] encoding proteins responsible for cell-cycle arrest, death, and inflammation."[19] Another study examining the genes of 100 citizens of Detroit zeroed in on 23 subjects who were suffering from post-traumatic stress disorder.[20] These people had six to seven times more epigenetic variations, most of which involved compromising the immune system.

Researchers at the UCLA AIDS Institute found that not only did HIV spread faster in patients who were the most stressed, but also the higher a patient's stress level, the less he or she responded to the antiretroviral drugs. The drugs worked four times better for those patients who were relatively calm, compared to those whose blood pressure, skin moisture, and resting heart rate indicated they were feeling the most stress.[21] Based on these findings, researchers concluded that the nervous system has a direct effect on viral replication.

Although the fight-or-flight response was originally highly adaptive (because it kept early humans alive), it's now clear that the longer that survival system is constantly activated, the longer your body shunts its resources for creating optimal health, so the system becomes maladaptive.

The Legacy of Negative Emotions

As we keep making stress hormones, we create a host of highly addictive negative emotions, including anger, hostility, aggression, competition, hatred, frustration, fear, anxiety, jealousy, insecurity, guilt, shame, sadness, depression, hopelessness, and powerlessness, just to name a few. When we focus on thoughts about bitter past memories or imagined dreadful futures to the exclusion of everything else, we prevent the body from regaining homeostasis. In truth, we're capable of turning on the stress response by thought alone. If we turn it on and then can't turn it off, we're surely headed for some type of illness or disease—be it a cold or cancer—as more and more genes get downregulated in a domino effect, until we eventually arrive at our genetic destiny.

For example, if we can anticipate a possible known future scenario and then focus on that thought to the exclusion of everything else even for just one moment, the body will physiologically begin to change in order to prepare itself for that future event. The body is now living in that known future in the present moment. As a consequence of this phenomenon, the conditioning process begins to activate the autonomic nervous system, and it creates the corresponding stress chemicals *automatically.* This is how the mind-body connection can work against us.

When this happens, we are demonstrating the three elements of the placebo effect in perfect symmetry. First, we start to condition the body to the rush of adrenal chemistry in order to feel a boost of energy. If we can associate a person, thing, or experience at a particular time and place in our outer reality with that rush of chemistry within us, we'll begin to condition the body to turn on the response just by thinking about that stimulus. In time, we'll be able to simply condition the body to be put in mind of that emotionally aroused state by thought alone—the thought of a *potential experience* with some*one* and some*thing* at some *time* and some *place.* If we can expect the future outcome based on the past experience, then the expectation of the event, when we emotionally embrace it, will change the body's physiology. And if we assign meaning to the behaviors and experiences, we're putting our conscious intention behind the outcome so that our bodies will change or not change equal to what we think we know about our reality and ourselves.

But whether or not you believe that the stress in your life is justified or valid, the effect of that stress on the body is never advantageous or health enhancing. Your body believes that it is being chased by a lion, is standing perched on a perilous cliff, or is fighting off a pack of angry cannibals. Here are a few examples from scientific studies demonstrating the effects of stress on the body.

Researchers at the Ohio State University College of Medicine confirmed that stressful emotions trigger hormonal and genetic responses, by measuring how stress affects the speed of healing minor skin wounds—a significant marker of gene activation.[22] A group of 42 married couples were given small suction blisters, and then their level of three proteins commonly expressed in wound healing was monitored for a total of three weeks. The couples were asked to have a neutral discussion for half an hour as a baseline and then, later, to talk about a previous marital argument.

The researchers found that after the couples discussed a previous disagreement, their level of healing-linked proteins was mildly suppressed (showing that the genes were downregulated). The suppression rose to an even greater degree—about 40 percent—in couples whose discussion ballooned into a significant conflict, peppered with sarcastic comments, criticism, and put-downs.

Research also supports the reverse effect—that reducing stress with positive emotions triggers epigenetic changes that improve health. Two key studies by researchers at the Benson-Henry Institute for Mind Body Medicine at Massachusetts General Hospital in Boston looked at the effects of meditation, which is known for eliciting peaceful and even blissful states, on gene expression. In the first study, conducted in 2008, 20 volunteers received eight weeks of training in various mind-body practices (including several types of meditation, yoga, and repetitive prayer) known to induce the relaxation response, a physiological state of deep rest (discussed in Chapter 2).[23] The researchers also followed 19 long-term daily practitioners of the same techniques.

At the end of the study period, the novices showed a change in 1,561 genes (874 upregulated for health and 687 downregulated for stress), as well as reduced blood pressure and reduced heart and respiration rates, while the experienced practitioners expressed 2,209 new genes. Most of the genetic changes involved improving the body's response to chronic psychological stress.

The second study, conducted in 2013, found that eliciting the relaxation response produces changes in gene expression after just *one session* of meditation among both novices and experienced practitioners alike (with the long-term practitioners, not surprisingly, deriving more benefit).[24] Genes that were upregulated included those involved in immune function, energy metabolism, and insulin secretion, while genes that were downregulated included those linked to inflammation and stress.

Studies like these underscore just how quickly it's possible to change your own genes. That's why the placebo response can produce physical changes in a matter of moments. In my workshops around the world, my colleagues and I have witnessed significant and immediate changes in our participants' health after only one session of meditation. They transformed themselves and activated new genes in new ways by thought alone. (You'll be introduced to some of them soon.)

When we're living in survival mode, with our stress response turned on all the time, we can really focus on only three things: our physical bodies (*Am I okay?*), the environment (*Where is it safe?*), and time (*How long will this threat be hanging over me?*). Constantly focusing on these three things makes us less spiritual, less aware, and less mindful, because it trains us to become more self-absorbed and more focused on our bodies, as well as on other material things (such as what we own, where we live, how much money we have, and so on), in addition to all of the problems we experience in our external world. This focus also trains us to obsess about time—to constantly brace ourselves for the worst-case future scenarios based on our traumatic past experiences—because there's never enough time and everything always takes too much time.

So we could say that just as stress hormones cause the cells of the body to become selfish to ensure that we survive, they endorse our ego to become more selfish, too—and we become materialists defining reality with our senses. We end up feeling separate from any new possibilities, because when we never leave that state of chronic emergency, that me-first mentality that pervades all our thinking strengthens and endures, leading us to become self-indulgent, self-serving, and self-important. Ultimately, the self becomes defined as a body living in the environment and in time.

As you have just read and now more fully understand, the reality is that you do indeed have some degree of control over your own genetic engineering—by way of your thoughts, choices, behaviors, experiences, and emotions. Like Dorothy in *The Wizard of Oz*, who had the power she sought all along but didn't know it, you also possess a power that you may not have previously realized was yours—the keys that can set you free of being chained to the limitations of your own genetic expression.

Chapter Five

How Thoughts Change the Brain and the Body

Now you can understand that whether it's joyful or stressful, with every thought you think, every emotion you feel, and every event you experience, you're acting as an epigenetic engineer of your own cells. You control your destiny. So this raises another question: If your environment changes and you then program new genes in new ways, is it possible—based on your perceptions and beliefs—to program the gene *ahead of the actual environment?* Feelings and emotions are normally the end products of experiences, but can you combine a clear intention with an emotion that begins to give the body a sampling of the future experience before it's been made manifest?

When you're truly focused on an intention for some future outcome, if you can make inner thought more real than the outer environment during the process, the brain won't know the difference between the two. Then your body, as the unconscious mind, will begin to experience the new future event in the present moment. You'll signal new genes, in new ways, to prepare for this imagined future event.

If you continue to mentally practice enough times this new series of choices, behaviors, and experiences that you desire, reproducing the same new level of mind over and over again, then your brain will begin to physically change—installing new neurological circuitry to begin to think from that new level of mind—to look as if the experience has already happened. You'll be producing epigenetic variations that lead to real structural and functional changes in the body by thought alone—just as do those who respond to a placebo. Then your brain and body will no longer be living in the same past; they'll be living in the new future that you created in your mind.

This is possible through *mental rehearsal.* This technique is basically closing your eyes and repeatedly imagining performing an action, and mentally reviewing the future you want, all the while reminding yourself of who you no longer want to be (the old self) and who you *do* want to be. This process involves thinking about your future actions, mentally planning your choices, and focusing your mind on a new experience.

Let's go over this sequence in greater detail so we can more thoroughly understand exactly what's happening in mental rehearsal and how it works. As you mentally rehearse a destiny or dream about a new outcome, you imagine it over and over again until it becomes familiar to you. The more knowledge and experience you have wired in your brain about the new reality you desire, the more resources you have to create a better model of it in your mental picturing, and so the greater your intention and expectation are (as with the hotel maids). You are "reminding" yourself of what your life will look like and feel like once you get what you want. Now you are putting an intention behind your attention.

Then you consciously marry your thoughts and intentions with a heightened state of emotion, such as joy or gratitude. (More on heightened states of emotion is coming up.) Once you can embrace that new emotion and you get more excited, you're bathing your body in the neurochemistry that would be present if that future event were actually happening. It could be suggested that you're giving your body a taste of the future experience. Your brain and body don't know the difference between having an actual experience in your life and just thinking about the experience—neurochemically, it's the same. So your brain and body begin to believe they're actually living in the new experience in the present moment.

By keeping your focus on this future event and not letting any other thoughts distract you, in a matter of moments, you turn down the volume on the neural circuits connected to the old self, which begins to turn off the old genes, and you fire and wire new neural circuits, which initiates the right signals to activate new genes in new ways. Thanks to the neuroplasticity discussed previously, the circuits in your brain begin to reorganize themselves to reflect what you're mentally rehearsing. And as you keep coupling your new thoughts and mental images with that strong, positive emotion, then your mind and body are working together—and you're now in a new state of being.

At this point, your brain and body are no longer a record of the past; they are a map to the future—a future that you've created in your mind. Your thoughts have become your experience, and you just became the placebo.

A Few Mental-Rehearsal Success Stories

Maybe you heard that story a while back about a major who was imprisoned in a concentration camp in Vietnam who mentally practiced playing golf on a particular course every day to keep himself sane—only to shoot a perfect score when he was finally released and returned home. Or perhaps you've heard the account of Soviet human-rights activist Anatoly Shcharansky, later known as Natan Sharansky, who spent more than nine years imprisoned in the Soviet Union after being falsely accused of spying for the United States in the 1970s. Sharansky—who spent 400 days of his prison term in a small, darkened, freezing-cold punishment cell—played a game of mental chess against himself every day, keeping track of the board coordinates and the positions of each piece in his mind. This enabled Sharansky to maintain many of his neural maps (which normally require external stimulation to stay intact). After his release, he immigrated to Israel and eventually became an Israeli cabinet minister. When world chess champion Gary Kasparov came to Israel in 1996 to play a simultaneous chess match against 25 Israelis, Sharansky beat him.[1]

Aaron Rodgers, quarterback for the Green Bay Packers, also imagines moves in his head that he often later executes with precision on the field. Leading up to the Packers' 2011 Super Bowl win, in a play-off game that the sixth-seeded Packers won 48 to 21 against the top-seeded Atlanta Falcons, Rodgers completed 31 of 36 passes (86.1 percent), the fifth-best postseason completion percentage of all time.

"In the sixth grade, a coach taught us about the importance of visualization," Rodgers told a sports reporter for *USA Today*.[2] "When I'm in a meeting, watching film, or [lying] in bed before I go to sleep, I always visualize making those plays. A lot of those plays I made in the game, I had thought about. As I [lay] on the couch, I visualized making them." Rodgers was also able to successfully spin out of three potential sacks in that game, later noting about those plays, "I visualized the majority before I made them."

Countless other professional athletes have also used mental rehearsal to stunning effect, including golfer Tiger Woods; basketball stars Michael Jordan, Larry Bird, and Jerry West; and baseball pitcher Roy Halladay. Champion golfer Jack Nicklaus wrote in his book *Golf My Way:*

> I never hit a shot, even in practice, without having a very sharp, in-focus picture of it in my head. It's like a color movie. First, I "see" the ball where I want it to finish, nice and white and sitting up high on the bright-green grass. Then the scene quickly changes, and I "see" the ball going there: its path, trajectory, and shape, even its behavior on landing. Then there's sort of a fade-out, and the next scene shows me making the kind of swing that will turn the previous images into reality. Only at the end of this short, private, Hollywood spectacular do I select a club and step up to the ball.[3]

As we can see from these examples alone (and there are many, many more just like them), plenty of evidence shows that mental rehearsal is extremely effective for learning a physical skill with minimal physical practice.

I can't resist adding one more example, this time from Jim Carrey, who tells an amazing story about what he did when he first came to Los Angeles in the late 1980s as a struggling actor looking for work. He'd written a paragraph-long affirmation on a piece of paper about meeting the right type of people, getting the right types of acting jobs, working on the right movie with the right casting, and being successful and contributing something worthwhile and making a difference in the world.

He would go up to Mulholland Drive in the Hollywood Hills every night and lean back in his convertible and look up at the sky. He'd say that paragraph to himself, committing it to memory, as he imagined that what he was describing was actually happening. And he wouldn't drive back down from that Hollywood overlook until he felt as though he was the person he'd been imagining, until it felt real for him. He even wrote a check to himself for $10 million, penning "for acting services rendered" on it and dating it "Thanksgiving 1995." He carried the check in his wallet for years.

Finally, in 1994, three movies were released that made Carrey a star. First, *Ace Ventura: Pet Detective* came out in February, followed by *The Mask* in July. And for his role in the third movie, *Dumb and Dumber,* released in December, Carrey received a check for exactly $10 million. He created *exactly* what he had envisioned for himself.

What all of these individuals have in common is that they eliminated the external environment, got beyond their bodies, and transcended time so that they could make significant neurological changes within. When they presented themselves to the world, they were able to get their minds and bodies to work together, and they created in the material world what they'd first conceived in the mental realm.

Scientific studies back this up. To start with, many experiments on mental rehearsal prove that when you concentrate on a particular region of the body, your thoughts stimulate the region in the brain that governs that part[4]—and if you keep doing it, physical changes in the brain's sensory area will then follow. It makes sense, because if you keep placing your awareness in the same place, you are firing and wiring the same networks of neurons. And as a result, you'll build stronger brain maps in that area.

In a Harvard study, research subjects who'd never before played the piano mentally practiced a simple, five-finger piano exercise for two hours a day for five days—and made the same brain changes as the subjects who physically practiced the same activities, but without ever lifting a finger.[5] The region of their brains that controls finger movements increased dramatically, allowing their brains to look as though the experience they'd imagined had actually happened. They installed the neurological hardware (circuits) and software (programs), thereby creating new brain maps by thought alone.

In another study of 30 people over a 12-week period, some regularly exercised their little fingers, while others just imagined doing the same thing. While the group that actually did the physical exercises increased the strength of their little fingers by 53 percent, the group that *only imagined* doing the same thing also increased the strength of their little fingers—by 35 percent.[6] Their bodies had changed to look as if they were having the physical experience in external reality over and over again—but they only experienced it in their minds. Their minds changed their bodies.

In a similar experiment, ten volunteers each imagined flexing one of their biceps as hard as they could five times a week. Researchers recorded the subjects' electrical brain activity during the sessions and measured their muscle strength every two weeks. Those who only imagined flexing increased their bicep muscle strength by 13.5 percent in just a few weeks, and they maintained the gain for three months after the training stopped.[7] Their bodies responded to a new mind.

A final example is a French study that compared subjects who either lifted or imagined lifting dumbbells of different weights. Those who imagined lifting heavier weights activated their muscles more than did those who imagined lifting lighter weights.[8] In all three of these studies on mental rehearsal, the subjects were able to measurably increase their body strength using *only their thoughts*.

You may well wonder if studies exist showing what happens when we follow the *entire* sequence—when we not only imagine what we want to create, but also connect with strong positive emotion. As a matter of fact, they do. And you'll be reading about them soon enough.

Signaling New Genes in the Body with a New Mind

To understand more fully why mental rehearsal works, we need to look at just a few points of brain anatomy for a moment and then briefly add some neurochemistry. Let's start by explaining that your *frontal lobe,* located right behind your forehead, is your creative center. This is the part of the brain that learns new things, dreams of new possibilities, makes conscious decisions, sets your intentions, and so on. It's the CEO, so to speak, and even more to the point, the frontal lobe also allows you to observe who you are and evaluate what you're doing and how you're feeling. It's the home of your conscience. This is important, because once you become more aware of your thoughts, ultimately you can better direct them.

As you practice mental rehearsal and truly concentrate and focus on the outcome you want, the frontal lobe is your ally, because it also lowers the volume on the outside world so that you're not as distracted by information coming in from your five senses. Brain scans show that in a highly focused state, such as mental rehearsal, the perception of time and space diminishes.[9] This happens because your frontal lobe dials down the input from your sensory centers (which allow you to "feel" your body in space), your motor centers (responsible for your physical movement), and your association centers (where your thoughts about your identity and who you are live), as well as your parietal-lobe circuits (where you process time). Because you can get beyond your environment, beyond your body, and even beyond time, you're better able to make the thought you're thinking more real than anything else.

The moment you imagine a new future for yourself, think about a new possibility, and start to ask specific questions—such as *What would it be like to live without this pain and limitation?*—your frontal lobe snaps to attention. In a matter of seconds, it creates both an *intention* to be healthy (so you can get clear on what you want to create and what you no longer wish to experience) and a *mental picture* of being healthy so that you can imagine what it will be like.

As the CEO, the frontal lobe has connections to all the other parts of the brain. So it starts selecting networks of neurons to create a new state of mind as an answer to that question. You might say it becomes a symphony conductor, silencing your old hard-wiring (the pruning function of neuroplasticity) and selecting different networks of neurons from different parts of the brain and wiring them together to create a new level of mind to reflect what you were imagining. It's your frontal lobe that changes your mind—that is, it makes the brain work in different sequences, patterns, and combinations. Once the frontal lobe can select different networks of neurons and seamlessly turn them on in tandem to create a new level of mind, a picture or internal representation appears in your mind's eye, or frontal lobe.

Now let's bring in some more neurochemistry. If your frontal lobe is orchestrating enough of these neural nets to fire in unison as you focus on a clear intention, there will come a moment when the thought will become the experience in your mind—that's when your inner reality is more real than your outer reality. Once the thought becomes the experience, you begin to feel the emotion of how the event would feel in reality (remember, emotions are the chemical signatures of experiences). Your brain makes a different type of chemical messenger—a neuropeptide—and it sends it out to the cells in your body. The neuropeptide looks for the appropriate receptor sites, or docking stations, on various cells so that it can deliver its message to the body's hormonal centers and, ultimately, the cells' DNA—and the cells get a new message that the event has occurred.

When the DNA in a cell gets this new information from the neuropeptide, it responds by turning on (or upregulating) some genes and turning off (or downregulating) others, all to support your new state of being. Think of the upregulating and downregulating as lights either heating up and getting brighter or cooling off and getting dimmer. When a gene lights up, it's activated to make a protein. When a gene turns off, it becomes deactivated and gets dimmer or weaker—and it doesn't produce as many proteins. And we see the effects with measurable changes in our physical bodies.

Take a look at Figure 5.1A and Figure 5.1B. They will help you follow the entire sequence of how to change your body by thought alone.

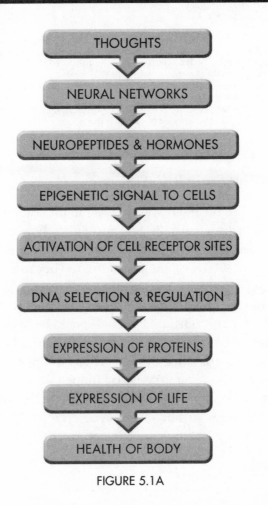

FIGURE 5.1A

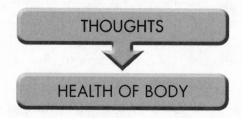

FIGURE 5.1B

In Figure 5.1A, the flowchart demonstrates how thoughts progress through a cascade of simple mechanisms and chemical reactions in a downward causation to change the body. By deduction, if new thoughts can create a new mind by activating new neural networks, creating healthier neuropeptides and hormones (which signal the cells in new ways and epigenetically activate new genes to make new proteins), and if the expression of proteins is the expression of life and is equal to the health of the body, then Figure 5.1B illustrates how thoughts can heal the body.

Stem Cells: Our Potent Pool of Potentials

Stem cells are the next layer we need to understand in the puzzle. They're at least partially responsible for how the seemingly impossible becomes possible. Officially, these are undifferentiated biological cells that become specialized. They're raw potential. When these blank slates are activated, they morph into whatever kind of cell the body needs—including muscle cells, bone cells, skin cells, immune cells, and even nerve cells in the brain—in order to replace injured or damaged cells in the body's tissues, organs, and systems. Think of stem cells as scoops of shaved snow-cone ice before the flavored syrup is pumped on top; lumps of clay waiting on the potter's wheel for their turn to be fashioned into plates, bowls, vases, or mugs; or maybe even a roll of silver duct tape that can fix a leaking pipe one day and be cleverly fashioned into a prom dress the next.

Here's an example of how stem cells work. When you cut your finger, the body needs to repair the break in the skin. The local physical trauma sends a signal to your genes from outside the cell. The gene turns on and makes the appropriate proteins, which then instruct stem cells to turn into healthily functioning skin cells. The traumatic signal is the information the stem cell needs to differentiate into a skin cell. Millions of processes like this occur all over our bodies all the time. Healing attributable to this type of gene expression has been documented in the liver, muscles, skin, intestines, bone marrow, and even the brain and the heart.[10]

In wound-healing studies where the subject is in a highly emotional, negative state like anger, the stem cells don't get the message clearly. When there's interference in the signal, as with static on the radio, the potential cell doesn't get the right stimulation in a coherent fashion to turn itself into a useful cell. As you know from reading the section about the stress response and living in survival mode, the healing will take longer because most of the body's energy is busy dealing with the angry emotion and its chemical effects. It's just not the time for creation, growth, and nurturing—it's the time for an emergency.

So when the placebo effect is at work, and you create the right level of mind with a clear intention and combine it with a nurturing, elevated emotion, the right type of signal can reach the cell's DNA. The message will not only influence the production of healthy proteins for better structure and function of the body, but also make brand-new, healthy cells from latent stem cells that are just waiting to be activated by the right message.

You could even think of these stem cells as "get out of jail free" cards, as in the game *Monopoly,* because once they're picked up or activated, they replace cells in damaged areas of the body, allowing for a fresh, clean start. In fact, stem cells help explain how healing occurs in at least half the placebo cases involving sham surgery, whether it's for an arthritic knee or a coronary bypass (as described in Chapter 1).

How Intention and Elevated Emotion Change Our Biology

We've already mentioned emotions and how they play a vital role in healing the body, but now let's take a deeper look at the subject. If we have a *heightened emotional response* to the new thoughts we're concentrating on in mental rehearsal, it's like turbocharging our efforts, because the emotions help us make epigenetic changes much faster. We don't *need* the emotional component; after all, the subjects who strengthened their muscles by imagining they were lifting weights didn't need to get blissed out to change their genes. However, they inspired themselves by using their imaginations with each mental lift, saying, "Harder! Harder! Harder!" The consistent emotion was the energetic catalyst that truly enhanced the process.[11] Maintaining such an elevated emotion allows us to get far more dramatic results much more quickly—the same kind of amazing results as we see in the placebo response.

Remember the laughter study from Chapter 2? Japanese researchers found that watching an hour-long comedy show upregulated 39 genes, 14 of which were related to natural killer cell activity in the immune system. Several other studies have shown increases in various antibodies after subjects watched a humorous videotape.[12] Research at the University of North Carolina at Chapel Hill further showed that increased positive emotions produced increases in *vagal tone,* a measure of the health of the *vagus nerve,* which plays a major part in regulating the autonomic nervous system and homeostasis.[13] In a Japanese study, when baby rats were tickled for five minutes a day for five days in a row to stimulate positive emotion, the rats' brains generated new neurons.[14]

In each of these cases, strong positive emotions helped the subjects trigger real physical changes that improved their health. Positive emotions cause the body and brain to flourish.

Now look at the pattern of many of the placebo studies: The moment someone starts getting a clear intention of a new future (wanting to live without pain or disease) and then combines it with a heightened emotion (excitement, hope, and anticipation of actually living without pain or disease) is the moment the body is no longer in the past. The body is living in that new future, because as we've seen, the body doesn't know the difference between an emotion created by an actual experience and one created by thought alone. So that heightened state of emotion in response to the new thought is a vital component of that process, because it's new information coming from outside the cell—and to the body, the experience from the outer environment or inner environment is the same.

Remember Mr. Wright from Chapter 1? He got very excited when he thought about taking the powerful new drug he'd heard about and imagined how it might cure him. He was so excited that he badgered his doctor to allow him to take it. When he actually did, he had no idea that it was inert. But because his brain didn't know the difference between his highly emotionally charged mental images of being well and actually being well, his body emotionally responded as if what he had imagined had already happened. His mind and his body were then working together to signal new genes in new ways, and *that,* rather than the "powerful new drug" he took, was what shrank his tumors and restored his health. That's what created his new state of being.

Then, when Mr. Wright learned that the drug trials showed that the drug didn't work, he reverted back to his old thoughts and old emotions—to his old programming—and not surprisingly, his tumors returned. His state of being changed once again. But when his doctors told him that he could get an improved version of the drug that had worked before, he got excited all over again. He really believed that this new version of the drug could work, because he'd seen it do so before (or at least that's what he thought he'd seen).

Naturally, when he reembraced the intention of health and started thinking new thoughts about possibility again, his brain went back to firing and wiring new neural connections, and he created a new mind. All his excitement and hope returned, and that emotion created the very chemicals in his body that supported his new thoughts. And so once more, his body didn't know the difference between his thoughts and feelings about being well and actually *being* well. And once more, his brain and body responded as if what he'd imagined had already happened—and his tumors disappeared again.

Once he read in the news that his "miracle drug" truly was a bust, he reverted to his old thinking and old emotions one final time—and his old personality-self, along with his tumors, returned. There was no miracle drug—*he* was the miracle. And there was no placebo—*he* was the placebo.

So it makes sense that we should concentrate not merely on avoiding negative emotions, like fear and anger, but also on consciously cultivating heartfelt, positive emotions, such as gratitude, joy, excitement, enthusiasm, fascination, awe, inspiration, wonder, trust, appreciation, kindness, compassion, and empowerment, to give us every advantage in maximizing our health.

Studies show that getting in touch with positive, expansive emotions like kindness and compassion—emotions that are our birthright, by the way—tends to release a different neuropeptide (called *oxytocin*), which naturally shuts off the receptors in the *amygdala*, the part of the brain that generates fear and anxiety.[15] With fear out of the way, we can feel infinitely more trust, forgiveness, and love. We move from being selfish to selfless. And as we embody this new state of being, our neurocircuitry opens the door to endless possibilities that we never could have even imagined before, because now we're not expending all our energy trying to figure out how to survive.

Scientists are finding areas in the body—like the intestines, the immune system, the liver, and the heart, as well as many other organs—that contain receptor sites for oxytocin. These organs are highly responsive to oxytocin's major healing effect, which has been linked to growing more blood vessels in the heart,[16] stimulating immune function,[17] increasing gastric motility,[18] and normalizing blood-sugar levels.[19]

Let's return to mental rehearsal for a moment. Remember how the frontal lobe is our ally in mental rehearsal? That's true because, as we established earlier, the frontal lobe helps us unplug from the body, the environment, and time—the three main focuses of someone who's living in survival mode. It helps us get past ourselves to a state of pure consciousness, where we have no ego.

In this new state, as we envision what we desire, our hearts are more open, and positive emotion can flood through us so that now the loop of feeling what we're thinking and thinking what we're feeling is finally working in our favor. The selfish mind-set we were in when we were in survival mode no longer exists, because the energy we channeled toward survival needs has now been freed up for us to create. It's as though someone paid our rent or mortgage payment for the month so that we have extra cash to play with.

Now we can understand exactly why it is that if we hold a clear intention of a new future; marry it to a state of expansive, elevated emotion; and repeat that over and over until we've created a new state of mind and a new state of being, these thoughts will seem more real to us than our previous, limited view of reality. We're finally free. And once we truly embrace that emotion, we can more easily fall in love with the possibility that we've been envisioning.

The symphony conductor (frontal lobe) feels like a kid in a candy store—excitedly and joyfully seeing all sorts of creative possibilities for new neural connections that can combine to form new neural nets. And as the conductor unplugs us from the old state of being and switches on the circuits in this new state of being, our neurochemicals begin delivering new messages to our cells, which are now prepared to make epigenetic changes that signal new genes in new, empowering ways—and because we've used heightened emotions to make it seem as though it's already happened, we're signaling the gene *ahead of the environment*. Now we're no longer *waiting* for the change and *hoping* for the change— *we are the change.*

Back to the Monastery

Let's revisit the study from the beginning of the last chapter, where the elderly men pretended to be younger and actually got physically younger. The question of how they did it has now been answered, and we've solved the mystery.

When these men arrived at the monastery, they retreated from their familiar lives. They were no longer reminded of who they thought they were based on their external environments. Then they began their retreat by holding a very clear intention: to pretend they were young again (using physical and mental rehearsal, because both change the brain and the body) and to make it as real as possible. As they watched the movies, read the magazines, and listened to radio and television programs from when they were 22 years younger, without modern-day interruptions, they were able to let go of the reality of being in their 70s and 80s.

They actually started living as though they were young again. As they experienced new thoughts and feelings about being younger, their brains started firing neurons in new sequences, new patterns, and new combinations—some of which hadn't been fired for 22 years. Because everything around the men, as well as their own excited imaginations, joyfully supported them in making the experience feel real, their brains couldn't tell the difference between actually *being* 22 years younger and just *pretending* that they were. So the men, in a matter of days, were able to start signaling the exact genetic changes to reflect who they were being.

In doing that, their bodies produced neuropeptides to match their new emotions, and when the neuropeptides were unleashed, they delivered new messages to the cells in their bodies. As the appropriate cells allowed those chemical messengers in, they ushered them straight to the DNA deep inside each cell. Once they arrived there, new proteins were created, and these proteins looked for new genes according to the information they were carrying. When they found what they were looking for, the proteins unwrapped the DNA, switching on the gene that was lying in wait and triggering epigenetic changes. These epigenetic changes resulted in the production of new proteins that resembled the proteins of men 22 years younger. If the men's bodies didn't happen to have the necessary parts to create whatever the epigenetic changes required, the epigenome simply called upon stem cells to make what was needed.

A cascade of physical improvements ensued as the men made more epigenetic changes and switched on more genes, until finally, the men who waltzed back out through the monastery gates were no longer the same men who had shuffled through those gates just one week earlier.

And if the process worked for these guys, I assure you that it can work for you, too. What reality do you *choose* to live in, and who are you *pretending* to be (or not be)? *Could it be that simple?*

Chapter Six

Suggestibility

Thirty-six-year-old Ivan Santiago stood patiently on a New York City street, along with a handful of paparazzi gathered behind a velvet rope outside a service entrance to a four-star Lower East Side hotel. They were awaiting a foreign dignitary who was about to exit the building and jump into one of two black SUV limos waiting at the curb. But Santiago wasn't clutching a camera. One hand held a brand-new red backpack, while the other reached inside the partially unzipped bag and took hold of the grip of a pistol outfitted with a silencer. Santiago, an imposing Pennsylvania corrections officer with a bald head that would make Vin Diesel proud, knew a thing or two about deadly weapons. He'd never had to fire one while on duty, but he was ready to fire one today.

Moments before, Santiago had been on his way home, without a single thought of guns, backpacks, foreign dignitaries, or assassination. But now here he was, finger on the trigger, brow knit into an intimidating scowl, and mere seconds from turning into a killer. The hotel door opened, and out sauntered his mark in a crisp, white dress shirt, sporting shades and carrying a leather briefcase. The man took only two or three strides toward the waiting limo before Santiago whipped his gun out of the backpack and fired three times. The man fell to the sidewalk, motionless, his shirt stained red.

Seconds later, a man named Tom Silver appeared out of nowhere, calmly put one hand on Santiago's shoulder and his other on Santiago's forehead, and said, "On the count of five, I'll say, 'Fully refreshed.' Open your eyes and wake up. One, two, three, four, five! Fully refreshed!"

Santiago had been hypnotized to shoot a stranger (actually a stuntman) using what turned out to be a harmless Airsoft prop gun in an experiment run by a handful of researchers who set out to test the unthinkable: Using hypnosis, was it possible to program a law-abiding, all-around good person to become a cold-blooded assassin?[1]

Hidden inside the SUV, eyes riveted to the scene, were the researchers working with Silver: Cynthia Meyersburg, Ph.D., then a postdoctoral fellow at Harvard specializing in experimental psychopathology; Mark Stokes, Ph.D., a neuroscientist at Oxford who studies the neural pathways of decision making; and Jeffery Kieliszewski, Ph.D., a forensic psychologist with Human Resource Associates in Grand Rapids, Michigan, who's done work in super-maximum-security prisons and hospitals for the criminally insane.

The day before, the researchers had started out with a group of 185 volunteers. Silver (a certified clinical hypnotherapist and forensic-hypnosis investigation expert who once helped the Taiwan Department of Defense bust open a $2.4 billion international arms-trading scandal) screened all 185 participants to determine how suggestible they were to hypnosis. Only about 5 to 10 percent of the population are considered very susceptible to hypnosis. In the test group, 16 passed muster and were given a psychological evaluation to weed out those who might suffer permanent psychological harm from the experiment. Eleven progressed to the next test, which determined whether, under hypnosis, they would reject deeply rooted social norms; this would show which were the most suggestible.

Divided into smaller groups, the subjects were taken to a fairly busy restaurant for lunch, but unbeknownst to them, they'd been given a posthypnotic suggestion that once they sat down, their chairs would feel very hot, to the point where they'd quickly become so warm that they'd strip to their underwear—right there in the restaurant. While all of the subjects complied with the instructions to varying degrees, the researchers eliminated seven who they felt either were playing along or just weren't suggestible enough to fully follow the prompt. The others stripped to their underwear within seconds; they really *thought* their chairs were extremely hot.

The four who progressed to the next level were invited to take a test no one would be able to fake. The subjects were to step into a deep metal bathtub filled with 35°F ice water, just 3° above freezing. One at a time, the subjects were wired to devices that monitored their heart rate, breathing rate, and pulse, while a special thermo-imaging camera monitored both their body temperature and the temperature of the water. Hypnotizing them, Silver told the subjects they would feel no discomfort from the cold water and, in fact, would feel as though they were stepping into a nice, warm bath. Anesthesiologist Sekhar Upadhyayula administered the test as emergency medical technicians stood by.

This test would make or break the experiment. Normally, when someone is exposed to water this cold, an involuntary gasping reflex happens as the water reaches nipple level. The heart rate and respiratory rate climb, the person starts to shiver, and the teeth begin to chatter. It's the autonomic nervous system taking over in an automatic attempt to maintain internal balance— something that's not under conscious control. Even if a person were in a deep state of hypnosis, the amount of sensation being sent to the brain under these extreme circumstances would normally be too overwhelming to maintain a hypnotic state. If any of the subjects passed this test, they were indisputably suggestible to a very high degree.

Three of the subjects were indeed in deep states of hypnosis, but not deep enough to withstand this kind of intense cold without their bodies losing homeostasis. The longest any of them could stay in the bath was 18 seconds. But the fourth subject, Santiago, stayed in for just over two full minutes before Dr. Upadhyayula called a halt to the test.

Although Santiago's heart rate was high *before* the experiment, once he stepped into the water, his heart rate calmed down immediately. There wasn't so much as a flutter on his EKG or a single blip in his respiratory rate. Santiago sat among ice cubes as though he were soaking in a warm bathtub; indeed, that's exactly what he believed he was doing. The man never flinched nor did his body fall into hypothermia, and the researchers knew they'd found the subject they were looking for.

Because Santiago was so suggestible under hypnosis that his body could overcome such an extreme environment for this amount of time and his mind could control his autonomic functions, he was ready for the final test.

Santiago's background check had shown he was a great guy, the researchers noted. He was a trusted employee, a devoted son, and a loving uncle. He was certainly not the type of man who would agree to kill somebody in cold blood. Would Silver succeed in getting such a man to turn into an assassin?

For this next phase of the experiment to be valid, Santiago couldn't know what was being staged; he couldn't make any connection between the experiments he was taking part in and the scene in front of the hotel next to where the study was taking place. As part of the plan, the television producers in charge of filming the experiments told him he hadn't been selected to continue in the program, although they wanted him to return the next day for a short exit interview. Before Santiago left, he was told he wouldn't be put under hypnosis again.

Santiago returned the following day. While he was chatting with a producer, the team went to work staging the scene outside. The stuntman strapped on blood packs; the Airsoft prop gun (which had the blast and recoil action of a real firearm) was placed inside a red backpack and laid on the seat of a parked motorcycle right outside the entrance to the building. A velvet rope line was set up outside the hotel service entrance, right next door, and staged paparazzi were in place with their film and video cameras. Two SUVs were parked on the street, looking ready to drive off with the "foreign dignitary" and his entourage.

Back upstairs, Santiago happily answered questions in his "exit interview," until the producer excused herself for a moment, saying she'd be right back. Soon after she left the room, Silver entered, saying he wanted to say good-bye to Santiago. As Silver shook Santiago's hand, he gave a little tug on his arm that prompted Santiago, by now well conditioned to this cue, to drop immediately into a hypnotic trance. He went limp on the couch.

Silver told him "a bad guy" was downstairs, adding, "He's gotta be erased. We've got to get rid of him, and you're the one to do it." He told Santiago that once he exited the building, he'd see a red backpack on a motorcycle, and inside would be a gun. He told Santiago that he was to grab the red backpack and walk over to the velvet rope, where he'd wait for the dignitary, who'd be carrying a briefcase, to emerge from the hotel. He told Santiago, "As soon as he comes out the doors, you're going to point the gun at his chest and fire that gun: Bang! Bang! Bang! Bang! Bang! But as soon as you do it, you'll simply, completely, totally forget that it ever happened."

Finally Silver implanted both an audible and a physical stimulation trigger that would send Santiago back into a hypnotic state, under which he'd follow the posthypnotic suggestion Silver had given him: He told Santiago that he'd recognize a segment producer outside the building, and the man would shake his hand and say, "Ivan, you did a spectacular job." Silver told Santiago to nod "yes" if he'd do what Silver had instructed, and Santiago complied. Then Silver brought him out of the trance and acted as if he were truly just saying good-bye.

The producer returned to the room after Silver left and thanked Santiago, telling him the exit interview was over and he could leave. Soon after, Santiago left the building, thinking he was going home.

Once he was outside, the segment producer walked up to him, shook his hand, and said, "Ivan, you did a spectacular job." That was the trigger. Immediately, Santiago looked around, saw the motorcycle, walked over to it, and calmly picked up the red backpack sitting on the seat. Seeing the velvet rope line and the paparazzi, he walked over next to them and slowly unzipped the bag.

In moments, a man carrying a briefcase strode out the door. Without flinching, Santiago pulled the gun out of the backpack and shot the man in the chest several times. The blood bags under the "dignitary's" shirt erupted, and he dramatically collapsed to the ground.

Silver almost immediately appeared on the scene and had Santiago close his eyes. The stuntman made a hasty exit as Silver then brought Santiago out of his trance. The psychologist Jeffery Kieliszewski appeared and suggested Santiago follow him inside with the others for a debriefing. Once inside, the researchers told a surprised Santiago what had happened and asked him if he had any memory of what he'd done or what had just unfolded outside. Santiago didn't remember a thing—that is, until Silver suggested to him that he would.

Programming the Subconscious

In the first few chapters, you read about many different individuals who accepted a possible imagined scenario, and like magic, their bodies responded to that picture in their minds: individuals who'd been trapped for years by the involuntary tremors of Parkinson's disease but increased their dopamine levels by thought alone, only to see their spastic paralysis mysteriously vanish; a chronically depressed woman who, over time, physically changed her brain and transmuted her debilitating emotional state into joy and well-being; asthmatics who experienced a full-blown bronchial episode brought on by nothing more than water vapor, but then reversed their bronchial constriction in seconds by inhaling exactly the same water vapor; and, of course, the men with severe knee pain and compromised range of motion who miraculously improved after having sham knee surgery and remained healed years later.

In all of these cases and more, it could be said that each subject first accepted and then believed in the *suggestion* of better health, and then surrendered to the outcome without further analysis. When these people accepted the potential of recovery, they aligned themselves with a future possible reality—and changed their minds and brains in the process. As they believed in the outcome, they emotionally embraced the idea of better health, and as a result, their bodies, as the unconscious mind, were living in that future reality during the present moment.

They conditioned their bodies to a new mind and so began to signal new genes in new ways and express new proteins for better health—and they moved into a new state of being. Once they surrendered to a new possible scenario, they no longer analyzed how it was going to happen or when it would manifest; they simply trusted in a better state of being and maintained that new state of mind and body for an extended period of time. It was that sustained state of being that switched on the right genes and programmed them to stay on.

Whether they took a regimen of daily sugar pills lasting weeks or even months, received a single saline injection, or submitted to fake surgery, these individuals reaffirmed their acceptance, belief, and surrender for the duration of the study they participated in. If they were taking a pill daily to relieve pain or depression, the pill was a constant *reminder* for them to condition, expect, and assign meaning to their intentional activity, thus reinforcing the internal process over and over again. If it was a weekly visit to the hospital to see a doctor and be interviewed about their improvement, the choice to interact in a particular environment with doctors, nurses, equipment, and waiting rooms triggered a host of sensory responses, and through associative memory, they were reminded of a possible new future. They were conditioned from past experiences that the place called "a hospital" was where people went to get well. They began to anticipate their future changes and, therefore, assigned intention to the whole healing process. Because all these factors had meaning, they helped make the placebo patients more suggestible to the outcomes they experienced.

So now let's address the elephant in the room: No real physical, chemical, or therapeutic mechanisms made these changes happen. None of these people had actual surgery, took active medication, or received any real treatment to create these significant alterations in health. The power of their minds so influenced their bodies' physiology that they became healed. It's safe to say that their real transformation happened independent of their conscious minds. Their conscious minds may have *initiated* the course of action, but the real work happened subconsciously, with the subjects remaining totally unaware of *how* it happened.

The same is true of Ivan Santiago. The power of his mind under hypnosis so influenced his physiology that even when he was sitting in a freezing ice-cube bath, he didn't so much as flinch. It was the power of his subconscious mind altered by a mere suggestion, however, not his conscious mind, that was responsible for this feat. If he hadn't accepted the suggestion, the outcome would have been very different. In addition, he did what he did without thinking about how he was able to do it; in fact, in his mind, he *wasn't* sitting in an ice bath. He was sitting in a perfectly pleasant tub of warm water.

So just as with hypnosis, the placebo effect is created by a person's consciousness somehow interacting with the autonomic nervous system. Quite simply, the conscious mind merges with the subconscious mind. Once the placebo patients accept a thought as a reality, and then believe and trust in the end result emotionally, the next thing that happens is that they get well.

A cascade of physiological events automatically carries out the whole biological change—without their conscious minds being involved. They're able to enter the operating system where these functions already happen routinely, and when they do, it's as if they've planted a seed in fertile ground. The system automatically takes over for them. In fact, it's not anyone's job to do anything. It just happens.

None of the subjects could *consciously* spike dopamine levels by 200 percent and control involuntary tremors with the mind, manufacture new neurotransmitters to combat depression, signal stem cells to morph into white blood cells to mount an immune response, or restore knee cartilage in order to reduce pain—just as Santiago couldn't have *consciously* avoided flinching when he lowered his body into that tub. Anyone trying to accomplish any of these feats would certainly be unsuccessful. These people would have to get help from a mind that already knows how to initiate all of these processes. To succeed, they'd have to activate the autonomic nervous system, the *subconscious mind,* and then assign it the task of making new cells and healthy new proteins.

Acceptance, Belief, and Surrender

I have mentioned the word *suggestibility* throughout this book as if being suggestible were something that all of us could simply do voluntarily on command. As you read in the story at the beginning of the chapter, it turns out that it's not that easy. Let's face it. Some of us—certainly Ivan Santiago—are more suggestible than others. And even those who are more suggestible respond to certain suggestions better than other suggestions.

For example, some of the hypnotism test subjects had no problem stripping to their underwear in public when given that posthypnotic suggestion, yet they were unable to subconsciously accept the idea that a tub of frigid ice water was really a warm Jacuzzi. This was true even though posthypnotic suggestions (including the suggestion that Santiago shoot the stranger) are generally more difficult to make stick, compared to suggestions that alter someone's state temporarily during the hypnotic trance itself.

And like hypnosis, the placebo response also doesn't just work for everyone. The placebo patients you've read about who were able to make positive changes last for years (like the men who had the sham knee surgery) respond much like hypnotherapy subjects who've been given posthypnotic suggestions. For some, like these men, such suggestions work beautifully. For others, not much happens.

For instance, when they're sick or suffering from a disease, many people simply can't accept the idea that even a drug, procedure, treatment, or injection can help them—let alone that a placebo might work. Why not? It takes thinking greater than how they feel—in turn allowing those new thoughts to drive new feelings, which then reinforce those new thoughts—until it becomes a new state of being. But if familiar feelings have become the means of familiar thinking and the person can't transcend that habituation, he or she is in the same past state of mind and body, and everything stays the same.

However, if those same people who can't accept that a drug or procedure could make them well could reach a new level of acceptance and belief, and then surrender to that end without constantly fretting, worrying, and analyzing, then they could reap greater rewards from the process. That's what suggestibility is: making a thought into a virtual experience and having our bodies consequentially respond in a new manner.

Suggestibility combines three elements: *acceptance, belief,* and *surrender.* The more we accept, believe, and surrender to whatever we're doing to change our internal state, the better the results we can create. Similarly, when Santiago was under hypnosis and his subconscious mind was in control, he could totally accept what Silver told him about the "bad guy" who needed to be eliminated, he could believe that Silver was telling the truth, and he could surrender to carrying out the detailed instructions Silver gave him, without ever analyzing or thinking critically about what he was about to do. There was no hand-wringing and asking for proof. There was no second-guessing. He just did it.

Adding in Emotion

So when we are presented with the idea of better health, and we can associate that hope or thought—that something outside of us is going to change something inside of us—with emotional anticipation of the experience, we're becoming suggestible to that end result. We condition, expect, and assign meaning to the whole delivery system.

But the emotional component is key in this experience; suggestibility isn't just an intellectual process. Many folks can intellectualize being better, but if they can't *emotionally* embrace the result, then they can't enter into the autonomic nervous system (as Santiago did using hypnotism), which is vital because that's the seat of the subconscious programming that's been calling all the shots (as discussed in Chapter 3). In fact, it's generally accepted in psychology that a person who experiences intense emotions tends to be more receptive to ideas and is therefore more suggestible.

The autonomic nervous system is under the control of the *limbic brain,* which is also called the "emotional brain" and the "chemical brain." The limbic brain, depicted in Figure 6.1, is responsible for subconscious functions like chemical order and homeostasis, for maintaining the body's natural physiological balance. It's your emotional center. So as you experience different emotions, you activate this part of the brain, and it creates the corresponding chemical molecules of emotion. And since this emotional brain exists below the conscious mind's control, the moment you feel emotion, you activate your autonomic nervous system.

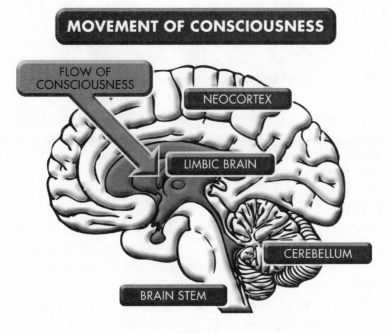

FIGURE 6.1

When you feel an emotion, you can ultimately bypass your neocortex—the seat of your conscious mind—and activate your autonomic nervous system. Therefore, as you get beyond your thinking brain, you move into a part of the brain where health is regulated, maintained, and executed.

So if the placebo effect requires you to embrace an elevated emotion ahead of the actual experience of healing, then when you amplify your emotional response (and come out of your normal resting state), you're activating your subconscious system. Allowing yourself to feel emotions is a way to enter the operating system and program a change, because you're now automatically instructing the autonomic nervous system to begin creating the corresponding chemistry as if you were getting better. And the body receives a blend of those natural alchemical elixirs from the brain and mind. As a result, the body is now becoming the mind emotionally.

As we've seen, these can't be just any emotions. The survival emotions that we already explored in the last chapter knock the brain and body out of balance and so downregulate (or shut off) the genes needed for optimal health. Fear, futility, anger, hostility, impatience, pessimism, competition, and worry won't signal the proper genes for better health. They actually do the opposite. They turn on the fight-or-flight nervous system and prepare your body for emergency. You're now losing vital energy for healing.

It's a similar situation with *trying* to make something happen, by the way. The moment you're trying, you're pushing against something because you're endeavoring to change it. You're struggling, attempting to force an outcome, even if you don't realize that's what you're actually doing. That knocks you out of balance, just as the survival emotions do, and the more frustrated and impatient you become, the more out of balance you get. Remember in *The Empire Strikes Back,* when Yoda said to Luke Skywalker that there is no try, only do (or do not)? The same is true with the placebo response: There is no try; there's only allow.

All those negative and stressful emotions are so familiar to us and connect to so many past known events that when we focus on them, those familiar emotions keep the body connected to the same past conditions—which, in this case, is poor health. No new information can then program your genes in any new ways. Your past reinforces your future.

On the other hand, emotions like gratitude and appreciation open your heart and lift the energy in your body to a new place—out of the lower hormonal centers. Gratitude is one of the most powerful emotions for increasing your level of suggestibility. It teaches your body emotionally that the event you're grateful for has *already happened,* because we usually give thanks *after* a desirable event has occurred.

If you bring up the emotion of gratitude *before* the actual event, your body (as the unconscious mind) will begin to believe that the future event has indeed already happened—or is happening to you in the present moment. Gratitude, therefore, is the ultimate state of receivership. Look at Figure 6.2 to review the difference between the expression of survival emotions and the expression of elevated emotions.

ELEVATED EMOTIONS
VS.
LIMITED EMOTIONS

CREATIVE EMOTIONS (SELFLESS)

- GRATITUDE
- LOVE
- JOY
- INSPIRATION
- PEACE
- WHOLENESS
- TRUST
- KNOWINGNESS
- PRESENCE
- EMPOWERMENT

SURVIVAL EMOTIONS (SELFISH)

- DOUBT
- FEAR
- ANGER
- INSECURITY
- WORRY
- ANXIETY
- JUDGMENT
- COMPETITION
- HOSTILITY
- SADNESS
- GUILT
- SHAME
- DEPRESSION
- LUST

FIGURE 6.2

Survival emotions are derived primarily from the stress hormones, which tend to endorse more selfish and more limited states of mind and body. When you embrace elevated, more creative emotions, you lift your energy to a different hormonal center, your heart begins to open, and you feel more selfless. This is when your body starts to respond to a new mind.

If you can bring up the emotion of appreciation or thankfulness, and combine it with a clear intention, you're now beginning to *embody* the event emotionally. You're changing your brain and body. Specifically, you're chemically instructing your body to know what your mind has philosophically known. We could say that you're in a new future in the present moment. You're no longer using familiar, primitive emotions to keep you anchored to the past; you're now using elevated emotions to drive you into a new future.

Two Faces of the Analytical Mind

Let's go back to the idea introduced earlier that we each have different levels of our own acceptance to a suggestion, resulting in a spectrum of suggestibility. Everyone has his or her own level of susceptibility to thoughts, suggestions, and commands—from both outer and inner realities—based on many different variables. Think of your level of suggestibility as being inversely related to your analytical thinking (as illustrated in Figure 6.3): the greater your analytical mind (the more you analyze), the less suggestible you are; and the lesser your analytical mind, the more suggestible you are.

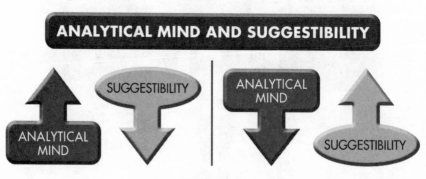

ANALYTICAL MIND AND SUGGESTIBILITY

SUGGESTIBILITY

ANALYTICAL MIND

ANALYTICAL MIND

SUGGESTIBILITY

FIGURE 6.3

The inverse relationship between the analytical mind and suggestibility.

The analytical mind (or the critical mind) is that part of the mind you consciously use and are aware of. It's a function of the thinking *neocortex*—the part of the brain that's the seat of your conscious awareness; that thinks, observes, and remembers things; and that resolves problems. It analyzes, compares, judges, rethinks, examines, questions, polarizes, scrutinizes, reasons, rationalizes, and reflects. It takes what it has learned from past experience and applies it to a future outcome or to something it hasn't yet experienced.

In the hypnosis experiment described at the start of this chapter, for example, 7 of the 11 subjects given the posthypnotic suggestion to peel their clothes off in the public restaurant didn't fully comply. It was the analytical mind that brought them "back to their senses." The moment they began to analyze—*Is this right? Should I do this? What will I look like? Who's watching? What will my boyfriend think?*—the suggestion was no longer as powerful, and they returned to their old, familiar state of being. The folks who immediately stripped to their underwear, on the other hand, did it without questioning what they were doing. They were less analytical (and so more suggestible) than their counterparts.

Since the neocortex is divided into two halves called *hemispheres,* it makes sense that we analyze and spend a lot of time thinking in duality: you know, good versus bad, right versus wrong, positive versus negative, male versus female, straight versus gay, Democrat versus Republican, past versus future, logic versus emotion, old versus new, head versus heart—you get the idea. And if we're living in stress, the chemicals we're pumping into our systems tend to drive the whole analytical process faster. We analyze even more in order to predict future outcomes so that we can protect ourselves from potential worst-case scenarios based on past experience.

There's nothing wrong with the analytical mind, of course. It has served us well for our entire waking, conscious lives. It's what makes us human. Its job is to create meaning and coherence between our outer worlds (the combined experiences of people and things at different times and places) and our inner worlds (our thoughts and feelings).

The analytical mind works best when we're calm, relaxed, and focused. This is when it's working *for* us. It simultaneously reviews many aspects of our lives and provides us with meaningful answers. It helps us choose from myriad options in order to make decisions, learn new things, scrutinize whether to believe in something, judge social situations based on our ethics, get clear on our purpose in life, discern morality with conviction, and evaluate important sensory data.

As an extension of our egos, the analytical mind also protects us so that we can cope and survive best in our external environments. (In fact, one of the ego's main jobs is protection.) It's always evaluating situations in the external environment and assessing the landscape for the most advantageous outcomes. It takes care of the self, and it also tries to preserve the body. Your ego will let you know when there's potential danger, and it will urge you to respond to the condition. For example, if you were walking down the street and saw the oncoming cars driving too close to the side of the road where you were walking, you might cross the street to protect yourself—that's your ego giving you that guidance.

But when our egos are out of balance due to a barrage of stress hormones, our analytical minds go into high gear and become overstimulated. That's when the analytical mind is no longer working for us, but *against* us. We get overanalytical. And the ego becomes highly selfish by making sure that we come first, because that's its job. It thinks and feels as though it needs to be in control to protect the identity. It tries to have power over outcomes; it predicts what it needs to do to create a certainly safe situation; it clings to the familiar and won't let go—so it holds grudges, feels pain and suffers, or can't get beyond its victimhood. It will always avoid the unknown condition and view it as potentially dangerous, because to the ego, the unknown is not to be trusted.

And the ego will do anything to empower itself for the rush of addictive emotions. It wants what it wants, and it will do whatever it takes to get there first, by pushing its way to the front of the line. It can be cunning, manipulative, competitive, and deceptive in its protection.

So the more stressful your situation, the more your analytical mind is driven to analyze your life within the emotion you're experiencing at that particular time. When this happens, you're actually moving your consciousness further away from the operating system of the subconscious mind, where true change can occur. You're then analyzing your life from your emotional past, although the answers to your problems aren't within those emotions, which are causing you to think harder within a limited, familiar chemical state. You're thinking in the box.

Then because of the thinking and feeling loop discussed earlier in the book, those thoughts re-create the same emotions and so drive your brain and body further out of order. You'll be able to see the answers more easily when you get beyond that stressful emotion and see your life from a different state of mind. (Stay tuned.)

As your analytical mind is heightened, your suggestibility to new outcomes decreases. Why? Because an impending emergency isn't the time to be open-minded: entertaining new possibilities and accepting new potentials. It's not the time to believe in new ideas and openly let go and surrender to them. It's not the time to trust; instead, it's the time to protect the self by measuring what you know against what you don't know in order to determine the greatest chances of survival. It's the time to flee from the unknown. So it makes sense that as the analytical mind is endorsed by the stress hormones, you'll narrow your thinking, be unlikely to trust and believe in anything new, and be less suggestible to believing in thought alone or in making any unknown thought known. Thus, you can use the analytical mind or ego to work for you or against you.

The Inner Workings of the Mind

Think of the analytical mind as a separate part of the conscious mind that divides it from the subconscious mind. Since the placebo works only when the analytical mind is silenced so that your awareness can instead interact with the subconscious mind—the domain where true change occurs—the placebo response is possible only when you can get beyond your *self* and so eclipse your conscious mind with your autonomic nervous system.

Look at Figure 6.4 for a simple illustration of this. Let the circle in the figure represent the total mind. The conscious mind is only about 5 percent of the total mind. It's made up of logic and reasoning as well as our creative abilities. These aspects give rise to our free will. The other 95 percent of the total mind is the subconscious mind. This is the operating system where all of the automatic skills, habits, emotional reactions, hardwired behaviors, conditioned responses, associative memories, and routine thoughts and feelings create our attitudes, beliefs, and perceptions.

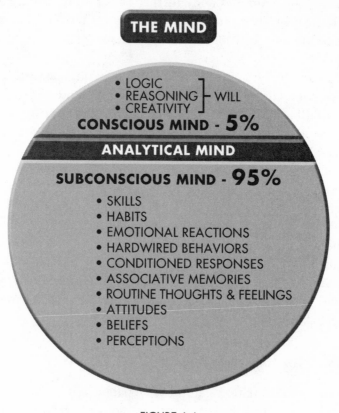

FIGURE 6.4

This is an overview of the conscious mind,
the analytical mind, and the subconscious mind.

The conscious mind is where we store our *explicit,* or *declarative, memories.* Therefore, declarative memories are memories that we can declare. They're the knowledge we've learned (termed *semantic memories*) and experiences we've had in this lifetime (*episodic memories*). You might be a woman who grew up in Tennessee; who rode horses in childhood until you fell off and broke your arm; who had a pet tarantula at age 10 that escaped from its cage, requiring you and your family to sleep at a hotel for two days; who won the state spelling bee at age 14 and now never misspells a word; who studied accounting in college in Nebraska; who presently lives in Atlanta so that you can be near your sister (who took a job for a large corporation); and who is now getting a master's degree in finance online. Declarative memories are the autobiographical self.

The other type of memories we have are *implicit,* or *nondeclarative, memories,* sometimes also called *procedural memories.* This kind of memory kicks in when you've done something so many times that you aren't even consciously aware of how you do it. You've repeated it so often that now your *body* knows it as well as your brain. Think of riding a bike, operating a clutch, tying your shoes, tapping a phone number or a PIN on a keypad, or even reading or speaking. These are the automatic programs that have been discussed throughout this book. You could say that you no longer have to analyze or consciously think about the skill or habit you've mastered, because it's now subconscious. This is the *programmed operating system,* which is depicted in Figure 6.5.

When you've mastered how to do something until it has become hardwired in your mind and emotionally conditioned to your body, then your body knows how to do it as well as your conscious mind. You've memorized an internal neurochemical order that has become innate. The reason is simple: Repeated experience enriches the brain's neural networks and then finally seals the deal when it emotionally trains the body. Once the event is neurochemically embodied enough times through experience, you can turn on the body and the corresponding automatic program just by accessing a familiar subconscious thought or feeling—and then you momentarily move into a particular state of being, which executes the automatic behavior.

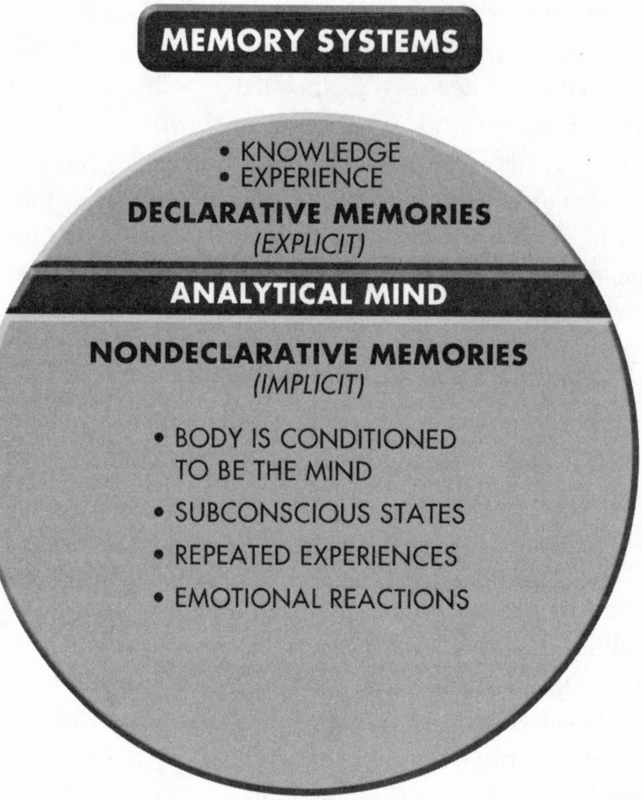

FIGURE 6.5

Memory systems are divided into two categories:
declarative memories (explicit) and *nondeclarative memories* (implicit).

Since implicit memories are developed from the emotions of experience, two possible scenarios explain how this unfolds: (1) A *highly charged one-time emotional event* can be immediately branded and stored in the subconscious (for example, a childhood memory of being in a big department store and getting separated from your mother), or (2) the *redundancy of emotions derived from consistent experience* will also be repeatedly logged there.

Since implicit memories are part of the subconscious system of memory and are routed there either by repeated experience or by highly charged emotional events, when you bring up any emotion or feeling, you're opening a door to your subconscious mind. Since thoughts are the language of the brain and feelings are the language of the body, the moment you feel a feeling, you're turning on your body-mind (because your body has become your subconscious mind). You've just entered the operating system.

Think about it like this: When you feel a certain familiar way, you're subconsciously accessing a series of thoughts derived from that particular feeling. You're autosuggesting thoughts on a daily basis equal to how you feel. These are the thoughts you accept, believe, and surrender to as if they were true. Therefore, you're *more* suggestible *only* to the thoughts that are matched to exactly the same feeling. As a result, those thoughts that you unconsciously think about are the ones you accept, believe, and surrender to over and over.

Conversely, it could also be said that you're much *less* suggestible to any thoughts that are *not* equal to your memorized feelings. Any new thought that reflects an unknown possibility just wouldn't feel right. Your self-talk (the thoughts that you listen to every day) slips by your conscious awareness on a moment-to-moment basis and stimulates the autonomic nervous system and the flow of biological processes, reinforcing the programmed feeling of who you think you are. Remember the study in Chapter 2, where researchers found that optimists responded more favorably to suggestions that were positive while pessimists responded more unfavorably to suggestions that were negative.

By the same means, if you were to change how you feel, could you become more suggestible to a new stream of thoughts? Absolutely! By feeling an elevated emotion and allowing a whole new set of thoughts to be driven by that new feeling, you'd increase your level of suggestibility to what you were feeling and then thinking. You'd be in a new state of being, and your new thoughts would then be the autosuggestions equal to that feeling. And when you feel emotions, you're naturally activating your implicit memory system and the autonomic nervous system. You can simply allow the autonomic nervous system to do what it does best: restore balance, health, and order.

Isn't that what many people did in the placebo studies mentioned earlier? Weren't they able to bring up an elevated emotion like hope or inspiration or the joy of being well? And once they saw a new possibility without ever analyzing it, wasn't their level of suggestibility influenced by those feelings? As they felt those corresponding emotions, didn't they enter the operating system and reprogram their autonomic nervous system with new orders—by thought alone—autosuggesting equal to those emotions?

Opening the Door to the Subconscious Mind

If there are different degrees of suggestibility, then that can be demonstrated visually by showing different thicknesses of the analytical mind. The thicker the barrier between the conscious mind and the subconscious mind, the more difficulty you'll have getting into the operating system.

Take a look at Figures 6.6 and 6.7 on the following two pages, which represent two people with different types of minds.

The person in Figure 6.6 has a very thin veil between the conscious and subconscious minds and therefore is very open to suggestion (like Ivan Santiago from the beginning of the chapter). This person will naturally accept, believe, and surrender to an outcome, because he or she doesn't analyze or intellectualize too much. Folks like this might be more innately prone to accept that a thought is a potential experience and embrace it emotionally so that the package becomes imprinted on the autonomic nervous system, ready to be executed as a reality. These people don't spend a lot of time trying to figure things out in their lives, and they don't overthink many things. If you've ever seen a hypnosis stage show, the subjects who make it to the front of the room usually fall into this category.

Now contrast this with Figure 6.7. If you look at the thicker analytical mind that separates the conscious and subconscious minds, you can easily see that this person is less prone to taking suggestions at face value without a significant degree of help from his or her intellectual mind in evaluating, processing, planning, and reviewing. People like this are highly critical and will make sure they've analyzed everything before simply surrendering and trusting.

FIGURE 6.6

A less analytical mind (represented by the thinner layer in the illustration) is more suggestible.

Bear in mind that some of us have a more built-up analytical mind even without constantly living by our stress hormones. We might have studied different subjects in college or lived with parents who reinforced the mechanisms of rational thought when we were young, or maybe it's just part of our nature. (Nevertheless, you can have a significantly broad analytical mind and still learn how to get beyond it—I certainly did—so there's hope.)

FIGURE 6.7

A more developed analytical mind (represented by the
thicker layer in the illustration) is less suggestible.

As I said before, neither of these types is more advantageous
than the other. I think a healthy balance between the two works
very well. Someone who's overanalytical is less likely to trust and
flow in his or her life. Someone who's overly suggestible might be
too gullible and less functional. The point I want to make is that
if you're continually analyzing your life, judging yourself, and obsessing about everything in your reality, then you'll never enter
the operating system where those old programs exist and reprogram them. Only when a person accepts, believes, and surrenders

to a suggestion does the door between the conscious and subconscious minds open. That information then signals the autonomic nervous system and—presto!—it takes over.

Now take a look at Figure 6.8. The arrow represents the movement of consciousness from the conscious mind into the subconscious mind, where the suggestion is biologically embossed into the programming system.

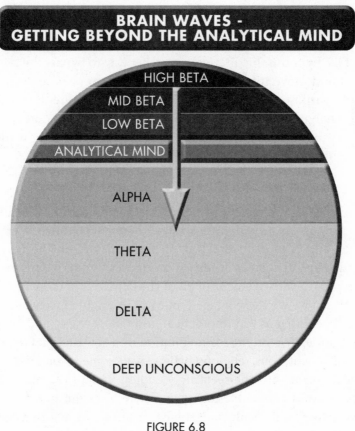

FIGURE 6.8

This figure represents the relationship between brain-wave states and the movement of awareness from the conscious mind to the subconscious mind, moving past the analytical mind during the practice of meditation.

A few additional elements can also silence the analytical mind and open the door to the subconscious mind in order to increase a person's level of suggestibility. For example, physical or mental fatigue increases your suggestibility. Certain studies have shown that the limited exposure to social, physical, and environmental cues in sensory deprivation can cause increased susceptibility. Extreme hunger, emotional shock, and trauma also weaken our analytical faculties, therefore making us more suggestible to information.

Demystifying Meditation

Like hypnosis, meditation is another way to bypass the critical mind and move into the subconscious system of programs. The whole purpose of meditation is to move your awareness beyond your analytical mind—to take your attention off your outer world, your body, and time—and to pay attention to your inner world of thoughts and feelings.

Many stigmas surround the word *meditation.* Most people conjure up images of a bearded guru on a mountaintop, immune to the elements and sitting in perfect stillness; a monk in a simple robe, his face adorned with a huge, mysterious smile; or even a young and beautiful woman, with flawless skin, on the cover of a magazine, dressed in stylish yoga clothes and looking serenely free from the enslavement of all of the demands of daily life.

When we see these images, many of us might perceive the discipline required as too impractical, too out of reach, and beyond our abilities. We might see meditation as a spiritual practice that doesn't fit into our religious beliefs. And some of us are simply overwhelmed with the seemingly endless varieties of meditation available and are unable to decide where to begin. But it doesn't have to be that difficult, "out there," or confusing. For this discussion, let's just say that the whole purpose of meditation is to move our consciousness beyond the analytical mind and into deeper levels of consciousness.

In meditation, we move not just from conscious mind to subconscious mind, but also from self*ish* to self*less*, from being some*body* and some*one* to being no *body* and no *one,* from being a materialist to being an immaterialist, from being some *place* to being no *place,* from being in time to being in no time, from believing that the outer world is reality and defining reality with our senses to believing that the inner world is reality and that once we're there, we enter "non-sense": the world of thought beyond the senses. Meditation takes us from survival to creation; from separation to connection; from imbalance to balance; from emergency mode to growth-and-repair mode; and from the limiting emotions of fear, anger, and sadness to the expansive emotions of joy, freedom, and love. Basically, we go from clinging to the known to embracing the unknown.

Let's reason this for a moment. If your neocortex is the home of your conscious awareness and it's where you construct thoughts, use analytical reasoning, exercise intellect, and demonstrate rational processes, then you'll have to move your consciousness beyond (or out of) your neocortex in order to meditate. Your consciousness would have to essentially move from your thinking brain into your limbic brain and the subconscious regions. In other words, in order for you to dial down your neocortex and all the neural activity that it performs on a daily basis, you'd have to stop thinking analytically and vacate the faculties of reason, logic, intellectualizing, forecasting, predicting, and rationalizing—at least temporarily. This is what's meant by "quieting your mind." (Revisit Figure 6.1, if you need to.)

According to the neuroscientific model that I outlined in the previous chapters, to quiet your mind would mean that you'd have to declare a "cease-fire" on all of the automatic neural networks in your thinking brain that you habitually fire on a regular basis. That is, you'd have to stop reminding yourself of who you think you are, repeatedly reproducing the same level of mind.

I know that sounds like a huge task that may well be overwhelming, but it turns out that practical, scientifically proven ways exist for us to accomplish this feat and make it a skill. In the workshops that I teach around the world, many ordinary people who'd never meditated before got pretty good at doing this—once they learned how. You'll learn these methods in the chapters that follow, but first, let's increase your level of intention so that when you get to the how-to, you'll reap greater rewards (just as did the aerobic exercisers in Quebec from Chapter 2 who were told that their well-being would be enhanced by their efforts and, thus, could assign meaning to what they were doing—and then got better results).

Why Meditation Can Be So Challenging

The analytical neocortex uses all of the five senses to determine reality. It's very preoccupied with putting all of its awareness on the body, the environment, and time. And if you're the least bit stressed, then your attention will be directed to and will amplify all three of these elements. When you're under the gun of the fight-or-flight emergency system and you switch on your adrenaline, just like any animal threatened in the wild, all of your attention will be placed on taking care of your body, finding escape routes in your environment, and figuring out how much time you have to make it to safety. You overfocus on problems, obsess about your looks, dwell on your pain, think about how little time you have to do what you need to do, and rush to get things done. Sound familiar?

Because you're so hyperfocused on this external world and your problems in it when you're living in survival, it's easy to think that what you see and experience is all there is. And without the external world, you're no *one*, no *body*, no *thing*, and in no *place*. How frightful that is for an ego that's trying to control all of its reality by constantly reaffirming an identity!

It might make it easier if you remind yourself that when you're living in survival, what you sense is truly just the tip of the iceberg, only a limited array of ingredients making up your external world. You identify with the many variations and combinations in your external world that reflect back to you who you think you are—but that doesn't mean there isn't more. In fact, every time you learn something new, you change how you see the world.

The world hasn't really changed; only your perception of it has changed. (We'll learn more about perception in the next chapter.)

For now, it's enough to keep in mind that if your goal is to effect change and you haven't been able to make it happen with all your external-world resources, then clearly you'll need to look outside the limits of what you see, sense, and experience for your answers. You'll need to pull from other sources you haven't yet identified—from the unknown. So in that sense, the unknown is your friend, not your foe. It's the place where the answer lies.

Another reason it becomes difficult for us to pull our attention away from all of the conditions of our outer world and place our attention on our inner world is that most people are addicted to stress hormones—to feeling the rush of chemicals that are the result of our conscious or unconscious reactions. This addiction reinforces our belief that our outer world is more real than our inner world. And our physiology is conditioned to support this, because real threats, problems, and concerns do exist that need our attention. So we become addicted to our present external environment. And through associative memory, we use the problems and conditions in our lives to reaffirm that emotional addiction in order to remember who we think we are.

Here's another way to say it: The stress hormones we experience while living in survival mode give the body a high dose of energy and cause the five senses—which plug us into external reality—to become heightened. So naturally, if we're continuously stressed, we'll define reality with our senses. We become materialists. When we try to go within and connect with the world of "non-sense" and the immaterial, it takes some effort to break our conditioned habit and our addiction to the chemical rush we get from our external reality. How, then, could we possibly believe that thought is more powerful than physical, three-dimensional reality? If that's how we see things, it becomes challenging to change anything by thought alone, because we've become enslaved to our bodies and our environments.

Maybe one antidote to that is rereading the stories in Chapter 1—and reading the stories from my workshops later, in

Chapters 9 and 10. Reinforcing new information that shows us that what we think should be impossible is indeed possible helps us remind ourselves that there's more to reality than what our senses perceive. Whether we want to admit it or not, we are the placebo.

Navigating Our Brain Waves

If meditation is about entering the autonomic system so that we can become more suggestible and overcome the challenges just mentioned, then we need to know how to get there. The short answer is that we get there on a brain wave. The brain state we happen to be in at any given time has a huge effect on how suggestible we are at that moment.

Once you learn what these different states are and how to recognize them when you're in them, you can train yourself to move from one state to another, up and down the scale of brain-wave patterns. It takes some practice, of course, but it is possible. So let's explore these different states to learn more about them.

When neurons fire together, they exchange charged elements that then produce electromagnetic fields, and these fields are what are measured during a brain scan (like an electroencephalograph, or EEG). Humans have several measurable brain-wave frequencies, and the slower the brain-wave state we're in, the deeper we go into the inner world of the subconscious mind. In order of slowest to fastest, the brain-wave states are *delta* (deep, restorative sleep—totally unconscious), *theta* (a twilight state between deep sleep and wakefulness), *alpha* (the creative, imaginative state), *beta* (conscious thought), and *gamma* (elevated states of consciousness).

Beta is our everyday waking state. When we're in beta, the thinking brain, or neocortex, is processing all of the incoming sensory data and creating meaning between our outer and inner worlds. Beta isn't the best state for meditation, because when we're in beta, the outer world appears more real than the inner world. Three levels of brain-wave patterns make up the beta-wave spectrum: *low-range beta* (relaxed, interested attention, like reading a book), *mid-range beta* (focused attention on an ongoing stimulus outside the body, like learning and then remembering), and *high-range beta* (highly focused, crisis-mode attention, when stress chemicals are produced). The higher the beta brain waves, the further away we get from being able to access the operating system.

Most days, we move back and forth between beta and alpha states. Alpha is our relaxation state, where we pay less attention to the outer world and start to pay more attention to our inner world. When we're in alpha, we're in a light state of meditation; you could also call that imagination or daydreaming. In this state, our inner world is more real than our outer world, because that's what we're paying attention to.

When we go from high-frequency beta to slower alpha, where we can pay attention, concentrate, and focus in a more relaxed manner, we automatically activate the frontal lobe. As the previous material has presented, the frontal lobe lowers the volume on the brain circuits that process time and space. Here, we're no longer in survival mode. We're in a more creative state that makes us more suggestible than we were in beta.

More challenging is learning how to drop down even further into theta, which is a kind of twilight state where we're half-awake and half-asleep (often described as "mind awake, body asleep"). This is the state we're shooting for in meditation, because it's the brain-wave pattern where we're the most suggestible. In theta, we can access the subconscious, because the analytical mind isn't operating—we're mostly in our inner world.

Think of theta as the key to your own subconscious kingdom. Take another look at Figure 6.8. It shows brain-wave states and how they correlate with the conscious and subconscious mind. Then take a look at Figure 6.9, which illustrates the different brain-wave frequencies.

You'll find this brief tour through brain-wave patterns even more useful when you get to the practice of meditation, later in the book. Don't expect that you'll necessarily be able to drop right into theta on command, of course, but having some knowledge of what the various brain states are and what effect they have on what you're trying to achieve will help.

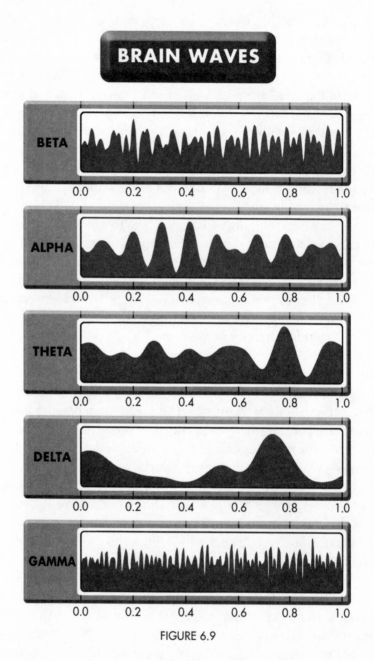

FIGURE 6.9

This illustration shows the different brain-wave states (during a one-second interval).
Gamma brain-wave patterns are included because they represent a
level of super-awareness, which reflects a heightened state of consciousness.

Anatomy of an "Assassination"

Now let's return to the story of Ivan Santiago and the other hypnosis subjects from the start of this chapter. Obviously, these folks have an easier time getting past their analytical minds than most of us. They seem to have both a neuroplasticity and an emotional plasticity that allow them to make their inner worlds more real than their outer worlds. In their normal waking states, they probably spend more time in alpha than in beta, so they have fewer stress hormones circulating that can pull them out of homeostasis. Their highly suggestible states better enable their conscious minds to control the autonomic functions of their subconscious minds.

Yet they're not all the same; several different degrees of suggestibility were demonstrated in this study. The 16 people who passed the initial evaluation were certainly suggestible, although they weren't all as suggestible as those who passed the next test by taking their clothes off in public after being given a posthypnotic suggestion to do so, going against deeply rooted social norms. The four who passed that test were certainly highly suggestible, able to be greater than their social environment. But when it came to immersing themselves in the ice water, three of those four couldn't go that far; they weren't able to be greater than their physical environment.

Only Santiago, who remained greater than his physical environment in extreme conditions for an extended period of time while having dominion over his body, demonstrated the highest level of suggestibility. He was able not only to withstand the frigid ice bath, but also to be greater than his moral environment, by following the posthypnotic suggestion to shoot the "foreign dignitary," despite the fact that his conscious personality was hardly one of a cold-blooded killer.

In terms of the placebo effect, it takes a similar high degree of suggestibility to be greater than the body and greater than the environment for an extended period of time—that is, to accept, believe, and surrender to the idea of your inner world being more real than your outer world. But in just a few chapters, you'll learn how you can not only change your beliefs and become more suggestible, but also use that state to program your subconscious mind—not to shoot a stuntman with a prop gun, fortunately, but to triumph over whatever health issues, emotional traumas, or other personal matters you may be dealing with.

Chapter Seven

Attitudes, Beliefs, and Perceptions

A 12-year-old Indonesian boy with a vacant stare opens his mouth to willingly accept shards of broken glass from people in a crowd gathered in a Jakarta park to watch traditional Javanese trance dancing called "kuda lumping." The boy chews on the glass and swallows it, as if it were nothing more than a handful of popcorn or pretzels, and he shows no ill effects. As a third-generation kuda lumper, this youth has been ingesting glass in similar mystical performances since he was nine. The boy and the other 19 members of his traditional dance troupe recite a Javanese spell before every performance, summoning the spirits of the dead to reside in one of them for the duration of that day's dance, protecting that dancer from pain.[1]

The boy and his fellow dancers are no different, in certain respects, from the Appalachian snake-handling preachers described in Chapter 1 who become anointed with the spirit and enthusiastically dance around the pulpit with venomous snakes coiled around their arms and shoulders. Bringing them dangerously close to their faces, they are seemingly immune to the venom if bitten. The dancers are also similar to the Fijian firewalkers from the Sawau tribe on the island of Beqa, who unflinchingly walk across white-hot stones that have been covered in flaming logs and glowing red coals for hours, an ability said to have been given to one of the tribe's ancestors by a god and then passed down within the tribe.

The glass-eating boy, the snake-handling preacher, and the Fijian firewalker never pause even for a moment to think, *I wonder if it will work this time?* There isn't an ounce of wishy-washiness in any of them. The decision to chew glass or handle copperheads or tread on searing stones transcends their bodies, the environment, and time, altering their biology to allow them to do the seemingly impossible. Their rock-solid belief in the protection of their gods leaves no room for second-guessing.

The placebo effect is similar in that very strong beliefs are part of the equation. Yet this component hasn't been examined much, because up to this point in mind-body research, most scientific studies have measured only the effects of the placebo instead of looking for the cause. Whether the shift in one's internal state has been the product of faith healing, conditioning, the release of suppressed emotions, a belief in symbols, or a specific spiritual practice, the question still remains: What has happened to create such profound alterations in the body—and if we discover what that is, can we cultivate it?

Where Our Beliefs Come From

Our beliefs aren't always as conscious as we think they are. We may very well accept an idea on the surface, but if deep down, we don't really believe it's possible, then our acceptance is just an intellectual process. Because calling upon the placebo effect requires us to truly change our beliefs about ourselves and what's possible for our bodies and our health, we need to understand what beliefs are and where they come from.

Let's suppose a person goes to the doctor with certain symptoms and is diagnosed with a condition based on the physician's objective findings. The doctor gives the patient a diagnosis, prognosis, and treatment options based on the average outcome. The moment the person hears the doctor say "diabetes," "cancer," "hypothyroidism," or "chronic fatigue syndrome," a series of thoughts, images, and emotions is conjured up based on his or her past experience. That experience could be that the patient's parents had the condition, that he or she saw a show on TV in which one of the characters died of that disease, or even that something the person read on the Internet scared him or her about the diagnosis.

Once the patient sees the doctor and hears a professional opinion, the patient automatically accepts the condition, then believes what the confident doctor has said, and finally surrenders to the treatment and possible outcomes—and this is done without any real analysis. The patient is suggestible (and susceptible) to what the doctor says. If the person then embraces the emotions of fear, worry, and anxiety, along with sadness, then the only possible thoughts (or autosuggestions) are those that are equal to how he or she feels.

The patient can *try* to have positive thoughts about beating the disease, but his or her body still feels bad because the wrong placebo has been given, resulting in the wrong state of being, the signaling of the same genes, and the inability to see or perceive any new possibilities. The patient is pretty much at the mercy of his or her beliefs (and the beliefs of the doctor) about the diagnosis.

So when people like the folks you'll read about in the next few chapters healed themselves using the placebo effect, what did they do differently? First, they didn't *accept* the finality of their diagnosis, prognosis, or treatment. Nor did they *believe* in the most probable outcome or future destiny that their doctors had authoritatively outlined. Finally, they didn't *surrender* to the diagnosis, prognosis, or suggested treatment. Because they had a different attitude from those who *did* accept, believe, and surrender, they were in a different state of being.

They weren't suggestible to the doctors' advice and opinions, because they didn't feel fearful, victimized, or sad. Instead they were optimistic and enthusiastic, and those emotions drove a new set of thoughts, which enabled them to see new possibilities. Because they had different ideas and beliefs about what was possible, they didn't *condition* their bodies to the worst-case scenario, they didn't *expect the same predictable outcome* as others who'd received the same diagnosis, and they didn't *assign the same meaning* to the diagnosis as everyone else with the same condition. They assigned a different meaning to their future, so they had a different intention. They understood epigenetics and neuroplasticity, so instead of passively seeing themselves as victims of the disease, they used that knowledge to become proactive, fueled by what they'd learned in my workshops and events. As a result, these folks also got different and better results than other people who'd received the same diagnosis—just as the hotel maids got better results after the researchers gave them more information.

Now think about the average person who receives a diagnosis and promptly announces, "I'm going to beat this." Someone may not accept the condition and the outcome the doctor outlines, but the difference is that most people haven't truly changed their beliefs about not being sick. Changing a belief requires changing a subconscious program—since a belief, as you'll soon learn, is a subconscious state of being.

Folks who use only their conscious minds to change never come out of the resting state to reprogram their genes, because they don't know how to do that. This is where their healing stops. They're unable to surrender to possibility, because they're not truly able to become suggestible to anything different from what the doctor tells them.

Is it possible that, whenever people don't respond to treatment or when their health stays the same, they're living by the same emotional state every day, accepting, believing, and surrendering to the medical model without too much analysis, based on the social consciousness of millions of other people who've done exactly the same thing? Does a doctor's diagnosis become the modern-day equivalent of a voodoo curse?

So now, let's dissect belief a little further, backing up just slightly to begin with the following idea: When you string a succession of thoughts and feelings together so that they ultimately become habituated or automatic, they form an *attitude*. And since how you think and feel creates a state of being, attitudes are really just shortened states of being. They can fluctuate from moment to moment as you alter how you think and feel. Any particular attitude can last for minutes, hours, days, or even a week or two.

For example, if you have a series of good thoughts that are aligned with a series of good feelings, you might say, "I have a good attitude today." And if you have a sequence of negative thoughts that's connected to a sequence of negative feelings, then you might say, "I have a bad attitude today." If you revisit the same attitude enough times, then it becomes automatic.

If you repeat or maintain certain attitudes long enough and you string those attitudes together, that's how you create a *belief*. A belief is just an extended state of being—essentially, beliefs are thoughts and feelings (attitudes) that you keep thinking and feeling over and over again until you hardwire them in your brain and emotionally condition them into your body. You could say that you become addicted to them, which is why it's so hard to change them and why it doesn't feel good on a gut level when they're challenged. Because experiences are neurologically etched into your brain (causing you to think) and chemically embodied as emotions (causing you to feel), most of your beliefs are based on past memories.

So when you revisit the same thoughts over and over by thinking about and analyzing what you remember from your past, these thoughts will fire and wire into an automatic unconscious program. And if you cultivate the same feelings based on past experiences and you feel the same as you did when the event originally occurred, you'll condition your body to subconsciously be the mind of that emotion—and your body will unconsciously be living in the past.

And if the redundancy of how you think and feel over time conditions your body to become the mind, and it becomes programmed subconsciously, then beliefs are subconscious and also unconscious states of being derived from the past. Beliefs are also more permanent than attitudes; they can last for months or even years. And because they last longer, they become more programmed within you.

A case in point is a story from my childhood that's stamped in my memory. I grew up in an Italian family, and when I was going into fourth grade, we moved to another city that had a mixture of both Italian and Jewish residents. On my first day of school that year, the teacher assigned me to a seat in a group of six desks along with three Jewish girls. That was the day the girls broke the news to me that Jesus wasn't Italian. It was one of the most memorable days of my life.

When I came home that afternoon, my little Italian mother kept asking me how my first day of school went, and I wouldn't talk to her. After I ignored her enough times, she finally grabbed me by the arm and insisted I tell her what was wrong.

"I thought Jesus was Italian!" I blurted out angrily.

"What are you talking about?" she responded. "He's Jewish!"

"Jewish?" I shot back. "What do you mean? He looks Italian in all those pictures, doesn't he? Grandma talks in Italian to him all day long. And what's the deal with the Roman Empire? Isn't Rome in Italy?"

So the belief that I had—that Jesus was Italian—was based on my past experiences, and how I thought and felt about Jesus had become my automatic state of being. This belief took some getting over, because changing deep-seated beliefs isn't easy. Needless to say, I succeeded.

Now let's move the concept forward a little further. If you string a group of related beliefs together, they form your *perception.* So your perception of reality is a sustained state of being that's based on your long-standing beliefs, attitudes, thoughts, and feelings. And since your beliefs become subconscious and also unconscious states of being (that is, you don't even know why you believe certain things, or you aren't really conscious of your beliefs until they're tested), your perceptions—how you *subjectively* see things—for the most part, become your subconscious and unconscious view of your reality from the past.

In fact, scientific experiments have shown that you don't see reality as it truly is. Instead, you unconsciously fill in your reality based on your memories of the past, which is what's neurochemically maintained in your brain.[2] When perceptions become implicit or nondeclarative (as was discussed in the last chapter), they become automatic or subconscious so that you automatically edit reality subjectively.

For example, you know your car is your car, because you've driven it so many times. You have the same experience of your car daily, because nothing much changes about it. You think and feel the same way about it most every day. Your attitude about your car has created a belief about it, which has formed a particular perception about your vehicle—that it's a good car, say, because it rarely breaks down. And although you automatically accept that perception, it's actually a subjective perception, because someone else may have the same make and model of car as you do, and that person's car may break down all the time, causing him or her to have a different belief and different perceptions about the same vehicle based on personal experience.

In fact, if you're like most people, you probably don't pay attention to several aspects of your car unless something goes wrong. You expect it to run as it did the day before; you naturally expect your future experience of driving your car to be like your past experience, yesterday and the day before—that's your perception. But when it malfunctions, you have to pay more attention to it (like listening to the sound of the motor more closely) and become conscious of your unconscious perception of your car.

Once your perception of your car is altered because something has changed about the way it drives, you'll now perceive your car differently. The same is true of relationships with your spouse and your co-workers, your culture and your race, and even your body and your pain. Actually, this is the way most perceptions about reality function.

Now, if you want to change an implicit or subconscious perception, you must become more conscious and less *un*conscious. In truth, you'd have to increase your level of attention to all of the aspects of yourself and your life that you've previously stopped paying much attention to. Better yet, you'd have to wake up, change your level of awareness, and become conscious of what you were once unconscious about.

But it's rarely that easy, because if you experience the same reality over and over again, then the way you think and feel about your current world will continue to develop into the same attitudes, which will inspire the same beliefs, which will expand into the same perceptions (as shown in Figure 7.1).

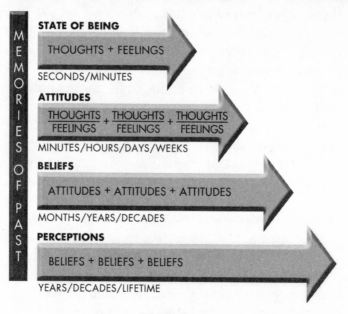

FIGURE 7.1

Your thoughts and feelings come from your past memories. If you think and feel a certain way, you begin to create an attitude. An attitude is a cycle of short-term thoughts and feelings experienced over and over again. Attitudes are shortened states of being. If you string a series of attitudes together, you create a belief. Beliefs are more elongated states of being and tend to become subconscious. When you add beliefs together, you create a perception. Your perceptions have everything to do with the choices you make, the behaviors you exhibit, the relationships you choose, and the realities you create.

When your perception becomes so second nature and so automatic that you really don't pay attention to the way reality truly is (because you automatically expect everything to be the same), you're now unconsciously accepting and agreeing to that reality—the way most people unconsciously accept and agree to what the medical model tells them about a diagnosis.

So the *only* way to change your beliefs and perceptions in order to create a placebo response is to change your state of being. You have to finally see your old, limited beliefs for what they are—records of the past—and be willing to let go of them so that you can embrace new beliefs about yourself that will help you create a new future.

Changing Your Beliefs

So then ask yourself: What beliefs and perceptions about you and your life have you been unconsciously agreeing to that you'd have to change in order to create this new state of being? This is a question that requires some thought, because as I said, with many of these beliefs, we aren't even aware that we believe them.

Often, we accept certain cues from our environment that then prime us to accept certain beliefs, which may or may not be true. Either way, the moment we accept the belief, it has an effect not only on our performance, but also on the choices we make.

Remember the study from Chapter 2 about the women taking the math test who first read fake research reports about men being better than women in math? Those who'd read that the advantage was due to genetics scored lower than those who'd read that the advantage was due to stereotyping. Although both reports were false—men are no better at math than women—the women in the group who'd read that they had a genetic disadvantage believed what they'd read and then scored lower. It was the same with the white men who were told that Asians score slightly better than whites on a test they were about to take. In both cases, when the students were primed to unconsciously believe they wouldn't score as well, they in fact didn't—even though what they were told was totally false.

With this in mind, take a look at this list of some common limiting beliefs and see which ones you may be harboring without being fully aware that you're doing so:

I'm not good at math. I'm shy. I'm short-tempered. I'm not smart or creative. I'm a lot like my parents. Men shouldn't cry or be vulnerable. I can't find a partner. Women are lesser than men. My race or culture is superior. Life is serious. Life is difficult, and no one cares. I'm never going to be a success. I have to work hard to make it in life. Nothing good ever happens to me. I'm not a lucky person. Things never go my way. I never have enough time. It's someone else's responsibility to make me happy. When I own this particular thing, then I'll be happy. It's hard to change reality. Reality is a linear process. Germs make me sick. I gain weight easily. I need eight hours of sleep. My pain is normal, and it'll never go away. My biological clock is ticking. Beauty looks like this. Having fun is frivolous. God is outside of me. I'm a bad person, so God doesn't love me. . . .

I could go on forever, but you get the idea.

Since beliefs and perceptions are based on past experiences, then any of these beliefs that you happen to hold about yourself came from your past. So are they true, or did you just make them up? *Even if they were true* at some point in time, that doesn't necessarily mean that they're true *now*.

We don't look at it that way, of course, because we're addicted to our beliefs; we're addicted to the emotions of our past. We see our beliefs as truths, not ideas that we can change. If we have very strong beliefs about something, evidence to the contrary could be sitting right in front of us, but we may not see it because what we perceive is entirely different. We've in fact conditioned ourselves to believe all sorts of things that aren't necessarily true—and many of these things are having a negative impact on our health and happiness.

Certain cultural beliefs are a good example. Remember the story about the voodoo curse from Chapter 1? The patient was convinced he was going to die, because the voodoo priest had put a hex on him. The hex only worked because he (and others in his culture) believed voodoo to be true—it wasn't the *voodoo* that had hexed him; it was the *belief* in the voodoo.

Other cultural beliefs can cause premature deaths. For instance, Chinese Americans who have a disease, combined with a birth year that Chinese astrology and Chinese medicine consider to be ill fated, die up to five years early, according to researchers at the University of California at San Diego who studied the death records of almost 30,000 Chinese Americans.[3] The effect was stronger in those who were more attached to Chinese traditions and beliefs, and the results also held consistent for nearly all major causes of death studied. For example, Chinese Americans born in years associated with susceptibility to diseases involving lumps and tumors died of lymphatic cancer four years younger than Chinese Americans born in other years or than non–Chinese Americans with similar cancers.

As these examples demonstrate, we're suggestible only to what we consciously or unconsciously believe to be true. An Eskimo who doesn't believe in Chinese astrology is no more suggestible to the idea that he's vulnerable to a certain disease because he was born in the year of the tiger or the year of the dragon than an Episcopalian would be suggestible to the idea that a hex from a voodoo priest could kill him or her.

But once *any of us* accepts, believes, and surrenders to an outcome without consciously thinking about it or analyzing it, then we'll become suggestible to that particular reality. In most people, such a belief is planted well beyond the conscious mind into the subconscious system, which is what creates the disease. So now let me ask you another question: How many personal beliefs based on cultural experiences do *you* have that may not be true?

Changing beliefs may be difficult, but it's not impossible. Just think what would happen if you were able to successfully challenge your unconscious beliefs. Instead of thinking and feeling, *I never have enough time to get everything done,* what if you instead thought and felt, *I live in "no-time," and I accomplish everything?* What if instead of believing, *The universe is conspiring against me,* you believed, *The universe is friendly and works in my favor?* What a great belief! How would you think, how would you live, and how would you walk down the street if you believed the universe works in your favor? How do you think that would change your life?

When you change a belief, you have to start by first accepting that it's possible, then change your level of energy with the heightened emotion you read about earlier, and finally allow your biology to reorganize itself. It's not necessary to think about how that biological reorganization will happen or when it's going to happen; that's the analytical mind at work, which pulls you back into a beta brain-wave state and makes you less suggestible. Instead, you just have to make a decision that has finality. And once the amplitude or energy of that decision becomes greater than the hardwired programs in your brain and the emotional addiction in your body, then you are greater than your past, your body will respond to a new mind, and you can effect real change.

You already know how to do this. Think about a time in your past when you made up your mind to change something about yourself or your life. If you recall, a moment came when you probably said to yourself, *I don't care how I feel* [body]*! It doesn't matter what's going on in my life* [environment]*!* And, *I'm not concerned how long it will take* [time]*! I'm going to do this!*

Instantly, you got goose bumps. That's because you moved into an altered state of being. The moment you felt that energy, you were sending your body new information. You felt inspired, and you came out of your familiar resting state. That's because, by thought alone, your body moved from living in the same past to living in a new future. In reality, your body was no longer the mind; *you* were the mind. You were changing a belief.

The Effect of Perception

Like beliefs, our perceptions of past experiences—whether positive or negative—directly affect our subconscious state of being and our health. In 1984, Gretchen van Boemel, M.D., then associate director of clinical electrophysiology at Doheny Eye Institute in Los Angeles, uncovered a striking example of this when she noticed a disturbing trend among Cambodian women referred to Doheny. The women, all between the ages of 40 and 60 and living in nearby Long Beach, California (known as Little Phnom Penh because of its roughly 50,000 Cambodian residents), were having severe vision problems, including blindness, in disproportionately high numbers.

Physically, the women's eyes were perfectly healthy. Dr. van Boemel did brain scans on the women to evaluate how well their visual systems were functioning and compared them to how well their eyes were seeing. She found that each of the women had perfectly normal visual acuity, often 20/20 or 20/40, although when they tried to read an eye chart, their vision tested at legally blind. Some of the women had absolutely no light perception and couldn't even detect any shadows—*even though there wasn't anything physically wrong with their eyes.*

When Dr. van Boemel teamed up with Patricia Rozée, Ph.D., of California State University, Long Beach, to do research on the women, they found that those who had the worst vision had spent the most time living under the Khmer Rouge or in refugee camps when communist dictator Pol Pot was in power.[4] The genocide perpetrated by the Khmer Rouge was responsible for the deaths of at least 1.5 million Cambodians between 1975 and 1979.

Of the women studied, 90 percent had lost family members (some as many as ten) during that time, and 70 percent were forced to watch their loved ones—sometimes even their entire families—being brutally murdered. "These women saw things that their minds just could not accept," Rozée told the *Los Angeles Times*.[5] "Their minds simply closed down, and they refused to see anymore—refused to see any more death, any more torture, any more rape, any more starvation."

One woman was forced to watch her husband and four children be killed right in front of her, and she lost her sight immediately afterward. Another woman had to watch a Khmer Rouge soldier beat her brother and his three children to death, which included seeing her three-month-old nephew being thrown against a tree until he died. She started losing her eyesight right after that.[6] The women also suffered beatings, starvation, untold humiliations, sexual abuse, torture, and 20-hour days of enforced labor. Although now they were safe, many of these women told the researchers that they preferred to stay in their homes, where they had to relive their memories of the atrocities over and over through recurring nightmares and intrusive thoughts.

Documenting a total of 150 cases of psychosomatic blindness in Cambodian women in Long Beach—the largest known group of such victims anywhere in the world—van Boemel and Rozée presented their research at the 1986 American Psychological Association annual meeting in Washington, D.C. The audience was riveted.

The women in this study became blind or nearly blind not because of some eye disease or physical malfunction, but because the events they lived through had such an emotional impact that they literally "cried until they could not see."[7] The heightened emotional amplitude from being forced to bear witness to the unbearable left them not wanting to see anymore. The event created physical changes in their biology—not in their eyes, but most likely in their brains—which altered their perception of reality for the rest of their lives. And because they kept replaying the traumatizing scenes over and over in their minds, their vision never improved.

While this is certainly an extreme example, our past traumatic experiences probably have similar effects on us. If you're having vision challenges, what things might you have chosen not to see because of painful or frightening past experiences? Similarly, if you're having hearing challenges, what in your life might you be unwilling to hear?

Figure 7.2 charts how all of this happens. The line in the chart reflects a relative measurement of a person's state of being, which starts out at a more or less normal or baseline level before the event occurs. When the line spikes, it indicates a strong emotional reaction to an event—such as when the women experienced the atrocities of the Khmer Rouge soldiers. That horrific experience neurologically branded their brains and chemically changed their bodies, as well as altered their state of being—their thoughts, their feelings, their attitudes, their beliefs, and ultimately their perceptions. Specifically, the women no longer wished to look at the world anymore, so through neurological rewiring and chemical resignaling, their biology complied.

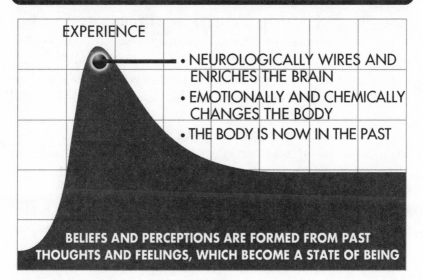

HOW AN EXPERIENCE BIOLOGICALLY CHANGES YOU

EXPERIENCE

- NEUROLOGICALLY WIRES AND ENRICHES THE BRAIN
- EMOTIONALLY AND CHEMICALLY CHANGES THE BODY
- THE BODY IS NOW IN THE PAST

BELIEFS AND PERCEPTIONS ARE FORMED FROM PAST THOUGHTS AND FEELINGS, WHICH BECOME A STATE OF BEING

FIGURE 7.2

A highly charged experience in our external reality will impress itself upon the circuitry of the brain and emotionally brand the body. As a result, the brain and body live in the past, and the event alters our state of being, as well as our perception of reality. We are no longer the same personality.

Although the line in the graph eventually falls and levels off, the place where it ends up is a different place from where it began—indicating that the person remains chemically and neurologically altered by the experience. At that point for the Cambodian women, they were effectively living in the past, because they remained affected by the neurological and chemical branding that had come from the experience. They were no longer the same women; the event changed their state of being.

The Power of the Environment

Just changing your beliefs and perceptions once isn't enough. You have to reinforce that change over and over. To see why, let's return for a moment to the Parkinson's patients mentioned earlier who improved their motor skills after receiving a saline injection that they thought was a powerful drug.

As you'll recall, the moment they moved into a state of better health, their autonomic nervous systems started to endorse this new state by producing dopamine in their brains. That didn't happen because they were praying or hoping or wishing their bodies would make dopamine; it happened because they *became* people who made dopamine.

Unfortunately, however, the effect doesn't stick for everyone. In fact, for some, the placebo effect only lasts for a certain amount of time, because they go back to who they were before: their old states of being. In this case, when the Parkinson's patients went back home and saw their caregivers, saw their spouses, slept in the same beds, ate the same food, sat in the same rooms, and maybe played chess with the same friends who complained about their pains, their same old environments reminded them of their same old personalities and their same old states of being. All of the conditions in their familiar lives reminded them of who they were before, so they just slipped right back into those identities, and their various motor problems recurred.[8] They *reidentified* with their environments. The environment is that strong.

The same thing happens with drug addicts who've been clean for many years. If you put them back in their same environments where they used to do drugs, even without their ingesting any drug, being there turns on the same receptor sites in their cells that the drugs did when they were using—and that in turn creates physiological changes in their bodies as if they've taken the drugs, increasing their cravings.[9] Their conscious minds have no control over that. It's automatic.

Let's examine this concept a bit further. You've learned that the conditioning process creates strong associative memories. You've also learned that associative memories stimulate subconscious automatic physiological functions by activating the autonomic nervous system. Think of Pavlov's dogs again. Once Pavlov conditioned the dogs to associate the bell with getting fed, the dogs' bodies were immediately physiologically changed, without much control from the conscious mind. It was the cue from the environment that (via associative memory) automatically, autonomically, subconsciously, and physiologically changed the dogs' internal states. They began to salivate and their digestive juices turned on, because they were anticipating a reward. The dogs' conscious minds couldn't do that. It was the stimulus from the environment that created the associative memory from the conditioned response.

Now let's revisit the Parkinson's patients and the former drug users. We could say that the instant any one of these individuals returned to the familiar environment, the body would automatically and physiologically return back to the old state of being—without the conscious mind having much control over it. In fact, that past state of being, which has been thinking and feeling the same way for years on end, has conditioned the body to become the mind. That is, the body is the mind that responds to the environment. That's why it's so hard for anyone in this situation to change.

And the greater the addiction to the emotion, the greater the conditioned response is to the stimulus in the environment. For example, let's say you were addicted to coffee and wanted to break your addiction to it. If you were visiting my house and I started making a java, and you heard the blast of the espresso machine, smelled the coffee brewing, and saw me drinking it, here's what would happen: The moment your senses picked up those cues from the environment, your body, as the mind, would subconsciously, automatically respond without much help from your conscious mind—because you conditioned it to be that way. Your body-mind would then be craving its physiological reward, waging a war against your conscious mind, trying to convince you to take a sip or two.

But if you truly broke the addiction to coffee and then I made a cup in front of you, you could have some or not, because you wouldn't have the physiological response you had previously. You'd no longer be conditioned (your body would no longer be the mind), and the associative memory of your environment would no longer have the same effect on you.

The same holds true for emotional addictions. For instance, if you have memorized guilt from your past experiences and unconsciously live that way every day in the present, then like most people, you'll use someone or something at someplace in your external environment to reaffirm your addiction to guilt. Try as you might to be consciously greater than it, the moment you see your mother (whom you use to feel guilty) at the house where you grew up, your body will autonomically, chemically, and physiologically return to the same past state of guilt in the present moment, without your conscious mind being involved. Your body, which has been subconsciously programmed to be the mind of guilt, is already living in the past in that present moment. So it's more natural to feel guilty when you're with your mother than to feel any other way. And just as in the drug addict, a conditioned response has altered your internal state based on your association with your present-past external reality. Break the addiction to guilt by changing the subconscious programming, and you can be in the presence of the same conditions and remain free from your present-past reality.

Researchers from the Victoria University of Wellington in New Zealand examined the effect of environment using a group of 148 college students who were invited to take part in a study set in a bar-like atmosphere.[10] The researchers told half the students that they would get vodka and tonic and told the rest they'd receive just tonic water. In reality, the bartenders in the study didn't pour a single drop of vodka; all the students got just plain tonic. The bar-like atmosphere the researchers fashioned looked very realistic, right down to the resealing of the vodka bottles that had been cleverly filled with flat tonic water. The bartenders rimmed glasses with limes dunked in vodka for a more realistic effect, before proceeding to mix and pour drinks as though they were serving the real thing.

The subjects became tipsy and acted drunk, with some even showing physical signs of intoxication. They didn't get drunk because they drank alcohol; they got drunk because the environment, by associative memory, cued their brains and bodies to respond in the same old, familiar way.

When the researchers eventually told the students the truth, many were amazed and insisted that they really did feel drunk at the time. They believed they were drinking alcohol, and those beliefs translated into neurochemicals, which altered their states of being.

In other words, their beliefs alone were sufficient to fire up a biochemical change in their bodies that was equal to being drunk. That's because the students conditioned themselves enough times to associate alcohol with a change in their internal chemical states. As the subjects expected or anticipated the future change in their inner states based on their past associative memories of drinking, they were cued by the environment to physiologically change, just as did Pavlov's dogs.

There's a flip side, too, of course. The environment can also signal healing. Hospital patients in Pennsylvania who recovered from surgery in a room with a view of a stand of trees in a natural suburban setting needed less-potent pain medications and were released seven to nine days earlier than patients in rooms facing a brown brick wall.[11] Our states of mind, created from the environment, can most definitely contribute to healing our brains and our bodies.

So, then, do you need a sugar pill or a saline injection or a sham procedure or a picture window—some*thing* or some*one* or some*place* in your external environment—to move into a new state of being? Or can you do it just by changing how you think and feel? Can you simply believe in a new possibility of health, without relying on any external stimulus, and make the thought in your brain a new emotional experience to the degree that it changes your body and you become greater than the conditioning in your external environment?

If so, what you've just read suggests that it would be a good idea to change your internal state every day—before you get up and face your same old environment so that it won't pull you, as it did the Parkinson's patients, back to your old state of being. Remember Janis Schonfeld, from Chapter 1, who made physical changes in her brain by thinking she was taking an antidepressant? Part of the reason the placebo worked so well for her was that taking that inert pill was a *daily reminder* to change her state of being (because she associated taking the pill with her optimistic thoughts and feelings about getting better—as do more than 80 percent of people who take an antidepressant placebo).

If you could access a new state of being through meditation by combining a clear intention with getting in touch with that heightened state of emotion that was mentioned earlier, and you got up jazzed and on fire about what you were creating every day, you'd finally start coming out of your resting state. You'd then be in a new state of being, with a different attitude, belief, and perception, no longer reacting to the same things in the same way, because now your environment would no longer control how you think and feel. You'd then be making new choices and demonstrating new behaviors, which would lead to new experiences and new emotions. And so you'd then turn into a new and different personality—a personality that doesn't have the arthritic pain or the Parkinson's motor issues or the infertility or whatever other condition you want to change.

I want to take a moment to point out here that not all sickness and disease starts in our minds, of course. Certainly, babies are born with genetic defects and conditions that clearly couldn't have been triggered by their thoughts, feelings, attitudes, and beliefs. And trauma and accidents do indeed happen. Furthermore, exposure to environmental toxins can definitely wreak havoc in the human body. My point is not that when these things come up, we've somehow asked for them—although it's true that our physical bodies can be weakened by stress hormones and made more susceptible to disease when our immune systems shut down. My point is that no matter what the source of our ills, there's a possibility that we can change our condition.

Changing Your Energy

So now we can see that if we want to change our beliefs and create a placebo effect to improve our health and our lives, we have to do the exact opposite of what the Cambodian women did by default. By holding a clear and firm intention and heightening our emotional energy, we have to create a new *internal* experience in our minds and bodies that's greater than the past *external* experience. In other words, when we decide to create a new belief, the amplitude or energy of that choice must be high enough that it's greater than the hardwired programs and emotional conditioning in the body.

To see what happens when we do just this, take a look at Figure 7.3 on the following page. Here, the energy of the choice in this new experience is *greater* than the energy of the trauma in the past experience (as we saw in Figure 7.2), which is why the peak in this graph is *higher* than the peak in the first graph. And as a result, the effects of this new experience *override* the residue of the neural programming and emotional conditioning from the past experience.

This process, if we do it right, actually repatterns our brains and changes our biology; the new experience will reorganize the old programming, and in so doing, it will *remove* the neurological evidence of that past experience. (Think of how a bigger wave breaking farther up on the beach erases any sign of whatever shell, seaweed, sea foam, or sand pattern was there before.) Strong emotional experiences create long-term memories. So this new internal experience creates new long-term memories that override our past long-term memories, thus the choice becomes an experience

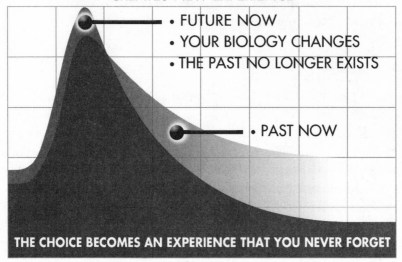

FIGURE 7.3

In order to change a belief or perception about yourself and your life, you have to make a decision with such firm intention that the choice carries an amplitude of energy that is greater than the hardwired programs in the brain and the emotional addiction in the body, and the body must respond to a new mind. When the choice creates a new inner experience that becomes greater than the past outer experience, it will rewrite the circuits in your brain and resignal your body emotionally. Since experiences create long-term memories, when the choice becomes an experience that you never forget, you are changed. Biologically, the past no longer exists. We could say that your body in that present moment is in a new future.

that we never forget. There should be no evidence of our pasts in our brains and bodies any longer, and the new signal then rewrites the neurological program and genetically changes the body.

Now look at Figure 7.3 again and notice how the slope of the line in the graph goes *all the way* back down (whereas in Figure 7.2, it descended but still remained higher than it was at the point where it started). That shows there's no trace left of the past experience; it no longer exists in this new state of being.

In addition to reorganizing your neurocircuitry, this new signal also begins to rewrite the body's conditioning by breaking the emotional attachment to the past. When that happens, in that second, the body is living fully in the present; it is no longer a prisoner of the past. That heightened energy is felt within the body and translated as a *new* emotion (which is just another way of saying "energy in motion," or "e-motion"), whether that emotion is feeling invincible, courageous, empowered, compassionate, inspired, or whatever. And it's *energy* that's changing our biology, our neurocircuitry, and our genetic expression—not chemistry.

A similar process happens with the firewalkers, the glass chewers, and the snake handlers. They get clear that they're going to move into a different state of mind and body. And when they hold that firm intention to make that shift, the energy of that decision creates internal changes in their brains and bodies that make them immune to the external conditions in the environment for an extended period of time. Their energy now is protecting them in a way that, in that moment, transcends their biology.

As it happens, our neurochemistry isn't the only thing that responds to heightened states of energy. The receptor sites on the outside of the body's cells happen to be a hundred times more sensitive to energy and frequency than they are to the physical chemical signals, like neuropeptides, that we know gain access to our cells' DNA.[12] Research consistently reveals that invisible forces of the electromagnetic spectrum influence every single aspect of cellular biology and genetic regulation.[13] Cell receptors are frequency-specific to incoming energy signals. The energies of the electromagnetic spectrum include microwaves, radio waves, x-rays, extremely low-frequency waves, sound harmonic frequencies, ultraviolet rays, and even infrared waves. Specific frequencies of electromagnetic energy can influence the behavior of DNA, RNA, and protein synthesis; alter protein shape and function; control gene regulation and expression; stimulate nerve-cell growth; and influence cell division and cell differentiation, as well as instruct specific cells to organize into tissues and organs. All of these cellular activities influenced by energy are part of the expression of life.

And if that's true, then it has to be true for some reason. Remember the 98.5 percent of our DNA that scientists call "junk DNA" because it doesn't seem to serve much of a useful purpose? Surely Mother Nature wouldn't place all of this encoded information in our cells, waiting to be read, without giving us the ability to create some type of signal to unlock it; after all, nature doesn't waste anything.

Could it be that your own energy and consciousness is what creates the right kind of signal outside of the cells to enable you to tap into that vast "parts list" of potentials? And if that was true, if you changed your energy the way you read about earlier in this chapter, could that help you access your true ability to authentically heal your body? When you change your energy, you change your state of being. And the rewiring in the brain and the new chemical emotions in the body trigger epigenetic changes, and the result is that you become quite literally *a new person.* The person you were before is history; a part of that person simply vanished along with the neurocircuitry, chemical-emotional addictions, and genetic expression that supported your old state of being.

Chapter Eight

The Quantum Mind

Reality can be a bit of a moving target—literally. We're used to thinking of reality as something fixed and certain, but as you'll soon see in this chapter, the way we've always been taught to see it isn't the way it really is. And if you're going to learn how to be your own placebo by using your mind to affect matter, it's vital that you understand the true nature of reality, how mind and matter are related, and how reality can shift—because if you don't know how and why those shifts occur, you won't be able to direct any outcomes according to your intentions.

Before we dive into the quantum universe, let's take a look at where our ideas about reality came from and where they've brought us so far. Thanks to René Descartes and Sir Isaac Newton, for centuries the study of the universe was divided into two categories: *matter* and *mind*. The study of matter (the material world) was declared the realm of science, because for the most part, the laws of the universe that govern the objective outer world could be calculated and therefore predicted. But the inner realm of the mind was considered too unpredictable and complicated, so it was therefore left to the auspices of religion. Over time, matter and mind became separate entities, and dualism was born.

Newtonian physics (also known as *classical physics*) deals with the mechanics of how objects function in space and time, including their interactions with each other in the material, physical world. Because of Newton's laws, we can measure and predict what path planets take around the sun, how quickly an apple accelerates when it falls from a tree, and how long it takes to go from Seattle to New York by plane. Newtonian physics is about the predictable.

It looks at the universe as if it functioned like an enormous machine or a huge timepiece.

But classical physics has its limitations when it comes to the study of energy, the actions of the immaterial world beyond space and time, and the behavior of atoms (the building blocks of everything in the physical universe). That realm belongs to quantum physics. And it turns out that this very tiny subatomic world of electrons and photons doesn't behave anything like the much larger world of planets, apples, and airplanes that we're more familiar with.

When quantum physicists began to look at the smaller and smaller aspects of an atom, like what makes up the nucleus, the closer they looked, the less distinct and clear the atom became, until eventually it just completely disappeared. Atoms, they tell us, appear to be 99.999999999999 percent empty space.[1] But that space isn't really empty. It's actually filled with energy. More specifically, it's made up of a vast array of energy frequencies that form a kind of invisible, interconnected field of information. So if every atom is 99.999999999999 percent energy or information, that means that our known universe and every *thing* in it—no matter how solid that matter may appear to us—is essentially just energy and information. That's a scientific fact.

Atoms do contain a smattering of matter, but when the quantum physicists tried to study it, they discovered something really strange: Subatomic matter in the quantum world doesn't behave anything at all like the matter we're used to dealing with. Instead of adhering to the laws of Newtonian physics, it appears somewhat chaotic and unpredictable, completely disregarding the boundaries of time and space. In fact, on the subatomic quantum level, matter is a momentary phenomenon. It's here one moment, and then it disappears. It exists only as a tendency, a probability, or a possibility. In the quantum, there are no absolute physical things.

That wasn't the only strange discovery that scientists made about the quantum universe. They also found that when they observed particles of subatomic matter, they could affect or change their behavior. The reason they're here and gone (and then here and gone again all the time) is that all of these particles actually exist simultaneously in an infinite array of possibilities or probabilities within the invisible and infinite quantum field of energy. It's only when an observer focuses attention on any one location of any one electron that the electron actually appears in that place. Look away, and the subatomic matter disappears back into energy.

So according to this "observer effect," physical matter can't exist or manifest until we observe it—until we notice it and give it our attention. And when we're no longer paying attention to it, it vanishes, going back from whence it came. So matter is constantly transforming, oscillating between manifesting into matter and disappearing into energy (about 7.8 times per second, as a matter of fact). And so because the human mind (as the observer) is then intimately connected to the behavior and appearance of matter, you could say that mind over matter is a quantum reality. Another way to look at it is this: In the tiny world of the quantum, the subjective mind has an effect on objective reality. Your mind can become matter; that is, you can *make your mind matter.*

Since subatomic matter makes up everything we can see and touch and experience in our macro world, then in a sense we— along with everything in our world—are also doing this disappearing and reappearing act all the time. And so if subatomic particles exist in an infinite number of possible places simultaneously, then in some way, so do we. And just as these particles go from existing everywhere simultaneously (wave, or energy) to existing precisely where the observer looks for them at the moment the observer is paying attention (particle, or matter), we're also potentially capable of collapsing an infinite number of potential realities into physical existence.

In other words, if you can imagine a particular future event that you want to experience in your life, that reality already exists as a possibility somewhere in the quantum field—beyond this space and time—just waiting for you to observe it. If your mind (through your thoughts and feelings) can affect when and where an electron appears out of nowhere, then theoretically, you should be able to influence the appearance of *any* number of possibilities that you can imagine.

From a quantum perspective, if you observed yourself in a particular new future that was different from your past, expected that reality to occur, and then emotionally embraced the outcome, you'd be—for a moment—living in that future reality, and you'd be conditioning your body to believe it was in that future in the present moment. So the quantum model, which states that all possibilities exist in this moment, gives us permission to choose a new future and observe it into reality. And because the entire universe is made of atoms, with more than 99 percent of an atom being energy or possibility, that means that there's *a lot* of potentials out there that you and I might be missing.

However, this also means that you create by default as well. If you, as the quantum observer, look at your life from the same level of mind every day, then according to the quantum model of reality, you're causing infinite possibilities to collapse into the same patterns of information day in and day out. Those patterns, which you call your life, never change, so they never allow you to *effect change*.

So the mental rehearsal I talked about earlier is certainly not idle daydreaming or wishful thinking. It is, in a very real sense, the way you can intentionally manifest your desired reality, including a life without pain or disease. By focusing more on what you do want and less on what you don't want, you can call into existence whatever you desire *and* simultaneously "fade away" what you don't want by no longer giving it your attention. Where you place your attention is where you place your energy. Once you fix your attention or your awareness or your mind on possibility, you place your energy there as well. As a result, you're affecting matter with your attention or observation. The placebo effect is not fantasy, then; it's quantum reality.

Energy on the Quantum Level

All atoms in the elemental world emit various electromagnetic energies. For example, an atom can give off invisible fields of energy at different frequencies that include x-rays, gamma rays, ultraviolet rays, and infrared rays, as well as visible light rays. And just as invisible radio waves carry a frequency with specific information encoded into it (whether it's 98.6 or 107.5 hertz), each different frequency likewise carries specific diverse information, as shown in Figure 8.1. For example, x-rays carry very different information than infrared rays do, because they are different frequencies. All of these fields are different energy patterns that are always giving off information at the atomic level.

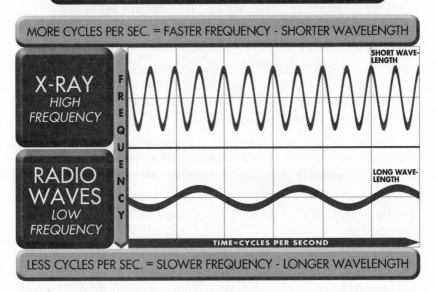

FIGURE 8.1

This chart shows two different frequencies that each carry different information and therefore have different qualities. X-rays behave differently from radio waves and thus have different inherent characteristics.

Think of atoms as vibrating fields of energy or small vortices that are constantly spinning. To better understand how that works, let's use the analogy of a fan. Just like a circular fan creates wind (a vortex of air) when it's turned on, each atom, as it spins, radiates a field of energy in a similar fashion. And just like a fan can spin at different speeds and so create stronger or weaker wind, atoms also vibrate at different frequencies that create stronger or weaker fields. The faster the atom vibrates, the greater the energy and frequency it emits. The slower the speed of the atom's vibration or vortex, the less energy it creates.

The slower a fan's blades spin, the less wind (or energy) is created and the easier it is to see the blades as material objects in physical reality. On the other hand, the faster the blades spin, the more energy is created and the less you see of the physical blades; the blades appear to be immaterial. Where the fan blades can potentially appear (like the subatomic particles the quantum scientists were trying to observe that kept popping in and out of view) depends on your observation—where and how you look for them. And so it is with atoms. Let's look at this in a little more depth.

In quantum physics, matter is defined as a solid *particle,* and the immaterial energetic field of information can be defined as the *wave.* When we study the physical properties of atoms, like mass, atoms look like physical matter. The slower the frequency that an atom is vibrating, the more time it spends in physical reality and the more it appears as a particle that we can see as solid matter. The reason physical matter appears solid to us, even though it's mostly energy, is that all of the atoms are vibrating at the same speed we are.

But atoms also display many properties of energy or waves (including light, wavelengths, and frequency). The faster an atom vibrates and the more energy it generates, the less time it spends in physical reality; it's appearing and disappearing too fast for us to see it, because it's vibrating at a much faster speed than we are. But even though we can't see the energy itself, we can sometimes see physical evidence of certain frequencies of energy, because the force field of atoms can create physical properties, such as the way infrared waves heat things up.

If you compare Figure 8.2A to Figure 8.2B, you can see how slower frequencies spend more time in the material world and thus appear as matter.

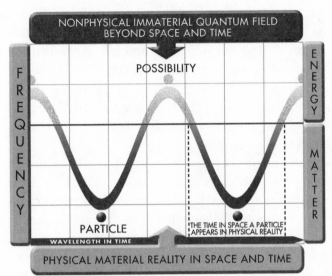

SLOWER FREQUENCY, SLOWER VIBRATION & LONGER
WAVELENGTH = MORE TIME IN PHYSICAL MATERIAL REALITY

FIGURE 8.2A

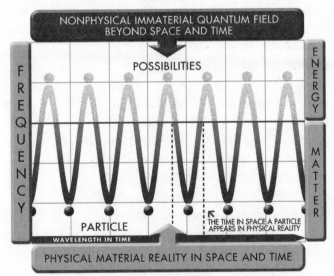

FASTER FREQUENCY, FASTER VIBRATION & SHORTER
WAVELENGTH = LESS TIME IN PHYSICAL MATERIAL REALITY

FIGURE 8.2B

When energy vibrates slower, particles appear in physical reality for longer periods of time and thus appear as solid matter. Figure 8.2A shows how matter manifests from a slower frequency with a longer wavelength. Figure 8.2B depicts particles spending less time in physical reality, therefore they are more energy and less matter. That's because they have shorter wavelengths, faster frequency, and a faster vibration.

So the physical universe may look as if it's made up of only material matter, but in truth, it shares a field of information (the quantum field) that unifies matter and energy so intimately that it's impossible to consider them as separate entities. That's because all particles are connected in an immaterial invisible field of information beyond space and time—and that field is made of consciousness (thought) and energy (frequency, the speed at which things vibrate).

Because each atom has its own specific field of energy or energy signature, when atoms assemble collectively to form molecules, they share their fields of information and then radiate their own unique combined energy patterns. If everything material in the universe radiates a specific unique energy signature because everything is made of atoms, then you and I radiate our own specific energy signatures as well. You and I are always broadcasting information as electromagnetic energy—based on our states of being.

So when you change your energy to alter a belief or perception about yourself or your life, you're actually increasing the frequency of the atoms and molecules of your physical body so that you're amplifying your energy field (as shown in Figure 8.3). You're turning up the speed on the atomic fans that make up your body. As you embrace a heightened, emotional creative state like inspiration, empowerment, gratitude, or invincibility, you're causing your atoms to spin faster, just like the fan blades, and to broadcast a stronger energy field around your body, which affects your physical matter.

So the physical particles that make up your body are now responding to an elevated energy. You're becoming more energy and less matter. You're now more wave and less particle. Using your consciousness, you're creating more energy so that matter can be lifted to a new frequency, and your body responds to a new mind.

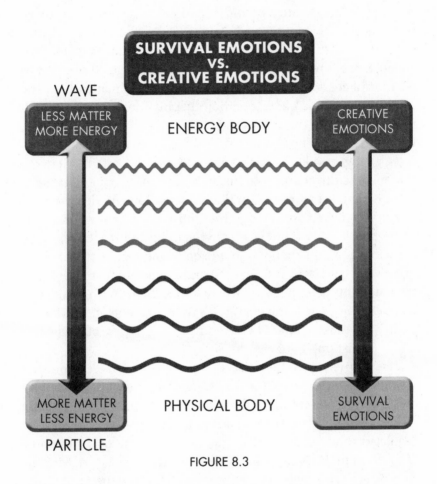

FIGURE 8.3

When you change your energy, you lift matter to a new mind, and your body vibrates at a faster frequency. You become more energy and less matter—more wave and less particle. The more elevated the emotion or the higher the creative state of mind, the more energy you have to rewrite the programs in the body. Your body then responds to a new mind.

Receiving the Right Energetic Signal

So how does matter become lifted to a new mind? Think of the preacher who moves into a state of religious ecstasy and drinks strychnine, with no biological effects. How did he overcome that chemistry that would normally poison the average person? It was his level of energy that transcended the effects of matter. He made a decision with such firm intention that his choice carried an amplitude of energy that transcended the laws of the environment, the effects on the body, and linear time. In that moment, he was more energy and less matter, and as a result, it was a new energy that rewrote the circuitry in his brain, the chemistry in his body, and his genetic expression. In that present moment, he wasn't his identity that was connected to his familiar environment, nor was he his physical body, nor was he living in linear time. His elevated consciousness and energy were the epiphenomenon of matter. In other words, it's both information and frequency that give rise to the blueprints of matter. And when we're demonstrating an elevated level of awareness and energy, it's these elements that influence matter—because matter is created from a lowering of frequency and information.

It's entirely possible that the preacher's cell-receptor sites weren't selectively open for the strychnine; the cells' doors were closed to poison and so were suspended from its effects. By being moved by the spirit—that is, moved by energy—he instantly upregulated the cells in his body for immunity and downregulated the cells in his body for poison. The same thing is at work with the firewalkers; once they change their state of being, their cell receptors are no longer open to the effects of heat. This is also what allowed the teenage girls to lift the 3,000-pound tractor to free their father, as you read about in Chapter 1. When they saw their father trapped and almost certain to die, their heightened state of energy turned off the cell receptors that normally would tell their bodies that the tractor was too heavy to lift and turned on the muscle-cell receptors to bear a greater load so that when they tried, their muscles responded and they were able to free their dad. It wasn't matter (body) that was moving matter (tractor); it was energy that was influencing matter.

You'd have to agree with me that your body is made up of a vast array of atoms and molecules and that these atoms and molecules form chemicals. Those chemicals organize into cells, which form tissues that further organize into organs, which create various systems within your body. For example, a muscle cell is made of different chemicals (proteins, ions, cytokines, growth factors), which are made of the different interactions of molecules, which are made of various atomic bonds; those atoms share an invisible field of information to form molecules.

The chemicals that make up a cell also share a field of information. It's that invisible field of information that orchestrates the hundreds of thousands of functions of the cell at any given second. Scientists are beginning to realize that a field of information exists that's responsible for myriad cellular functions existing beyond the boundaries of matter.

It's this invisible field of consciousness that orchestrates all of the functions of the cells, tissues, organs, and systems of the body. How do certain chemicals and molecules of your cells know what to do and interact with such precision? There's an energetic field surrounding the cell that's the summation of energy from atoms, molecules, and chemicals working together in balance that gives birth to matter, and it's that vital field of information that matter draws from.

For instance, the muscle cells in the previous example can further organize and specialize into tissues called "muscle tissue." Let's say that the particular type of muscle tissue in this example is called "cardiac muscle." Cardiac muscle tissue forms an organ called the "heart." The tissues, which are made of cells, share a field of information that allows the heart to function in a coherent manner. The heart is part of the cardiovascular system of the entire body. As it shares this field of information, it organizes matter to function in a harmonic, holistic way. So the field that's created that gives birth to matter is what *controls* matter. The greater the field, the faster the atoms vibrate—or the faster your subatomic fan blades spin.

The Newtonian model of biology is based on linear events in which chemical reactions occur in a sequence of steps. But that's not actually how biology works; you can no longer explain something even as simple as how a cut heals without the understanding of the interconnected coherent information pathways you just read about. Cells share an intercommunication of information in a nonlinear way. The universe and all the biological systems within it share an integration of independent, entangled energy fields that, in turn, share information beyond space and time on a moment-to-moment basis.

Research confirms that most interactions between cells happen faster than the speed of light[2]—and since the limit of this physical reality *is* the speed of light, that means that cells must communicate via the quantum field. The interactions between atoms and molecules form an intercommunication that unifies the physical, material world and the energy fields that make up the whole. In the quantum, the linear, predictable characteristics of the Newtonian world do not exist. Things interact in a holistic, cooperative manner.

So according to the quantum model of reality, we could say that all disease is a lowering of frequency. Think about stress hormones. When your nervous system is under the control of fight-or-flight mode, the chemicals of survival cause you to be more matter and less energy. You become a materialist, because you're defining reality with your senses; you overuse the vital energy surrounding the cell by mobilizing it for an emergency; and all of your attention goes toward the outer world of the environment, the body, and time. If you keep the stress response turned on for extended periods of time, the long-term effects keep slowing down the frequency of the body such that it becomes more and more particle and less and less wave. That means that there's less consciousness, energy, and information available for atoms, molecules, and chemicals to share. As a result, you become matter trying futilely to change matter—you are a body trying without success to change a body.

All of the individual subatomic fans making up your body start spinning not only slower, but also out of rhythm with one another. This creates incoherence among the body's atoms and molecules, which causes a weakened signal of communication such that the body begins to break down. The more your body is matter and the less it is energy, the more you're at the mercy of the second law of thermodynamics—the *law of entropy*—where material things in the universe tend to move toward disorder and breakdown.

Think what would happen if you had hundreds of fans in one enormous room, all working together and spinning in harmony, humming away in unison. That coherent humming would be like music to your ears, because it would be rhythmic and consistent. That's what it's like in our bodies when the signals between our atoms, molecules, and cells are strong and coherent.

Now imagine how different it would be if there weren't enough electricity (energy) getting to each of the fans, resulting in their spinning at different speeds or frequencies. The room would then be filled with a cacophony of incoherent clanking, wobbling, stopping, and starting. That's what it's like when the signals between our bodies' atoms, molecules, and cells are weaker and incoherent.

When you change your energy because you made a decision with firm intention, you increase the frequency of your atomic structure and create a more intentional, coherent electromagnetic signature (as depicted in Figure 8.4). You're now affecting the physical matter of your body. By increasing your energy, you increase the electricity flowing to your atomic fans. The elevated frequency begins to entrain or to organize the cells of your body to become less particle (matter) and more wave (energy). Or to put it another way, all of your matter has more energy—or more information. Think of *coherence* as rhythm or orderliness, and *incoherence* as the lack of rhythm, lack of orderliness, or lack of synchrony.

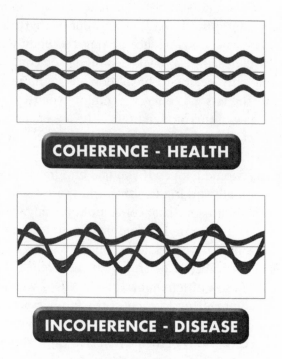

COHERENCE - HEALTH

INCOHERENCE - DISEASE

FIGURE 8.4

From a quantum perspective, a higher, more coherent frequency is called health, and a slower, more incoherent frequency is called disease. All disease is a lowering of frequency, as well as the expression of incoherent information.

Imagine a group of a hundred drummers with no rhythm banging on drums all at the same time. That's incoherence. Now imagine that a group of five professional drummers shows up among the mob of wannabe drummers, spreads out to different locations in the crowd, and starts to create a very rhythmic beat. In time, the five would entrain the entire hundred other drummers into perfect rhythm, orderliness, and synchrony.

That's exactly what happens when your body responds to a new mind, when the hair on the back of your neck stands up because you feel more like energy and less like matter. In that moment, you're lifting matter to a new mind. You're entraining the disease that exists as a lowering of frequency to an elevated frequency. At the same time, you're also causing the incoherent information that existed among the atoms and molecules, chemicals and cells, tissues and organs, and systems of the body to instead function from a field of more organized information.

It's like hearing static on your radio and then tuning in to a clear signal where, all of a sudden, the static disappears and you can hear the music. Your brain and nervous system do the same by tuning in to higher, more coherent frequencies. Once that occurs, you're no longer subject to the law of entropy. You experience *reverse entropy*, and the coherent signature of the energy field around your body causes you to be immune to the typical laws of physical reality. Now all of the atomic fans are spinning at a faster coherent frequency, and the physical molecules, chemicals, and cells that make up your body are receiving new information so that your energy is having a positive effect on your body.

Figures 8.5A, 8.5B, and 8.5C on the following page illustrate how a higher, more coherent frequency of energy entrains a slower, more incoherent frequency of matter, lifting matter to a new mind.

The more organized and coherent your energy, the more you entrain matter at an organized frequency, and the faster that frequency, the better and the more profound the electromagnetic signal the cell receives. (Remember, as you learned in the previous chapter, cells are a hundred times more sensitive to electromagnetic signals—energy—than to chemical signals, and it's these signals that change DNA expression.) The more incoherent and unsynchronized your energy is, on the other hand, the less able your cells are to communicate with one another. You'll learn the science of how to create coherence very shortly.

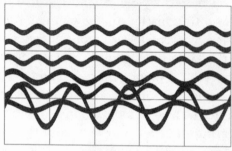

FIGURE 8.5A

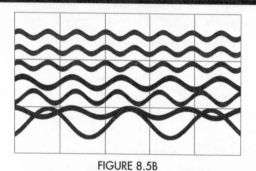

FIGURE 8.5B

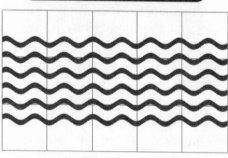

FIGURE 8.5C

When higher, more coherent energy interacts with slower, more incoherent energy, it begins to entrain matter to a more organized state.

Beyond the Quantum Doorway

Since the quantum field is an invisible field of information, is frequency beyond space and time that all things material come from, and is made of consciousness and energy, then everything physical in the universe is unified within and connected to this field. And since all things material are made of atoms, which are connected beyond space and time, then you and I, along with all things in the universe, are connected by this field of intelligence—personal and universal, both within us and all around us—that gives life, information, energy, and consciousness to all things.

Call it what you will, but this is the universal intelligence that's giving you life right now. It organizes and orchestrates the hundreds of thousands of notes in the harmonious symphony that is your physiology—those things that are part of your autonomic nervous system. This intelligence keeps your heart beating more than 101,000 times a day to pump more than two gallons of blood per minute, traveling more than 60,000 miles in each 24-hour period. As you finish reading this sentence, your body will have made 25 trillion cells. And each of the 70 trillion cells that make up your body execute somewhere between 100,000 to 6 trillion functions per second. You'll inhale 2 million liters of oxygen today, and each time you inhale, that oxygen will be distributed to every cell in your body within seconds.

Do you consciously keep track of all that? Or does something that has a mind so much greater than your mind, and a will so much greater than your will, do it for you? That's love! In fact, that intelligence loves you so much that it loves you into life. It's the same universal mind that animates every aspect of the material universe. This invisible field of intelligence exists beyond space and time, and it's where all things material come from.

It causes supernovas to be born in distant galaxies and roses to bloom in Versailles. It keeps the planets revolving around our sun and the tides rising and falling at Malibu. Because it exists in all places and at all times, and it's both within you and all around you, this intelligence must be both personal and universal. So there's a subjective, freewill consciousness (the individual aware-ness) called "you," and there's an objective consciousness (the universal awareness) that's responsible for all life.

If you were to close your eyes and take your attention off your body and all of the people, things, and events arising at different times and places in your external environment, letting go of time for a moment, you, as the quantum observer, would be removing your energy from your familiar life and investing your awareness into the unknown field of possibilities. Since where you place your attention is where you place your energy, then if you keep placing your awareness on your known life, your energy is invested in that familiar life. But if you were to invest your energy in the unknown field of possibilities beyond space and time, and you instead became a consciousness (a thought in quantum potential), you'd be drawing a new experience to yourself. As you enter a meditative state, your subjective, freewill consciousness would merge with the objective, universal consciousness, and you'd be planting a seed in possibility.

The self-organizing autonomic nervous system is your connection to that innate intelligence I mentioned that performs all of those automatic functions for you. It's certainly not your thinking neocortex that's responsible for the functions mentioned previously. Instead, it's the lower brain centers below the neocortex that subconsciously run the show. This loving intelligence is what you merge with in meditation when you lay down the ego and go from selfish to selfless, when you become pure consciousness—no longer a body in the environment or in linear time but, instead, no *body,* no *one,* no *thing,* in no *place* and no *time.* That's when you become simply an awareness in an infinite field of possibility.

You're in the unknown. And from the unknown, all things are created. You're in the quantum field. And you and I already have all the biological machinery we need to accomplish this feat of becoming pure consciousness.

Chapter Nine

Three Stories of Personal Transformation

In this chapter you'll meet a few folks who put the energy of their consciousness into the immaterial world beyond the senses and repeatedly embraced a possibility until it materialized into their lives.

Laurie's Story

At age 19, Laurie was diagnosed with a rare degenerative bone disease, called *polyostotic fibrous dysplasia.* In this debilitating condition, the body replaces normal bone with a cheaper, fibrous tissue, and the skeleton's supportive protein scaffolding becomes uncharacteristically thin and irregular. The atypical growth process associated with the syndrome causes bones to swell, weaken, and then fracture. Fibrous dysplasia can occur in any part of the skeleton, and in Laurie's body, it manifested in her right femur, right hip socket, right tibia, and some of the bones of her right foot. Her doctors told her the disease had no cure.

Fibrous dysplasia is a genetic condition that usually doesn't manifest until adolescence. In Laurie's case, she spent a whole year limping painfully around her college campus with what turned out to be a femoral fracture, before any sign of the disease surfaced. She was shocked to hear she'd broken a bone, because she hadn't suffered any trauma. Other than one foot being anatomically larger than the other, Laurie hadn't seen any evidence that

anything was wrong with her until that point. She'd lived a relatively active youth filled with activities like running, dancing,
and playing tennis. At the time she began limping, she'd even
begun training as a competitive bodybuilder.

After the diagnosis, Laurie's life changed overnight. Her orthopedic surgeon warned her that she was fragile and extremely
vulnerable. He insisted that she walk only with crutches until he
could schedule her for surgery: first a bone graft, followed by the
insertion of a Russell-Taylor femoral nail down the bone shaft.
After hearing that news, both Laurie and her mother spent an hour
crying in the hospital cafeteria. It was like some sort of nightmare;
Laurie's life, as she knew it, seemed to be suddenly over.

Laurie's perception of her limitations—both real and imagined—began to dominate her life. To avoid additional fractures,
she followed the surgeon's orders and dutifully used the crutches.
She had to quit the marketing internship she'd recently begun
with a major Manhattan product manufacturer and, instead,
began filling her days with medical appointments. Her father insisted she see as many orthopedic specialists as possible, so her
weeping mother drove Laurie from doctor's office to doctor's office over the next several weeks.

Each time she saw a new doctor, Laurie would patiently wait
for a different medical opinion, only to receive the same bad news
again. In just a few months, ten surgeons had weighed in on her
condition. The last physician she saw did have a different opinion:
He told Laurie that the surgery the other doctors had recommended absolutely wouldn't help her, because inserting the nail would
strengthen the diseased bone only in the weakest location and
would actually cause more fractures in the next most vulnerable
area above or below the nail. He advised Laurie to forget about
surgery and continue using crutches or a wheelchair—or simply
become sedentary for the rest of her life.

From then on, Laurie remained still most of the time for fear
she might break a bone. She felt powerless, small, and fragile, and
she was filled with anxiety and self-pity. She did return to college
a month later, but stayed largely cooped up in an apartment that

she shared with five other women. She cultivated an impressive ability to cloak a severe and mounting clinical depression.

Fearing Her Father

Laurie's father had been a violent man for as long as she could remember. Even once his children were grown, each member of the family had to be prepared for the wrath of this man's quick-moving fists at the most unexpected of moments. Everyone was constantly in a state of vigilance, wondering when his temper would flare next. Although Laurie certainly didn't know it at the time, her father's behavior was intrinsically connected to her condition.

Newborns spend the vast majority of their days in the delta brain-wave state. During the first 12 years, children gradually progress to a theta state and then to an alpha state, before they get to the beta state they'll spend most of their adulthood in. As you read earlier, theta and alpha are highly suggestible brain-wave states. Young children don't yet have an analytical mind to edit or to make sense of what happens to them, so all of the information they absorb from their experiences is encoded directly into their subconscious minds. Because of their increased suggestibility, the moment they feel emotionally altered from some experience, they pay attention to whoever or whatever caused it and so are conditioned to form associative memories connecting that cause to the emotion of the experience itself. If it's a parent, then over time, children will attach to that caregiver and think that the emotions they feel from the experience are normal, because they don't yet have the ability to analyze the situation. This is how early-childhood experiences become subconscious states of being.

Although Laurie didn't know this when her condition was diagnosed, the emotionally charged events she experienced growing up with her father had been branded into her implicit memory system beyond her conscious mind, programming her biology. Her reaction to her father's anger—feeling weak, powerless, vulnerable, stressed, and fearful every single day—then became part of her autonomic nervous system so that her body chemically memorized these emotions and the environment signaled the genes associated with her disorder to turn on. Because that response was autonomic, she wouldn't be able to change it as long as she stayed trapped in her emotional body. She could only analyze her state of being equal to the emotions of her past, even though the answers she needed existed beyond those emotions.

Once Laurie received the fibrous dysplasia diagnosis, her mother immediately proclaimed to the entire family that Laurie had been officially pronounced "fragile" by modern medicine—so she was safe from her father's physical violence. Although he continued to emotionally and verbally abuse Laurie (right up until his death 15 years later), her disease, ironically, protected her from further physical abuse.

Cementing Her Identity in Disease

This perverse sense of safety that Laurie created became a vehicle of survival for her. As a result, she began to benefit from special treatment (which she almost always needed). Whether getting a seat on the bus or subway when there was standing room only, getting her friends to wait in line for events while she sat on a nearby bench, or getting a seat quickly in a crowded restaurant, Laurie found that her disease began to *work for her.* She started relying heavily on her ailment to get what she wanted. She was now able to manage better in a world that she'd never before viewed as safe. The emotional benefit of manipulating her reality to get what she wanted in this way became very convenient, and Laurie received far more than she really needed to take stress off her body to prevent injury. Before long, her disease became her identity.

Laurie next developed a late-adolescent rebellion against the life that she thought had been thrust upon her by her doctors, her parents, and fate. By the next semester after her diagnosis, she went into a solid state of denial about her disease. She decided to become the first "gimpy" bodybuilder, returning to the sport with complete devotion. Blindly obsessive, while white-knuckling it and forcing a positive attitude solely with her conscious mind, Laurie found creative ways to bear weight that wouldn't twist her limbs.

She thought that by trying to push through the pain, she'd become healthier—although in truth, her efforts backfired, because she felt awful most of the time and her pain worsened. As sometimes happens with polyostotic fibrous dysplasia patients, Laurie also developed scoliosis and suffered from severe back pain daily. By the time she was in her 20s, she began to develop arthritis in her spine and elsewhere.

After she graduated from college, despite shuttling herself between a new house and a new job, Laurie became very sedentary and felt even more removed from life. Her fear, anxiety, and depression remained. She envied most of her peers and lost friendships and romantic interests because she lived more like her elderly parents than like a young adult.

By her late 20s, Laurie used a cane all the time to get around, even when she wasn't nursing one of the 12 serious fractures she'd eventually endure. As if those issues weren't enough, she also experienced dangerous microfractures. Her bones were so weak that bigger stress fractures would appear beneath the microscopic fissures and connect to other areas of weakened bone to form even bigger fractures that could be seen on an x-ray.

By age 30, Laurie had more back problems than her 72-year-old father, and she essentially became old before her time. She rested in bed for days and missed so many weeks of work that she was forced to quit jobs. She put graduate school on hold, because the school that accepted her didn't have a working elevator. She had to forgo parties, museum outings, shopping, traveling, concerts, and other activities that would have involved a lot of standing or walking. She was caught in the thinking-and-feeling loop I talked about earlier: thinking that she was limited and fragile on the inside, while her body manifested limitedness and fragility on the outside. The more she felt vulnerable and weak, the more vulnerable and weak she became—while continuing to experience fractures that reinforced her belief that she was frail, and further reaffirming her identity and validating her state of being.

She adjusted her diet and took various vitamins and supplements in addition to bone-strengthening drugs, but nothing seemed to stop the fractures. She could fracture a bone from just walking up a flight of stairs or even stepping off a curb. It was like waiting for the next nightmare in a series.

Ironically, when Laurie wasn't using crutches or limping, she looked perfectly healthy. Most people assumed that her cane was some sort of eccentric accessory, and many didn't believe Laurie really had a debilitating condition, which made it difficult and frustrating at times to receive the special treatment she often needed. Trying to convince people that she really had a disease further solidified her identity as a sick person, set her intention to prove she was handicapped, and anchored her belief about her disabled status. While the rest of the world seemed to work very hard to hide their weaknesses and vulnerabilities, Laurie found that she was constantly announcing hers.

She spent a lot of energy trying to control as much as possible in her environment. She paid careful attention to everything she ate and drank, measuring everything she consumed. Every walk around her neighborhood was calculated. She even weighed how much she could carry home from the supermarket: ten pounds, which was also the limit of the weight she could gain before her bones would worsen.

It was exhausting, but it was all Laurie knew to do. Her range of options got narrower and narrower as she kept limiting the scope of things that she could do physically in an attempt to keep from fracturing. As her lifestyle became narrower, her mind became narrower along with it. Laurie's fears increased, her depression worsened, and eventually, she tried to work again but couldn't even hold down a job.

This same woman who'd once been a runner, dancer, and competitive bodybuilder was now limited to doing only yoga for fitness, and by her late 30s, even hatha yoga had come to be too much for her. For years, her exercise was limited to sitting in a chair and doing vigorous breathing (although in her early 40s, her doctor finally allowed her to take up lap swimming).

She did make some attempts at healing through therapists, holistic doctors, energy healers, sound healers, and homeopaths—always seeking solutions outside of herself. A few times, she'd feel better after an energy healing and go straight to the orthopedist and demand new x-rays—only to be deflated when the results came back unchanged. She thought, *Maybe this is as good as it's ever going to get.* She awoke overwhelmed each morning, overcome with a feeling of dread, convinced she couldn't handle whatever the world had in store for her.

Laurie Learns What's Possible

Laurie and I met in 2009, after she had seen *What the Bleep Do We Know!?* and become transfixed by the concept that a person could possibly create a totally new life. I happened to meet her while eating dinner before a workshop I was teaching at a retreat center near New York. We talked about the courses I gave on personal change, and she immediately registered for my next class that August.

When Laurie came to her first event, she heard that it was absolutely possible to change your brain, your thoughts, your body, your emotional state, and your genetic expression. During the workshop, I talked about physical change, but Laurie's beliefs about her disease and her body were tenacious and her emotions were stuck quite firmly in her past. She had absolutely no intention of healing her body, mostly because she didn't really believe it was even possible. She came because she just wanted to feel better on the inside.

Laurie immediately applied the principles I taught as best she could, even though she couldn't seem to feel different by choice. The very first thing she did, almost immediately after that first weekend course, was to stop sharing her diagnosis with others.

Even though she couldn't control her emotions, she figured that she still had control over what she said out loud. So unless she needed to ask for a chair at a party or explain to a date why she couldn't take a walk with him, she stopped acknowledging her condition altogether. Laurie chose to focus on where she was headed in her future: toward a happy inner self, a deep connection to some unknown divine source, a wonderful job that she excelled at, a life partner, and close and healthy relationships with friends and relatives.

Laurie next concentrated on changing a few simple behaviors. She watched her thoughts and words, and reminded herself repeatedly to stop her old, repetitive, destructive patterns. She kept doing the meditations and taking my courses. In order to assign meaning to what she was doing, she reread her class notes religiously and kept in touch with as many fellow students as she could. In time, some small but perceptible percentage of the day, Laurie felt better, taller, abler, and stronger. She'd say "Change" to herself 20 times a day, whenever she noticed her mind drifting to her past. Although negative thoughts sneaked through a hundred times a day, little by little, Laurie created a few new thoughts, wrote them down, and attempted to believe them deeply.

Laurie worked hard at it, but it took almost two years before she could really *feel* those new thoughts. Instead of getting frustrated during that waiting period, Laurie reminded herself that it had taken quite a long time to *create* the disease from her emotional state, so it might take some time to *uncreate* it. She also reminded herself that she'd have to go through a biological, neurological, chemical, and genetic death of the old self before the new self emerged.

The circumstances in her external environment got worse before they got better. A flood trashed Laurie's home, and other situations in her apartment building created some new health problems. Laurie told me that every time she'd sit down to do her meditation and rehearse her ideal life, she felt as if she were telling herself a lie—and afterward, opening her eyes to her current circumstances felt like a slap in the face. I encouraged her to stop defining reality with her senses and to keep crossing the river of change.

Laurie kept limping in to the workshops, grumpy at times and grateful at others, and she kept at the work. She also assembled as many local fellow students as she could to meditate together. Hardly any situations in Laurie's life were pleasing, so she thought, *What the hell, I may as well have one hour a day behind my own eyelids where reality looks different, where I have a pain-free body, a safe and quiet home, and a full and loving relationship with the outside world and with my friends and family.*

In early 2012, during one of my progressive workshops, Laurie had a significant deepening in her meditation experience. She was literally and figuratively rocked to her core. Physically, it was like a disturbance and then a release. Her body shook, her face contorted, and her arms flew up as she tried her best to stay rooted to her chair. Emotionally, it was inexplicable joy. She cried, she laughed, and sounds came out of her mouth that she couldn't explain. All of the fear and control that she'd previously used to hold herself together was finally loosening. For the first time, she felt a divine presence and knew she was no longer alone.

Laurie told me, "I sensed something, someone, some divine presence, and this consciousness wasn't ignorant to my existence and unconcerned with my welfare, as I apparently previously believed. This consciousness has actually been paying attention. Realizing that was an overwhelming change for me." All the energy she'd been putting into controlling her physical movements and her life in general finally began to relax and unwind, and the energy she'd been using to maintain that control started to free up.

At the next event, I noticed that Laurie was walking without a cane or any limp. She was happy, smiling, and laughing to herself, instead of irritated, frowning, and wincing in pain. She was transmuting fear into courage, frustration into patience, pain into joy, and weakness into strength. She was beginning to change— on the inside *and* the outside. Free from the addiction of those limiting emotions, her body was now living less in the past as she moved toward a new future.

In early spring of 2012, Laurie's orthopedist told her during a regular checkup that about two-thirds of the length of a fracture she'd had in her femur since she was 19 (a fracture that had shown up on every one of the hundred or so x-rays she'd had so far) had vanished. He had no explanation to offer but, instead, suggested she begin riding a stationary bicycle at the gym for ten minutes, twice a week. The message was music to Laurie's ears, and off she went.

Success and Setbacks

All of Laurie's work in crossing the river of change was now starting to pay off. She was finally getting feedback that let her know she was making some type of physical progress. Each day, as Laurie got beyond her body, her environment, and time, she was also getting beyond the personality that was connected to her present and past external reality, beyond her emotionally addicted and habituated body, and beyond the predictable future that she'd always expected, based on her memory of the past. All of her effort to supersede her analytical mind, change her brain waves to those of a more suggestible state, find the present moment, and venture into the programming system where she was emotionally altered earlier in her life was finally changing her.

Laurie started to really believe that her mind was healing her body by thought alone. And the old fracture that was connected to the old self was healing, because she was literally becoming someone else. She was no longer firing and wiring the circuits in her brain that were connected to the old personality, because she was no longer thinking and acting in the same ways. She stopped conditioning her body to the same mind by reliving her past with the same emotions. She was "unmemorizing" being her old self and remembering being a new self—that is, firing and wiring new thoughts and actions in her brain by changing her mind and emotionally teaching her body what her future self would feel like.

Laurie was signaling new genes in new ways during her daily meditation by simply changing her state of being. Those genes were making new proteins that were healing the proteins responsible for the fractures related to her "dis-ease." From what she learned in the workshops, she reasoned that her bone cells needed to get the right signal from her mind in order to turn off the gene of fibrous dysplasia and turn on the gene for the production of a normal bone matrix.

Laurie explained:

> I knew that over the years, all of those fractures had manifested structurally from the unhealthy protein expression in my bone cells, because I had been living by the survival emotions of fear, victimization, and pain—and I felt weak. I was powerful enough to manifest weakness perfectly in my body. I had programmed the genes to stay on, because I'd memorized those emotions subconsciously in my body. And my body, as my mind, was always living in the past. So I figured, if bones are made of collagen— which is a protein—and I wanted my bone cells to make some healthy collagen, I'd have to enter my autonomic nervous system, get beyond my analytical mind, enter into the subconscious mind, repeatedly reprogram my body with new information, and allow it to receive new orders every day. When I received the good news, I felt like I was halfway across the river of change.

Laurie kept her meditations going and continued to take my workshops. She continued to have times of physical pain, but the frequency, intensity, and duration decreased considerably. She changed as many things as she possibly could. She changed gyms just for a different environment. She put her deodorant on the right side first instead of the left. She folded her arms left over right instead of the more natural right over left, whenever she could remember to do so. She sat in a different chair in her apartment. She slept on the other side of the bed (even though it meant walking all the way around to the far side of the room to get in and out of bed).

She reported, "Ridiculous as that may sound, I was just intent on giving my body as many new and different signals as possible, and since moving to a big house in the Hamptons wasn't realistic, these tiny things would have to do."

Laurie even put notes everywhere in her environment to remind herself to stay conscious and to elicit thoughts and feelings about her future. She wrote, "I am grateful," "Elevate!" and "Love!" on painter's tape and stuck the notes on the backs of several doors. She stuck a sticky note on her dashboard that read, "Your thoughts are incredibly powerful. Choose yours wisely." Encouraging notes and affirmations weren't new to her, but she'd never had the capacity to believe them before because she hadn't known how to change her beliefs.

In late January 2013, when she saw her orthopedist again, he told her for the first time in 28 years that she had *no* evidence of fractures—none. Her bones were whole and undamaged. She wrote to me, "I cannot convey in words the joy this brought me. I now felt empowered and lifted. I know I am *more* than halfway across the river of change."

Her bone cells were now programmed to make new, healthy proteins. Her autonomic nervous system was restoring balance within her body physically, chemically, and emotionally. It was doing the healing for her, through a greater intelligence, and she knew she could trust and surrender more to it now. Her body was continuing to respond to a new mind.

The month after her appointment with the orthopedist, Laurie flew to Arizona for one of my advanced workshops. An hour after she arrived, she received a phone call from the doctor's assistant, who told her that the results from her blood and urine tests were back and they indicated that her disease was actually still quite active. Her doctor recommended that she resume intravenous bisphosphonate therapy for the first time in many years.

Laurie was heartbroken. The x-rays had left her with the impression that she was whole again, but the lab tests indicated otherwise. Within seconds, she had lost perspective and was certain she'd failed. When she told me the news, I reassured her that her body was still living in the past and just needed more time to catch up with her mind. I suggested she continue to do the work for a few more months and retake the urine test then.

Inspired by some of the folks in our workshops who'd changed their health, Laurie went home and did her practice in earnest, feeling more vividly and intensely in her meditations the life that she could have. She stopped imagining herself with healed bones per se, and just imagined herself as whole in general—vital, glowing, resilient, youthful, and in energetic, good health. She mentally rehearsed and emotionally embraced having everything she wanted, which included a functional, walking body. She told herself that the old lady she'd been from ages 19 to 47 was just a story from the past.

New Mind, New Body

Over the next few months, Laurie simply began to feel happier, more joyful, freer, and healthier. She began to think with more clarity about her future. She rarely felt pain in her body and walked without any assistance.

When May 2013 arrived, she was feeling some trepidation about her appointment to retake the lab test. She postponed the appointment until June. Then Laurie discussed her hesitation and anxiety with an experienced workshop student, who asked her to think about some good things she could imagine related to walking into the hospital and taking the test. At this point, Laurie realized she had lots of positive, life-giving emotional resources to draw on. She began reciting a long list, including how clean the hospital was, how helpful all the staff always were, what an easy place it was to go to just be taken care of. It was exactly the shift in focus she needed.

On the day of the appointment, as she drove to the hospital, Laurie gave thanks for the sunshine, for how well traffic was moving, for her car, for her leg that was helping to operate the car, for her perfect eyesight, for the parking spot she easily found, and so on. As she later described to me, "I went inside, gave them my name, shut my eyes, and meditated in the waiting room until it was my turn. I peed in a cup, handed the nurse the bag, and walked out, giving thanks for the simple act of walking. And I let go of the result—entirely. I was okay, deep down inside, with either outcome. It enabled me to forget about it entirely, because I wasn't expecting anything. I felt happy, in fact, obsessively grateful. I stopped analyzing and just trusted."

She remembered my saying that the moment she began to analyze how or when her healing would happen, it would mean she was just returning back to the old self, because the new self would never think in that unsure way. Laurie continued, "And so, for no reason, I was simply grateful in the present moment *ahead* of the actual experience. I wasn't waiting for the results to make me happy or thankful; I was in a state of authentic gratitude and in love with life as if it had already happened. I no longer needed something outside of me to make me happy. I was already whole and happy, because something *inside* of me was more whole and complete."

She had almost nothing on any external "grand scale" by which to measure success, satisfaction, and security—not income, a house, a partner, a business, a child, not even any recent volunteer work she was particularly proud of. But Laurie had the love of her friends and those family members whom she could connect with. And she had a newfound love for herself. She'd realized that she'd never had self-love before—only self-interest. She told me later that it was a distinction that she never could have understood in her previous, narrow state of mind. She felt quite content with herself and her life. She said, "And for the first time since I began this journey, I just didn't care about the test. I was happy with myself."

Two joyful weeks later, the test results came back. The doctor's assistant told Laurie, "Your results are perfectly normal. You scored a 40. Your values are down from an abnormal, elevated level of 68, just five months ago."

Laurie had crossed the river and was on the shores of a new life. There was no evidence of her past living in her body any longer. She was free—born anew.

Laurie told me later:

> It occurred to me in an instant that my identity as "patient" and "sick person with a disease" had become stronger than any other role I'd played in life. I had pretended to be that person, but all along I knew I wasn't. All of my attention and energy were consumed with being a patient instead of with being a woman, a girlfriend, a daughter, an employee, or even just a happy and whole person. I now know that I had no available energy to be anyone else until I took my attention off my old personality and old self, and reinvested my attention and energy into a new self. I'm so grateful that now I'm me instead of that!

Laurie now has no regrets and no significant resentments, and she feels no loss over the past. As she puts it, "I wouldn't want to judge or hold a grudge or feel forsaken from my past, because that choice would take away this feeling of wholeness. It's as if my past condition was actually a blessing, because I overcame my own limitations and now I'm in love with who I am. I'm at peace. I am truly changed on the biological and cellular level. I am proof of the message that your mind can heal your body, and believe me, *no one* is more surprised than I am."

Candace's Story

Candace's relationship, barely a year old, just wasn't working. After their first few months together, she and her boyfriend became deeply embroiled in incessant fighting, volatile accusations, constant mistrust, and ceaseless acts of blame. They both felt jealous and insecure, so their communications were frustrating, at best. They each were haunted by unfulfilled expectations that the other had no hope of satisfying. In a rage she'd never known, Candace found herself in violent screaming matches, throwing uncontrollable tantrums. These fits left her feeling more unworthy, more victimized, and more insecure. All of this behavior was new to her; she hadn't been an angry, frustrated, or upset person before, and she'd never thrown a tantrum in all the 28 years of her life.

Although she knew on a gut level that staying in those circumstances wasn't benefiting her, Candace couldn't escape the emotional attachment to this unhealthy relationship. Yet as she became addicted to her stressful emotions, this became her new identity. Her personal reality was creating her new personality. Candace's external environment was controlling how she was thinking, acting, and feeling. She'd become a victim trapped in her own life.

Flooded with the strong energy of survival emotions, Candace began to operate like an addict, needing that emotional rush of feelings and believing that it was something *out there* that was causing her to feel and think and react in certain ways. She couldn't think or act greater than how she felt. Imprisoned in this emotional state, she was re-creating the same thoughts, the same choices, the same behaviors, and the same experiences over and over again.

Candace was actually using her boyfriend and all of the conditions in her outer world to reaffirm who she thought she was. Her need to feel anger, frustration, insecurity, unworthiness, fear, and victimization was associated with that relationship. Even though it wasn't serving her greatest ideal, she was too afraid of change to remedy the situation. In fact, she became so bonded to those emotions, because they reaffirmed her identity, that she would rather feel those familiar toxic feelings constantly than leave and embrace the unfamiliar—to step from the known into the unknown. Candace began to believe that she *was* her emotions, and as a result, she memorized a personality based on the past that she'd created.

About three months after things began to really go downhill, Candace's body couldn't sustain the stress of that heightened emotional state, and her hair started falling out in very large chunks;

within weeks, almost a third of it was gone. She began experiencing severe migraines, chronic fatigue, gastrointestinal issues, poor concentration, insomnia, weight gain, consistent pain, and myriad other debilitating symptoms—all of them quietly destroying her.

An intuitive young woman, Candace innately felt that this "dis-ease" was a self-inflicted product of her own emotional issues. Just *thinking* about her relationship would physiologically knock her out of balance in preparation for another conflict. Candace was turning on stress hormones and her autonomic nervous system by thought alone. And when she thought about her partner, or talked or complained about their relationship to her family and friends, she was conditioning her body to the mind of those emotions. It was the ultimate mind-body connection, and because she couldn't turn off the stress response, eventually she began downregulating genes. Her thoughts were literally making her sick.

Six months into the relationship, Candace was still living in utter dysfunction, at the highest levels of stress. Even though she was sure by now that the symptoms in her body were a warning sign, she subconsciously continued to choose the same reality, which was now her normal state of being. Barraging her body with negative survival emotions, Candace was signaling the wrong genes in the wrong ways. She felt that she was slowly dying from the inside out, and she knew she needed to take control of her life but had no idea how to go about doing it. She couldn't find the courage to leave the relationship, so she remained in it for over a year, living in a habitual mire of resentment and anger the entire time. Justified or not in feeling those emotions, Candace watched her body pay the price.

Candace Pays the Piper

In November 2010, Candace finally saw a medical doctor, who diagnosed her with Hashimoto's disease (also referred to as *Hashimoto's thyroiditis* or *chronic lymphocytic thyroiditis*), an autoimmune disease in which the immune system attacks the thyroid gland.

The condition is marked by hypothyroidism (an underactive thyroid) with occasional bouts of hyperthyroidism (an overactive thyroid). Symptoms of Hashimoto's include weight gain, depression, mania, sensitivity to heat and cold, numbness, chronic fatigue, panic attacks, abnormal heart rate, high cholesterol, low blood sugar, constipation, migraines, muscle weakness, joint stiffness, cramps, memory loss, vision problems, infertility, and hair loss—many of which Candace was experiencing.

During the consultation, the endocrinologist told Candace that her condition was genetic and she could do nothing about it. She would have Hashimoto's for the rest of her life and would need to take thyroid medication indefinitely, because her antibody count would never change. Although Candace discovered later that she actually had no family history of this illness, the die seemed cast.

Having an actual diagnosis gave Candace the unexpected gift of awareness. She'd clearly needed a wake-up call, and this was it. The physical breakdown of her body had caused her to reflect on her past and really see the truth of who she was being. It dawned on her that she was single-handedly responsible for creating an autoimmune illness that was slowly destroying her physically, emotionally, and mentally. She was living a life in constant-emergency fashion. All of her body's energy was going toward keeping her safe in her external environment, and no energy was left for her internal environment. Her immune system couldn't manage itself any longer.

Despite the gut-wrenching fear of change and of the unfamiliar, Candace finally chose to leave the relationship five months later. She fully understood that the relationship had been unhealthy and not served her. She asked herself, *What's the trade-off? Stay in the dysfunction and propel myself deeper into darkness? Or choose freedom and possibility? This is my chance for a new and different life.*

Candace's adversity became the genesis for her personal evolution, self-reflection, and expansion. She found herself standing on the edge of the cliff, wanting to leap into the unknown. Her decision to jump and to change became a passionate experience. So jump she did, into what she saw as endless possibilities and potentials, compelled by a desire to finally stop doing what was no longer loving to her so that she could rewrite her biological code.

This was a turning point in Candace's life. She'd read my two previous books and been to one of my beginning workshops, so she knew that if she embraced her diagnosis and the emotions of fear, worry, anxiety, and sadness it inspired, she would be autosuggesting and believing only in thoughts equal to those feelings. She could try to think positively, but her body was feeling bad, so that would have real consequences. Making that choice would be the wrong placebo, the wrong state of being.

So Candace chose instead not to accept her illness. She respectfully declined the physician's diagnosis, reminding herself that the mind that creates illness is the same mind that creates wellness. She knew she had to change her beliefs about the condition given to her by the medical community. Candace chose not to be suggestible to her doctor's advice and opinions, because she wasn't fearful, victimized, or sad.

In fact, she was optimistic and enthusiastic, and those emotions drove a new set of thoughts that allowed her to see a new possibility. She didn't *accept* her diagnosis, prognosis, or treatment; *believe* hastily in the most probable outcome or future destiny; or permanently *surrender* to the diagnosis or treatment plan. She didn't *condition* her body to that future worst-case scenario, *expect* the same predictable outcome that everyone else did, or *assign the same meaning* that everyone else with the condition did. She had a different attitude, so she was now in a different state of being.

Candace Gets Busy

Even though Candace didn't accept her condition, she had a lot of work ahead of her. She knew that to change her belief about her disease, she'd have to make a choice with an amplitude of energy that was greater than the hardwired programs in her brain and the emotional addictions in her body so that her body could respond to a new mind. Only then could she experience the necessary change in energy that she needed to rewrite her subconscious programs and erase her past neurologically and genetically—which is exactly what began to happen.

Although she had heard me say all of this before and knew the material intellectually, Candace had never embraced the information from personal experience. In the first workshop she attended after getting the diagnosis, she looked exhausted and kept falling asleep in her chair. I knew she was struggling.

When she came to her next workshop, she'd been taking thyroid medication to regulate her imbalanced chemical state for a little over a month, and she was more alert and interested. Candace was incredibly inspired by the stories I told during the weekend. When she heard that others weren't going to be victims of the circumstances in their external worlds and that uncommon healings could happen, she decided that she was going to be her own science project.

So Candace embarked on the journey. Having an understanding of epigenetics and neuroplasticity from my workshops, she knew she was no longer a victim of the disease and, instead, used her knowledge to become proactive. She assigned a different meaning to her future and so had a different intention. She awoke every day at 4:30 A.M. to do her meditation and began to emotionally condition her body to a new mind. She worked on finding the present moment, which she realized had been lost to her before.

Candace wanted to be happy and healthy, so she fought hard to regain her life. Even so, she struggled in the beginning and got very frustrated when she couldn't sit for any extended period of time. Her body had been trained to be the mind of frustration, anger, impatience, and victimization, and it understandably rebelled. As though she were training an undisciplined animal, Candace had to keep settling her body down to the present moment. Every time she went through that process, she was reconditioning her body to a new mind and freeing herself a bit more from the chains of her emotional addiction.

Every day in her meditations, Candace worked on overcoming her body, her environment, and time. She refused to get up as the same person who'd sat down to do the meditation, because the old Candace was the one who became angry and frustrated and was so chemically addicted to her external circumstances. She didn't want to be that person anymore. She listened to her meditations, emulated a new state of being, and wouldn't stop until she was in love with life—in a true state of gratitude for no particular reason.

Candace applied all the knowledge that she'd learned from my workshops and from listening to every audio CD, reading every book (more than once), and studying her notes from the courses. She was wiring new information into her brain to prepare herself for a new experience of healing. More and more often, she found that she could refrain from firing and wiring the old neural connections of anger, frustration, resentment, arrogance, and mistrust and that she could begin to fire and wire the new neural connections of love, joy, compassion, and kindness. In doing so, Candace knew she was pruning away the old connections and sprouting new ones. And the more times she made the effort with a level of mental fortitude, the more she would transform.

In time, she became incredibly grateful to be alive, realizing that where harmony existed, incoherence couldn't abide. She told herself, *I am not the old Candace, and I'm not reaffirming that existence any longer.* For months on end, she persevered. And if she found herself being driven to that lowest common denominator, being angry or frustrated at the conditions in her external world, or feeling sick or unhappy, she would very quickly make a conscious shift. By swiftly changing her state of being, she could shorten the periods in which those emotions had a hold on her so that she was overall less moody, less temperamental, and less like her old personality.

Some days Candace felt so bad that she didn't want to get out of bed, but she got up anyway and meditated. She told herself that whenever she transmuted those lower emotions into elevated emotions, she was removing herself biologically from her past and priming her brain and body to a new future. She began to realize how worthwhile doing her inner work was, and it soon became less like effort and more like a gift.

Thanks to her daily persistence, Candace noticed a huge shift very quickly, and she started feeling better. She started communicating with others differently once she stopped looking at the world through a mind of fear and frustration, and instead looked through a lens of compassion, love, and gratitude. Her energy increased, and she was able to think more clearly.

Candace realized that she didn't react the same way to the familiar conditions in her life, because the old fear-based emotions were no longer within her body. She was overcoming her knee-jerk reactions, because she now saw that the people and conditions that used to upset her existed only in relation to how she was feeling. She was becoming free.

Part of her process of change included becoming conscious of the unconscious thoughts that typically slipped by her awareness during the day. In her meditations, she became determined that those thoughts would never go unnoticed again. Under no circumstances would she allow herself to return to the behaviors and habits connected to her old self. She erased the chalkboard biologically, neurologically, and genetically, making room to create a new self, and her body began to liberate energy. In other words, she was going from particle to wave by releasing the stored emotions as energy in her body. Her body was no longer living the past.

With this newly available energy that she'd freed up, Candace began to see the landscape of a new future. She asked herself, *How do I want to behave? How do I want to feel? How do I want to think?* By getting up every day for months on end in a state of gratitude, she was emotionally instructing her body that her new future had already arrived, which signaled new genes in new ways, moving her body back into homeostasis. Right on the other side of Candace's anger, she found compassion. Right on the other side of her frustration, she discovered patience and gratitude. And right on the other side of her victimization was a creator, waiting to create joy and wellness. It was the same intense energy on either side, but she was now able to liberate it as she moved from particle to wave, from survival to creation.

Sweet, Sweet Success

When Candace returned to her doctor seven months after her diagnosis, he was amazed by the change in his patient. Her blood tests had come back perfect. In her initial round of tests in February 2011, her thyroid-stimulating hormone (TSH) had been 3.61 (which is high), and her antibody count had been 638 (showing a major imbalance). But by September 2011, Candace's TSH had dropped to a normal 1.15, and her antibody count was a healthy 450, even though she was no longer taking any medication. She'd healed herself in less than one year.

The doctor wanted to know just what she'd been doing to get these great results. It seemed almost too good to be true. Candace explained that she knew she'd created this condition, so she'd decided to conduct an experiment on herself to *uncreate* it. She told the doctor that by meditating daily and maintaining an elevated state of emotion, she had been epigenetically signaling new genes instead of letting unhealthy emotions continue to signal the old genes. She explained that she'd worked regularly on who she wanted to become and that she'd stopped responding to everything in her external environment like an animal in survival mode: fighting, fleeing, kicking, or screaming. Everything around her was basically the same; she was just responding in a way that was more loving to herself.

The doctor told her, looking absolutely amazed, "I wish all my patients were like you, Candace. It's just incredible to hear your story."

Candace doesn't really *know* how her healing happened. She doesn't need to. She just knows that she has become someone else.

I had dinner with Candace a while after all this happened, at a point when she had been off her medication for months and had no symptoms at all. Her health was fantastic, all her hair had grown back, and she felt great about herself. She mentioned over and over again that she was so in love with her present life.

I told her, laughing, "You're in love with life, and it's loving you back. You *should* be in love with your life—*you* created it every day for months that way!"

Candace explained that she just trusted in an infinite field of potentials and knew that something else was going on beyond her that had helped her heal. All she really had to do was to get beyond herself and enter into the autonomic nervous system, and then keep planting the seeds for a new life. And without knowing how it happened, it just happened—and when it did, she felt better than she'd ever felt before.

Candace's life is now completely different from her life when she was diagnosed with Hashimoto's. She's a business partner in a personal development program that teaches self-development work, and she also maintains a corporate job. She has a loving relationship, new friendships, and new business opportunities. A new personality ultimately creates a new personal reality.

A state of being is a magnetic force that draws events equal to that state of being, so when Candace fell in love with herself, she drew a loving relationship to herself. Because she felt worthy and felt respect for herself and all of life, conditions began to show up for her in which she had opportunities to contribute, to be respected, and to make a difference in the world. And of course, when she moved into a new personality, the old personality became like another lifetime. That new physiology began to drive her to greater levels of joy and inspiration—and the disease then belonged to the old personality. She was someone else.

It's not that she became addicted to joy; she was just no longer addicted to being unhappy. When she started experiencing greater levels of happiness, she found that there's always *more* bliss, *more* joy, and *more* love to experience, because every experience creates a different blend of emotions. She started really wanting the challenges in her life so that she could find out to what extent she could take this information into transformation.

The ultimate lesson that Candace learned was that her disease and her challenges were never about someone else—they were always about her. In her old state of being, she'd had the firm belief that she was a victim of her relationship and of her external circumstances and that life was always happening *to* her. Becoming aware of this work and taking full responsibility for herself and her life—and realizing that what had happened never had anything to do with what was outside of her—was not only a huge empowerment, but also one of the greatest gifts Candace could've ever asked for.

Joann's Story

Joann lived most of her life in the fast lane. The 59-year-old mother of five was also a committed wife, a successful businesswoman, and an entrepreneur who constantly juggled her home life, family dynamics, growing career, and thriving business. Although her goal was to stay sane, healthy, and balanced, she couldn't imagine her life any other way than intense, fast paced, and busy; she was living on the edge and proving to everyone that her mind was active and sharp. Joann constantly pushed herself to take on as much as possible, all the while maintaining exceptionally high standards. She was a leader, admired by many and regularly sought out for advice. Her peers called her "Superwoman," and she was—or so she thought.

All that ended abruptly in January 2008, when Joann stepped off the elevator in her apartment building and then just collapsed, about 50 feet from her front door. She hadn't felt well that day, so she'd gone to a walk-in clinic for help and been on her way back home. In a matter of moments, everything in her world had changed, and she found herself clinging to life.

After eight months of testing, the doctors diagnosed her with *secondary progressive multiple sclerosis* (SPMS), an advanced stage of multiple sclerosis (MS), a chronic disease in which the immune system attacks the central nervous system. Symptoms vary widely depending on the individual, but can start with conditions such as numbness in a leg or an arm, progressing as far as paralysis and even blindness. These symptoms can include not only physical but also cognitive and psychiatric problems.

Joann's symptoms had been so vague and sporadic over the previous 14 years that she'd easily brushed them off as by-products of a hectic lifestyle. But now her condition had a label, and it felt like a life sentence—with no chance of parole. She found herself thrown into the depths of the Western medical world, challenged by its strong belief that MS is a permanent disease.

A few years before the diagnosis, Joann had put the family business in Calgary on hold and made a life-changing move to Vancouver, on the west coast of Canada, something her family had wanted to do for years. After the move, Joann struggled with one challenge after another as the family's eroding finances and resources put them in a very precarious situation. Joann's self-esteem, confidence, and health all took a nosedive. Once she found herself unable to become greater than her environment, her mental and physical state began to decline. Money became tighter and tighter as other stressors began to increase. Soon, the family couldn't even meet their basic needs of food and shelter. In early 2007, the woman everyone else had always seen as Superwoman hit bottom, and before the end of the year, the family returned to Calgary.

MS is an inflammatory disease in which the insulating coverings of nerve cells in the brain and spinal cord are damaged, along with the nerve fibers themselves. The condition disrupts the nervous system from communicating and sending signals to various parts of the body. The type of MS Joann developed is a progressive type that builds up over time, often causing permanent neurological problems, especially as the disease advances. Her doctors told her it was incurable.

Initially, Joann was determined that her MS wouldn't define her. Yet she quickly spiraled downward into physical disability and cognitive decline. Joann had to depend on others for basic care as her limitations increased. Because of her sensory and motor problems, she began to rely on crutches, walkers, and a wheelchair. Eventually she had to rely on a mobility scooter to get around.

It wasn't much of a surprise that she crashed when her life did. Joann's body finally did her the favor she wouldn't do herself—that is, to stop and say, "No more!" She'd pushed herself too hard. Even though she'd achieved success in her early years, deep down inside, she felt like a failure most of the time because she constantly judged herself and thought that she could always do a better job. She was never satisfied. Whatever she did or achieved was *never good enough*.

Most important, Joann didn't want to stop doing, because then she would have to attend to that impending feeling of failure. So instead, she stayed busy by putting all of her attention on her outer world—various experiences with people and things at different times and places—so that she wouldn't have to put any attention on her inner world of thoughts and feelings.

The majority of Joann's life had been filled with supporting others, by celebrating their successes and encouraging them, yet she'd never allowed anyone to see what wasn't working in her own life. She hid her pain from everyone. Joann constantly gave but never received—because she never *allowed* herself to receive—so she'd spent a lifetime denying herself her own personal evolution by never expressing herself. It makes sense that when Joann tried to change her inner world by using the conditions in her outer world, she would inevitably manifest only failure.

When she finally collapsed, Joann was so weak and defeated that she barely had the strength to fight for her life. All that time spent living in emergency mode, constantly reacting to the conditions in her external world, had robbed Joann of her life force, draining all the energy from her internal world—the place for repair and healing. She was simply tapped out.

Joann Changes Her Mind

The one thing Joann knew without a doubt was that the damage that the MRIs showed was riddling her brain and spinal column hadn't appeared overnight. Her body had slowly been eaten away at her core—the central nervous system. After all those years of ignoring symptoms, she'd become *unnerved* because she was afraid to look inside herself. Those daily toxic chemicals were repeatedly knocking on the door of her cells, and finally the gene for the disease answered the door and switched on.

Bedridden, Joann made her first goal to slow down the progression of the MS in her body. She knew from reading my first book that the brain doesn't know the difference between what she could make real internally by thought alone and the real external experience, and she knew that mental practice could change her brain and her body. She started mentally rehearsing doing yoga, and after just a few weeks of daily practice, she was able to do some actual physical poses—even some standing ones. These results highly motivated her.

Every day, Joann primed her brain and body by thought alone. Just like the piano players in Chapter 5 who mentally rehearsed playing the piano and grew the same neurological circuits as the subjects who physically practiced the exercises, Joann was installing the circuits in her brain to look as if she were already physically walking and moving. Remember the subjects in the various weight-lifting studies who increased their strength just by mentally practicing lifting weights or flexing their biceps? Just like them, Joann knew she could make her body look as if the experience of healing had already started to happen—by literally changing her mind.

Soon she was able to stand briefly, and then she could walk with support. Joann was quite wobbly and otherwise still dependent on a mobility scooter, but at least she was no longer confined to bed and feeling sorry for herself. She had turned a corner.

When Joann began to meditate regularly to simply quiet her mind chatter, she became aware of how sad and angry she really was. The floodgates opened. Joann realized she felt weak, isolated, rejected, and unworthy most of the time. Out of balance, ungrounded, and disconnected, she felt as though she'd lost a vital part of herself. She observed how she denied herself by pleasing others and how she couldn't acknowledge herself without feeling guilty. She recognized that she was always trying to control what seemed to be a spiraling chaos around her, yet it never worked. On a deeper level, she had known this all along but had chosen to ignore it, pushing herself relentlessly and pretending that everything was okay.

Painful as it was, Joann was now looking at how she'd created her disease. She decided to become conscious of all of those subconscious thoughts, actions, and emotions that were defining her as the same personality who'd created this particular personal reality. She knew that once she could look at who she was being, it meant that she'd be able to change those aspects of herself. The more she became conscious of her unconscious self and aware of her state of being, the more she gained dominion over what she'd hidden from view.

By early 2010, Joann felt that the progression of the MS had indeed slowed. Her goal then became to stop it altogether. In May, when she mentioned this idea to a neurologist who asked what her goals were with her disease, the doctor abruptly terminated her appointment. Instead of becoming discouraged, Joann was more intent after this incident.

Taking Her Healing to the Next Level

When Joann attended a workshop in Vancouver, she couldn't walk on her own. During the weekend, I asked the participants to set a firm intention in their minds and combine it with an elevated emotion in their bodies. The goal was to recondition the body to a new mind, instead of continuing to condition it with survival emotions. I wanted participants to open their hearts and teach their bodies emotionally what their future would feel like.

This was the missing ingredient to Joann's daily mental practice. Embracing thoughts of walking across a 20- to 25-foot floor with only her cane for support excited her beyond belief. She was now adding the second element of the placebo effect to the equation: expectation with emotion.

It was this combination—convincing her body emotionally that the future event of healing was happening to her in the present moment—that would take Joann to the next level. Her body, as the unconscious mind, had to believe it for it to be so. If she were to embrace the joy of being well and give thanks *before* the healing occurred, then her body would be getting a sampling of her future in the present moment.

I suggested to Joann that she really pay attention to her thoughts, because it was her thoughts that had truly made her sick. I pressed her to get beyond the personality that was connected to her condition, which was necessary before she could create a new personality and a new personal reality. Now she could apply meaning and intention to what she was doing.

Two months after that workshop, Joann attended a second, more advanced workshop in Seattle. Her scooter had broken down the day before she left for that event, so she used her motorized wheelchair to get around. Despite initially feeling more vulnerable because of that, at the workshop, Joann soon felt better able to move. Her associative memory related to the positive experience of the last event, and the expectation of getting better in the current event, was what initiated that process. If 29 percent of chemo patients can experience anticipatory nausea before their chemo treatments (as you read in Chapter 1), then maybe it's possible for some of the workshop participants to experience anticipatory wellness when they're back in the workshop setting. Whatever the trigger, Joann saw a new possibility and, with enthusiasm, began once again to emotionally embrace that future in the present moment.

During the last meditation of that workshop, the magic happened for her. Joann experienced a huge internal shift, and she felt something that moved her profoundly. She felt her body changing automatically, once she entered her autonomic nervous system and it received the new instructions and took over. She felt lifted, overjoyed, and free. After the meditation, Joann got up from her chair a different person than she'd been when she'd sat down—she was in a new state of being. She then walked to the front of the room—without any support, not even her cane. She strutted across the room wide-eyed, laughing like a child. She could feel and move her legs, which had been dormant for years.

She'd gotten out of the way—and it felt incredible! To my amazement, Joann had signaled new genes in new ways right during that one meditation. She'd actually changed her condition in just one hour!

When she got beyond her MS identity, she became a different person, and that's when she stopped trying to slow, stop, or reverse her MS. She no longer tried to prove anything to herself, her family, her doctors, or anyone else. She understood and experienced for the first time that her true journey was always about wholeness, which is what verifiable healing is always about. She forgot that she had an official disease, and she dissociated from that identity for a moment. The freedom that doing so engendered and the amplitude of that elevated emotion were strong enough to switch on a new gene. Joann knew that MS was simply a label, like "mother," "wife," or "boss." She had changed that label by simply giving up her past.

More Miracles

When Joann arrived back home three days later, unbeknownst to her, the miraculous continued to unfold. While doing yoga, a practice she'd begun physically—not just mentally—after attending the second workshop, she noticed that she could lift one foot off the ground. She tried to lift the other—success! She then noticed that she could flex her feet for the first time in years. And she could wiggle her toes, which she hadn't done in a long time.

She was stunned and in absolute awe as tears of joy flowed from her eyes. She knew in that instant that anything was possible, not because of some external medication or procedure, but because of the internal changes she'd made. Joann knew she could be her own placebo.

Within a very short time, Joann taught herself how to walk again. Two years later, she is still walking unassisted and is more playful and full of life. Her body strength has improved, and she's now able to do many things that she thought she'd never again be able to do. Most important, she feels alive and filled with boundless joy. Joann feels whole, and because she can now *receive,* she continues to receive healing.

Joann recently told me, "My life is magical, full of incredible synergies, abundance, and unexpected gifts of every sort. It bubbles, sparkles, and tingles with a new and lighter reflection of myself. It's the new me—actually, the *real* me that I'd tried to keep under control and hidden for most of my life!"

Joann now lives most of her day in gratitude. She still takes the time to be aware of her thoughts and feelings; that is, she cultivates her state of being every day, paying attention to what she tells herself and what she thinks about others, too. In her meditations, she observes herself and becomes familiar with how she acts. Very rarely does a thought get past her conscious mind that she doesn't want to experience.

Joann's current neurologist supports her choices and has been astounded by what she has seen. Her physician has had to acknowledge the power of the mind, which Joann demonstrated right before her eyes with medical reports and blood tests that show no signs of MS.

Laurie, Candace, and Joann accomplished their dramatic remissions using no resources outside of themselves. They changed their health from the inside out—without the use of medication, surgery, therapy, or anything other than their own minds. They became their own placebos.

Now, let's take a scientific look into the brains of some other people from my workshops who were able to make similar dramatic changes so that we can see exactly what was going on in the process of these remarkable transformations.

Chapter Ten

Information to Transformation: Proof That You *Are* the Placebo

This book is about making your mind matter. You now understand that the placebo works because a person accepts and believes in a *known* remedy—a fake pill, injection, or procedure substituted for its real counterpart—and then surrenders to the outcome without overanalyzing how it's going to happen. We could say that a person associates her future experience of a particular *known* person (say, a doctor) or thing (a medication or procedure) at a specific time and place in her external environment with a change in her internal environment—and in doing so, she alters her state of being. After a few consistent experiences, the person will expect her future to be exactly like her past. Once that link is in place, the process becomes highly effective. It's about a *known* stimulus automatically producing a *known* response.

The bottom line is this: In the classic placebo effect, our belief lies in something outside of us. We give our power away to the material world, where our senses define reality. But can the placebo work by creating from the *immaterial* world of thought and making that unknown possibility a new reality? That would be a more prudent use of the quantum model.

The three workshop participants you read about in the last chapter accomplished this feat. They all chose to believe in *themselves* more than they believed in anything else. They changed *from the inside* and moved into the same state of being as someone who'd taken a placebo—without any material thing causing the phenomenon. That's what many students continue to do to get better. Once they know how the placebo really works, the pill, injection, or procedure can be taken away, and the same outcome unfolds.

Because of the research in these workshops, as well as the constant testimonials I've received from people around the world, I now know that *you are the placebo.* My students demonstrate that instead of investing their belief in the known, they can place their belief in the *unknown* and make the unknown *known.*

Think about this for a moment. The idea of verifiable healing exists as an unknown potential reality in the quantum field, until it is observed and realized, and has materialized. It lives as a possibility in an infinite field of information defined as no*thing* physically but all material possibilities combined. So the potential future of experiencing a spontaneous remission from a disease exists as an unknown located *beyond space and time,* until it's personally experienced and made known in *this space and time.* Once the unknown *beyond* the senses becomes a known experience *with* your senses, you're on the path of evolution.

So if you can experience a healing over and over again in the inner world of thoughts and feelings, then in time, that healing should finally manifest as an outer experience. And if you make a thought as real as the experience in the external environment, shouldn't there be evidence in your body and brain sooner or later? In other words, if you mentally rehearse that unknown future with a clear intention and an elevated emotion, and do it repeatedly, then based on what you've learned, you should have real neuroplastic changes in your brain and epigenetic changes in your body.

And if you keep moving into a new state of being each day by reminding your brain and conditioning your body to that same mind, then you should see the same structural and functional changes within you as if you took the placebo. Figure 10.1 gives a simple graphic showing how this process unfolds.

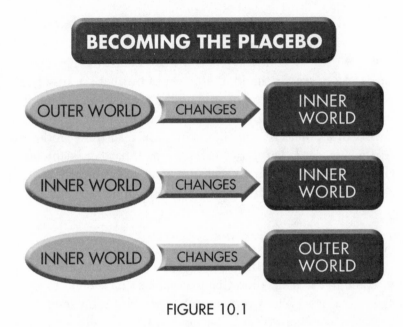

FIGURE 10.1

Most change starts with the simple process of something outside of us altering something inside of us. If you begin the inward journey and start to change your inner world of thoughts and feelings, it should create an improved state of well-being. If you keep repeating the process in meditation, then in time, epigenetic changes should begin to alter your outer presentation—and you become your own placebo.

So instead of aligning your faith (which I define as believing in a thought more than anything else) and your belief in something known, can you place your attention on an unknown possibility and then, by the principles discussed in this book, make that unknown reality known? By emotionally embracing the experience in your mind enough times, can you move from the immaterial to the material—from thought to reality?

By now, you should understand that you don't need any fake pills, holy shrines, ancient symbols, witch doctors (whether of the modern-day or traditional variety), sham surgery, or sacred ground in order to heal you. This chapter introduces the scientific evidence showing how our students did just that. They changed their biology by thought alone. It wasn't just in their minds—it was in their brains.

All of the supporting evidence in this chapter is provided to inspire you to see, firsthand, the power of meditation. It's my desire that once you see proof of what's possible, you'll apply the same principles to your own personal transformation and reap the benefits in all areas of your life. After you read these stories, by the time you get to Part II of the book, you'll have more intention behind your inward journey, because you'll assign more meaning to what you're doing—and therefore you'll get better results.

From Knowledge to Experience

I've learned something very important in teaching this work. I've come to the realization that everyone secretly believes in his or her greatness. When you get right down to it, on some level, everyone—whether you're a corporate CEO, a janitor at an elementary school, a single mother of three, or a prison inmate—innately believes in him- or herself.

We all believe in possibility. We all imagine a better future for ourselves than the reality where we currently reside. So I thought that if I could offer sincere individuals vital scientific information and then provide them with the necessary instruction on how to apply that information, they could experience varying degrees of personal transformation. Science is, after all, the contemporary language of mysticism. It transcends religion, culture, and tradition. It demystifies the mystical and unifies a community. I've seen it occur time and time again in my seminars around the world.

In my advanced workshops where my colleagues and I measure biological as well as energetic changes in participants, individually and in the group as a whole, I use several principles outlined in this book (and many additional ones as well) to teach people the scientific model of transformation. The model continues to progress as students evolve their skill sets. I constantly tie in more quantum physics to help people understand possibility. I then combine it with the latest information in neuroscience, neuroendocrinology, epigenetics, cellular biology, brain-wave science, energy psychology, and psychoneuroimmunology. We see new possibilities manifest as a result of learning new information.

Once our students learn and embrace this information, they can assign more meaning to their meditations and contemplative practices. But it's not enough for the students to merely understand the information intellectually or conceptually. They must be able to repeat what they've learned on command. Once they can explain the advancing knowledge, the progressing model will become more wired in their brains—and they can then install the neurological hardware. By then repeating what they've learned enough times, they create a hardwired software program. If they apply this new knowledge correctly, it can then serve as the forerunner to a new experience.

That is, once they align their minds and bodies, they'll gain wisdom from a novel experience by embracing the associated new emotion. Now they'll start to *embody* the information, because they are chemically instructing their bodies to emotionally understand what their minds intellectually understand. At this point, they'll begin to believe and know that it's the truth. But my desire is that instead of just doing it once, my students repeat the experience over and over again at will, until it becomes a new skill, habit, or state of being.

Once we achieve consistency, we're on the precipice of a new scientific paradigm—because anything that's repeatable *is* science. When you and I arrive at the level of competence where we can change our internal states by thought alone, and this is repeatedly observed, measured, and documented, we're on the verge of a new scientific law. Now we can contribute new knowledge about the nature of reality to the overall scientific model that the world presently embraces so that we can empower more people. This has been my ambition for years.

I've gone to great lengths to teach our workshop participants the specifics of how inward practices biologically change the brain and body so that they understand explicitly what they are doing. When nothing is left to conjecture, dogma, or supposition, we're more suggestible to a quantum possibility. And great strides result from great efforts. Nevertheless, the measurements are only as good as the students' abilities.

So in my workshops, the students retreat from their lives for three to five days to help them no longer define themselves by their present-past personal reality. They practice moving into new states of being. By no longer reaffirming aspects of their old-personality self that don't belong to their future and by pretending to be someone else—or by reinventing a new-personality self—they become the new self they envision, so they should produce epigenetic changes, just as did the older men in Chapter 4 who pretended they were 22 years younger.

It's my desire that workshop participants get beyond themselves—and their identities—in their meditations to become no *body,* no *one,* no *thing,* and to be in no *place* and in no *time*—so that they become pure consciousness. Once this occurs, I've seen them change their brains and bodies ahead of their environments (their familiar lives) so that when they return to their lives after the workshop is over, they're no longer the victims of unconscious conditioning from the external world. This is the domain where the uncommon and the miraculous happen.

Because I want to give students the right kind of instruction and provide them with opportunities to personalize all of the novel information they're learning so that they can ultimately produce some type of personal transformation, I created a new kind of event in 2013. If you remember, I discussed the evolution of this idea in the Preface. In this new workshop offering (held first in February of that year in Carefree, Arizona, and again in July in Englewood, Colorado), I wanted to measure the transformation as it was happening in real time.

My intention was that once these measurements were obtained, the data would then become more information that I could use to teach participants about the transformation they'd just experienced. And with *that* information, they could have *another* transformation, which could be measured, and on it would go as people began to close the gap between the two worlds of knowledge and experience. I call these workshops "Information to Transformation." It's where my passion lies.

Measuring Change

When I began the journey, I discovered a brilliant and talented neuroscientist named Jeffrey Fannin, Ph.D., who selflessly helped me measure what students' brains were doing. Dr. Fannin, the founder and executive director of the Center for Cognitive Enhancement in Glendale, Arizona, has worked in the field of neuroscience for more than 15 years and has extensive experience in training the brain for optimal performance. He specializes in head trauma, stroke, chronic pain, attention deficit disorder (ADD) and attention deficit hyperactivity disorder (ADHD), anxiety disorders, depression, and trauma recovery, as well as high-performance training that includes brain mapping for sports, enhancing leadership skills through brain-wave entrainment, improving brain function, enhancing mental and emotional dexterity, and personal transformation.

Over the years, he has been involved in cutting-edge research using electroencephalograph (EEG) technology (which measures the electrical activity of neurons) to accurately assess how balanced a person's brain-wave energy is, a measurement he calls the person's *whole-brain state*. His research focuses on subconscious belief patterns and merging personal success with balanced brain performance.

Dr. Fannin has also worked as part of a research team at Arizona State University, studying neuroscience and leadership using data gathered at the United States Military Academy at West Point. This research allowed him to co-develop and co-teach a unique course at Arizona State University called "The Neuroscience of Leadership." He also served for several years on the faculty at Walden University near Phoenix, teaching cognitive neuroscience at the master's and doctoral levels.

I invited Dr. Fannin and his whole team to both of these new workshop events, where we measured specific brain qualities and elements like coherence versus incoherence (the orderliness or disorderliness of brain waves), amplitude (the energy of the brain waves), phase organization (the degree to which the different parts of the brain are working together in harmony), the relative time it takes for a person to enter deep meditation (how long it takes to change brain waves and move into a more suggestible state), the theta/alpha ratio (the degree to which the brain functions in a holistic state and how different brain compartments communicate with each other across entire regions—the front with the back and the left side with the right side), the delta/theta ratio (the ability to regulate and control mind chatter and intrusive thoughts), and sustainability (the brain's ability to consistently maintain a state of meditation over time).

We also created four brain-scan stations equipped with EEG machines to measure participants both before and after the workshop so that we could observe how students' brain-wave patterns changed. We scanned more than a hundred participants in each of the two events. I also randomly selected four participants to measure during each of three meditation sessions per day, scanning their brains in real time. Altogether, in both 2013 workshops, we recorded a total of 402 EEGs. This is a safe, noninvasive procedure that takes measurements from 20 locations on the outside of the head. Those brain-wave measurements provide a host of information regarding the brain's current ability to perform.

The EEGs were then converted into quantitative EEGs (QEEGs), which is a mathematical and statistical analysis of EEG activity that's depicted as a brain-map graphic. This graphic features color gradations indicating how the activity recorded from the EEG compares to normal baseline activity. The various colors and patterns depicted at different frequencies offer greater information about how the brain-wave patterns affect a person's thoughts, feelings, emotions, and behaviors.

For starters, our overall data demonstrated that 91 percent of the individuals whose EEGs we recorded presented a significantly improved state of brain function. The majority of our students moved from a less coherent (or less orderly) state to a more co-herent state by the end of the transformational meditation ses-sions. Furthermore, more than 82 percent of the QEEG brain maps we recorded in both events demonstrated that participants were functioning within the healthy normal range of brain activity.

I learned that when your *brain* works right, *you* work right. When your brain is more coherent, you're more coherent. When your brain is more whole and balanced, you're more whole and balanced. When you can regulate your negative and intrusive thoughts every day, you're less negative and intrusive. And that's exactly what we witnessed with the students at these events.

The national average for someone to move into and sustain a meditative state is a little over one and a half minutes.[1] That is, it takes that long for most people to change their brain waves and move into a meditative state. The average time for *our* students to enter and sustain a meditative state in the 402 cases that we measured was only 59 seconds. That's under a minute. Some of our students were able to alter their brain waves (and their state of being) in as few as four, five, and nine seconds each.

To be clear, I'm not interested in making this a competition (which would defeat our purpose). However, this data does illus-trate two important points. First, moving beyond the analytical mind of beta brain waves and entering into a more suggestible state is a skill that you can improve if you keep practicing it. Sec-ond, students are able to use the methods my colleagues and I are teaching to get beyond their thinking brains and enter into the operating system of the subconscious mind relatively easily.

Interestingly, our research also shows a noticeable, consistent patterning in the way our students' brains work holistically. We see significant alternating alpha/theta patterns (how different brain compartments communicate with each other) in the fron-tal lobes when a person meditates. That means the two halves of the brain are talking in a more balanced and unified fashion. The dual frontal-lobe ratio patterns we repeatedly observe seem to produce the experience of high-level thankfulness and grati-tude, which appear over and over again in a rhythmic, wavelike manner. So when students are in this heightened state of gratitude during mental rehearsal, this data suggests that their inner experience is so real that they believe that the events are happening to them in real time—or that the events have already happened. They're thankful, because that's the emotion we feel when what we want happens.

Experienced meditators also showed an increase in theta and lower-range alpha brain-wave ratios, which means that they can spend quite a bit of time in altered states. Of particular significance was the increase in slow-wave regulation; these students, while in a theta brain-wave state, have higher-than-normal coherence, or brain-wave orderliness, between the activity in the front of the brain and the regions in the back of the brain. We saw the left-frontal region, which is associated with positive emotion, get activated repeatedly, which is consistent with inducing a state of meditative bliss.

In other words, when these students enter a meditation, they produce slower, more coherent brain waves that suggest they're in deep states of relaxation and heightened awareness. In addition, the unification between the front and the back of the brain, as well as between the left and right sides of the brain, indicates that they're feeling happier and more whole.

I Have a Brainstorm

Finally, while I was observing a student who was being brain mapped in real time during a meditation at the first of the two events, I understood something quite remarkable. As I was watching her brain on the scan, I saw how hard she was working and how her brain was moving further and further away from balance and from the deeper meditative states of alpha and theta. I saw how she was analyzing and judging herself and her life within the emotion she was experiencing at that time—as evidenced by the higher, more incoherent brain waves associated with a high-range beta state (indicating high stress, high anxiety, high arousal, high emergency, and general imbalance).

I witnessed how she was futilely trying to use her brain to change her brain—and it wasn't working. I knew that she was also using her ego to try to change her ego, which also wasn't working. In using one program to try to change another program, she was only endorsing her program, not rewriting it. She was still in her conscious mind, trying to change her subconscious mind, so she was keeping herself separate from the operating system, where true change resides. I approached her afterward, and when we spoke for a few minutes, she admitted to me that she was having a difficult time. The lights went on for me in that moment, and I knew exactly what I had to teach next.

She had to become detached and move beyond her body in order to change her body, move beyond the ego in order to change the ego, move beyond the program in order to change the program, and move beyond the conscious mind in order to change the subconscious mind. She had to become the unknown in order to create the unknown. She had to become an immaterial new thought in *nothing* materially in order to create a new experience materially. She had to move beyond space and time in order to change space and time.

The student had to become pure consciousness. She had to get beyond her associations with an identity that was associated with her known environment (her home, her job, her spouse, her kids, her problems), beyond her body (her face, her gender, her age, her weight, and her looks), and beyond time (the predictable habit of living in the past or the future, always missing the present moment). She had to get beyond her current self to create a new self. She had to get out of her own way so that something greater could take over.

When we are matter trying to change matter, it never works. When we are the particle trying to change the particle, nothing will happen, because we're vibrating at the same speed as matter and so can't have any significant effect on it. It's our consciousness (our intentional thought) and our energy (our elevated emotion) that influences matter. Only when we are consciousness can we alter our brains, our bodies, and our lives and create a new future in time.

And because it's consciousness that gives form to all things and that uses the brain and body to produce different levels of mind, once you arrive in the place where you are pure consciousness, you're free. So I began to let students linger for extended periods of time in their meditations and become no *one*, no *body*, no *thing*, and be in no *place* and in no *time*, until they were comfortable in the infinite field of possibilities.

I wanted students' subjective consciousness to merge with the objective consciousness of the field for long periods of time. They had to find the sweet spot of the present moment and invest their energy and awareness in a void that is not really empty space but is actually filled with an infinite number of possibilities, until they were comfortable in the unknown. Only once they were truly present in this potent place beyond space and time—the place from where all things materially come—could they start to create. This was when the real changes during the workshops began to happen.

A Quick Overview of the Brain Scans Used

I want to introduce you to two types of brain-scan readings so that you can see and understand the changes I'm about to show you. Let's make it simple. The first type of scan we used measures degrees of activity between brain areas (see Figure 10.2, located along with the rest of the figures for this chapter in the full-color insert pages). The scans map two relative types of this activity. *Hyperactivity* (or overregulation) is depicted by red lines connecting different locations in the brain. Imagine telephone lines connecting one place to another in order to establish communication between those areas. Having too many red lines at any one time indicates too much action taking place within the brain. *Hypoactivity* (lack of regulation) is depicted by blue lines indicating that minimal information is being communicated between the different brain areas.

The thickness of the lines represents the *standard deviation,* or how much *dysregulation* (or abnormal regulation) exists between the two locations the line connects. For example, the thin red lines indicate that the level of activity between those locations is 1.96 standard deviations (SD) above normal. The thin blue lines indicate that the level of activity between those locations is 1.96 SD below normal. The medium lines indicate 2.58 SD either above (red) or below (blue) normal. And the thick lines indicate 3.09 SD above or below normal. So when you see a lot of thick red lines in a scan, it means the brain is working too hard. When you see a lot of thick blue lines, it suggests there's little communication between different areas of the brain and, therefore, the brain is underactive. Think of it like this: The thicker the red line, the higher the volume of data the brain is processing, and the thicker the blue line, the lower the volume of data the brain processing.

The second type of scan we used comes from the QEEG analysis and is called a *Z-Score report. Z-Score* is a statistical measure that tells us not only whether a point is above or below average, but also how far from normal the measurement is. The scale on this report ranges from −3 to +3 SD. The darker blue represents 3 or more SD below normal, while the lighter blues range from about 2.5 to 1 SD below normal. Blue-green is approximately 0 to 1 SD below normal, while green is baseline normal. Light green registers at the outer area of normal but is considered from 0 to 1 SD above normal, while yellow and light orange are approximately 1 to 2 SD above normal, darker orange is about 2 to 2.5 SD above normal, and red is 3 or more SD above normal. (See Figure 10.3.)

The Z-Score report that will be used is called *relative power,* and it shows information about the amount of energy in the brain at different frequencies. Because green, as explained previously, indicates the normal range, the more green there is in a scan, the more the person is conforming to normal brain-wave activity. Each colored circle (resembling a person's head when viewed from the top) represents what one person's brain is doing at each brain-wave frequency. The circle in the upper-left region of each scan shows the lowest brain-wave frequency (in delta brain waves), and each circle after that depicts a higher and higher brain-wave state, moving progressively up to the highest beta brain waves at the bottom-right region. A cycle per second in brain-wave frequency is known as hertz, or Hz. From left to right and from top to bottom, it progresses from 1 to 4 cycles per second (delta) to 4 to 8 cycles per second (theta) to 8 to 13 cycles per second (alpha) to 13 to 30-plus cycles per second (low mid-range and high-range beta). The beta activity can be broken down into different frequency bands, such as 12 to 15 Hz, 15 to 18 Hz, 18 to 25 Hz, and 25 to 30 Hz.

Therefore, the relative colors in each area show what's happening in each different brain-wave state. For example, a lot of blue in a majority of the brain in 1 cycle per second of delta suggests that there's little activity of the brain in that delta range. And if there's a lot of red in 14 Hz alpha in the frontal lobe, it means that there's heightened alpha activity in that area of the brain.

It should also be understood that these measurements could be interpreted differently depending on what the subject is doing when the scan is taken. For example, if 1 Hz delta were depicted in blue, that would suggest that the energy in the brain at that frequency is 3 SD below normal. In a clinical sense, that might be interpreted as being abnormally low. But because it was recorded when the subject was meditating, such a scan would actually suggest that the 1 Hz delta had opened the door to a stronger connection to the collective conscious energy field. In other words, as the energy in the neocortex is turned way down, the autonomic nervous system is more readily accessed. In just a bit, you'll see several examples that will make all of this clear. In the meantime, glance at Figure 10.3 again. It will give you an overview to illustrate what I've just explained.

Coherence vs. Incoherence

Now look at Figure 10.4. The image to the left (labeled "before meditation") represents a brain that has a lot of chatter. It's functioning in a high level of arousal (high-range beta) and is quite incoherent. The thickness of the red lines shows that this brain is 3 SD above normal (because the thicker the red line, the more revved up and imbalanced the brain is). By looking at the red lines, you can see excessive incoherent activity happening throughout the entire brain. The blue in the front of the brain represents hypoactivity (2 to 3 SD below normal) in the frontal lobes, showing that the frontal lobes are shut down or turned off and so aren't restraining the hyperactivity in the rest of the brain.

This is a brain with attention problems; it's so overloaded that it has no leader to control the chatter. It's like a TV satellite system with 50 channels where the volume is turned up really loud and the channels are changing every second. Too many quick shifts in attention span occur from one thought process to the next, so the brain is overly vigilant, highly aroused, overworked, and over-regulated. We call this an incoherent brain pattern, because the different parts of the brain are not working together at all.

Now take a look at the second image (labeled "after meditation"). You don't have to be a neuroscientist to see the difference between the first image and this one. Here, you see hardly any red or blue lines, demonstrating normal brain activity—with very little hyperactivity or hypoactivity. The chatter has stopped, and the brain is working more holistically. This person's brain is now in balance, so we can say that this brain demonstrates a more coherent pattern. (The remaining activity in blue and red, as indicated by the arrow, represents sensory-motor activity, which probably means the person is twitching or blinking and in a state of rapid eye movement, or REM, which typically happens in very light sleep.) This change took place in one of the students after only *one* meditation.

Now let's explore some more case studies of students from the workshops. For each, I'll first give you a bit of background so that you can see what state of being students were in when they began the workshop, then I'll explain what their scans showed, and finally I'll describe the new state of being each student created.

Healing Parkinson's Disease Without a Placebo or Drug

Michelle's old self: Michelle is in her 60s and was diagnosed with Parkinson's disease in 2011, after she noticed progressive involuntary shaking of her left arm, left hand, and left foot. In November 2012, she became a patient at Barrow Neurological Institute in Phoenix. Her attending physician told her that she'd probably had Parkinson's for 10 to 15 years already and that she'd have to live with the symptoms. Her plan was to cope with the progression of the bodily limitations as she aged. She began taking Azilect (rasagiline mesylate), a medication used for Parkinson's disease that stops the uptake of dopamine at the receptor-site level, slowing its breakdown in the body. The drug produced very few noticeable changes.

Michelle became a student in November 2012. The month of December was outstanding. Her daily meditation routine brought a feeling of peace and joy, which began to reduce her symptoms to a noticeable degree. Michelle was certain that this course of action would assist her in overcoming Parkinson's.

She continued experiencing great meditation sessions through early February 2013. In mid-February, however, Michelle's mother was admitted to intensive care in Sarasota, Florida, so Michelle flew to Florida to be with her. The day Michelle flew back to Arizona for our February 2013 workshop, her mother was placed in hospice care. Michelle's plane landed in Phoenix about an hour and a half before her first brain scan. Needless to say, she was both physically and emotionally exhausted at the time of the brain scan, which indeed showed the extreme stress she was experiencing.

By the end of that workshop, she was certainly in a calmer, more positive state of being, with barely noticeable Parkinson's symptoms. Following the workshop, Michelle returned to Florida to be with her mother again. Although she and her mother always had a difficult relationship, as a result of her efforts in the workshop, Michelle felt sufficiently strengthened to be supportive, loving, and totally free of any old issues that could have interfered with the love she felt for her mother.

Nevertheless, because of her mother's illness and eventual passing, as well as her sister in Texas having a major stroke, Michelle was forced to fly back and forth to Florida and Texas to deal with her family challenges. Her routine was greatly affected, and by June, she stopped doing her meditations. Life had gotten in the way, and she had too many responsibilities. Stopping her meditations was like stopping taking the placebo. When she noticed her symptoms returning, she started meditating again and made significant strides.

Michelle's scans: Because Michelle lives close to Dr. Fannin's clinic in Arizona, we were able to track her progress for more than five months, by taking a series of six periodic brain scans. I want to explain her evolution during that time.

Take a look at the "before meditation" part of Figure 10.5. This is her scan at the February 2013 event after she came home from Florida, stressed and exhausted from her mother's illness. The thick red lines indicate her brain in all areas is 3 SD from normal. She's displaying too much brain activity, hyperincoherence, and overregulation. In Parkinson's disease, this is quite common. The lack of the proper neurotransmitters (specifically dopamine) causes the neurons to display an erratic communication system between each region of the brain, with neural networks firing out of control. The result is a type of spastic or hyperactive neuronal firing, which affects the brain and the body. As a result, involuntary motor functions interfere with normal movement.

Now review the "after meditation" part of the same figure. This is Michelle's brain after four days of changing her state of being during meditation. This is very close to a normal brain, with very little hyperactivity, incoherence, or overregulation. At the end of our event, she was experiencing no involuntary tremors, twitches, or motor problems—and her brain scan confirms this change.

Now let's look at the QEEG readings in Figure 10.6A, labeled "before meditation." If you look from the middle of the second row all the way to the last row—the images in blue—you'll see that Michelle's brain is showing no alpha or beta brain-wave functioning.

Remember that blue means cooled-off brain activity. With Parkinson's, this is typically represented by lessened cognitive activity, compromised learning, and a loss of engagement. Here, you can see that Michelle can't consolidate new information. She has no ability to sustain an internal picture, because she's not producing alpha brain waves. Her very low-range beta patterns also show that she is having difficulty with sustaining levels of awareness. All of the energy in her brain is going toward dealing with her hyperincoherence, so it's like a lightbulb going from 50 watts to 10 watts. The volume of energy in the brain is turned down.

If you look at the "after-meditation" part of the graphic, you'll see what looks like a much-improved and balanced brain. All of those green areas in most of the images indicated with arrows represent normal and balanced brain activity. Her brain can now function in alpha, and she can move into internal states more easily, cope with stress better, and enter into the subconscious operating system to influence autonomic functions. Even her beta activity returned back to normal (green), indicating that she is more conscious, alert, and attentive. The balanced activity resulted in very few motor problems.

The red areas circled at the bottom in higher-range beta signify anxiety. This is the attitude that Michelle struggles with and is working on changing from an internal perspective. Coincidentally, anxiety is exactly what has amplified her Parkinson's symptoms in the past. As she lowers her anxiety, she lowers the symptoms of Parkinson's. To Michelle, her tremors now represent when she's out of balance in her life. When she regulates her internal states, she produces changes in her external reality.

Three months later, Michelle again had her brain scanned at Dr. Fannin's office. The May 9, 2013, scan in Figure 10.6B still shows her brain improving, which is exactly what Michelle reported. She's still getting better in the midst of all of the different stresses in her life. Because she does her meditations every day (think of it as taking her placebo daily), Michelle is continually changing her brain and body to be greater than the conditions in her environment. The scan shows that she's dropped almost another standard deviation from her previous scan at the bottom of the graph. You can clearly see that her anxiety is still getting better, and as a result, so is her condition. Less anxiety means fewer tremors. She's sustaining and thus memorizing that state of being for a longer period of time—and her brain is showing the changes.

If you look at Michelle's brain scan from June 3, 2013, in Figure 10.6C, you'll see a slight regression of her progress—although she's still better than when she started. Here, she'd stopped doing her meditation (and therefore stopped taking the placebo), so her brain slightly regressed to what it knew before. The brain with the arrow at the blue area of 13 Hz means she's hypoactive in the sensory-motor area and, thus, has less ability to control her involuntary tremors. In this brain-wave pattern, Michelle has less energy to control her body. You can also see the red areas circled again in the bottom of the scan returning in higher-range beta, which correlate with her anxiety.

By her June 27, 2013, scan shown in Figure 10.6D, Michelle had gone back to her meditations at the beginning of that month, and her brain scan showed a significantly better brain. She had less overall anxiety, as demonstrated in red at the bottom row at 17 to 20 Hz. Now compare that scan to her next one, on July 13, 2013, after our workshop, as depicted in Figure 10.6E. There's even less red, and the blue that showed up in her first scan in February during alpha (indicating hypoactivity) is completely gone. Michelle continues to improve, and her changes are becoming more consistent.

Michelle's new self: Today, Michelle hardly ever has any of the involuntary motor symptoms associated with Parkinson's disease. Very minor twitches do present themselves when she gets stressed or overtired at times, but for the most part, she's high functioning and normal. When Michelle is balanced and joyful, doing her meditations daily, her brain is working well—and so is she. From both our continued scans and her own reports, Michelle isn't merely maintaining her condition; she continues to *get better and better.* She keeps meditating, because she understands that she has to be the placebo *every day.*

Changing Traumatic Brain and Spinal-Cord Injury by Thought Alone

John's old self: In November 2006, John broke his neck at the seventh cervical and first thoracic vertebrae while he was a passenger in a car that spun out of control and rolled at high speed. Due to the impact, he suffered a severe head injury as well. The doctors were quick and sure about his prognosis. He would be a quadriplegic for the rest of his life. He would never walk again and would have very limited use of his arms and hands. His vertebrae were 100 percent dislocated, resulting in spinal-cord damage. It wasn't until John had surgery that his doctors saw the exact extent of his injuries. Two days later, the neurologist told John's wife that his spinal cord was somewhat "intact" but that his type of injury could have the same outcome as a complete cord severing. It would be, as with all spinal-cord injuries, a waiting game.

When you're caught up in the day-to-day reality of living in the intensive care unit, and later a rehab center, it can be extremely difficult not to get swept away by conventional thinking. When John and his family asked about his possible recovery, the doctors said that given the injury and the lack of return to any kind of normal functioning up to that point, they should begin accepting the inevitable. John would be physically handicapped for the rest of his life. His doctors hammered this message home over and over, as a necessary part of "moving on." But somehow, both John and his wife couldn't accept it.

I met John while he was in his wheelchair in 2009, along with his wife and family and an amazing physical therapist who understands neuroplasticity. They are some of the most energetic and optimistic people I've ever met, and we eagerly began our journey together.

John's scans: Take a look at John's "before meditation" brain scan in Figure 10.7. His first picture demonstrates quite a bit of hypoactivity. It's more than 3 SD below normal. John's coherence measurement, with such significant thick blue lines, is the opposite of our study of Michelle's Parkinson's condition, which showed thick red lines. This scan reveals a diminished capacity for different parts of the brain working well together. His brain here is on idle and has no energy, and he has limited ability to respond to anything for any length of time. He couldn't sustain attention, and his awareness was limited. Because of his traumatic brain injury, his brain was in a state of super-low arousal, and it showed a high degree of incoherence.

Now look at his brain scan after four days of meditation. In the first image on the upper-left margin at 1 Hz delta, he has some more activity demonstrated in red. In this case, it's a good sign, because more coherence is happening in delta in both hemispheres. Here, John is starting to show more balanced dual-brain processing. Because his traumatic brain injury is most visible in delta and theta, the hyperactivity in delta suggests that his brain is waking up. The rest of his brain in alpha and beta is showing more balanced activity and better cognitive function. This shows he has more access to control his mind and body.

Now view Figure 10.8. The blue color starting from about the middle of the second row until the end of the bottom row once again indicates that John has no alpha or beta brain waves. This blue color distributed throughout the alpha and beta realms in the left and right hemispheres suggests that he's vegetating and working on limited resources. The blue shows less cognitive ability and less capacity to control his body. John's mind is just not there.

After four days of meditation, 90 percent of John's brain has returned back to normal, as shown by all the green. That's pretty good! He still has some hypoactivity in his left hemisphere, where the arrows are pointing, indicating some problems with verbal skills and expressing himself, but it's still so much better than his first scan. John continues to do his meditations, and his brain continues to show more energy, more balance, and more coherence.

John has regained access to the latent neuropathways that were there before. His brain woke up, remembered how to work again, and now has the energy to work better.

John's new self: John stood up at the end of our February 2013 event. He has regained full control of his bowels and his bladder. To date, he is now standing in a more normal and integrated posture. His movements are more coordinated. The frequency, intensity, and duration of his spastic tremors have diminished considerably. He's even doing a total gym workout on a regular basis, thanks to the help of his amazing therapist, B. Jill Runnion (director of Synapse–Center for Neuro Re-Activation in Driggs, Idaho), who also studies my work and has the skills and unlimited mind to challenge John by setting up the right conditions. His unassisted vertical-squat exercises have progressed from a 10-degree angle to a 45-degree angle.

John is now in complete control of lowering his body to a seated position. He can also perform a specific physical therapy exercise that involves loading his leg and torso muscles and pushing a sled away from his body with resistance. John is now going from lying facedown to supporting himself on all fours, completely under his own power, and he's now starting to crawl.

Just months after the workshop, John astounded his medical team with all of his improvements in cognitive functioning. His advances exceeded anything any of the specialists had ever seen in a spinal-cord-injury patient. It was as if John finally woke up, and his scans show that he now has more access to his brain and body. John is still demonstrating more control over dormant areas of his brain and body, because he now has more capacity to regulate his body.

John's overall integration and coordinated movement patterns progressed considerably, enabling him to sit up at a table unassisted, with his feet planted on the floor. John's fine motor skills improved to the point where he can now hold a pen and sign his name, use a smartphone to send a text message, grip the steering wheel to drive, and hold a regular toothbrush. His cognitive changes demonstrate more self-confidence and greater inner joy. He has a much greater sense of humor and is more aware than ever.

During the summer of 2013, John was able to go on a white-water rafting trip, where he held himself unassisted in a raft for six hours a day and slept in a tent on the ground. He managed to live in the Idaho wilderness, away from contact with the outside world, for seven days and six nights. He couldn't have done this a year ago. Every time John and I talk, he always says the same thing: "Dr. Joe, I have no idea what's happening."

I always give him the same response: "The moment you know what's happening, John, it's all over. The unknown is beyond our comprehension. Welcome it."

I'd like to make one final point about John's case. Everyone knows that a spinal-cord injury doesn't heal with typical conventional approaches. I'm sure that it's not *matter* that's changing *matter* for John. That is, it's not chemistry or molecules that are altering his damaged spinal cord. From a quantum perspective, he'd have to be in a coherent frequency of heightened energy that would have to consistently lift or entrain matter to a new mind. He'd have to display an elevated energy or wave that vibrates at a frequency faster than matter, combined with a clear intention, in order to alter the particles of matter. So it's *energy*, which is the epiphenomenon of matter, that is rewriting the genetic program and healing his spinal cord.

Overcoming the Analytical Mind and Finding Joy

Kathy's old self: Kathy is the CEO of a large company, an attorney, and a committed wife and mother. She has been trained to be highly analytical and rational. She uses her brain every day to anticipate outcomes and to be prepared for every possible forecasted scenario based on her experience. Before she was introduced to my work, she'd never actually meditated. In the beginning, Kathy became very aware of how much she was analyzing everything in her life. She had a huge daily to-do list and described her brain as never shutting off. In hindsight, she confesses that she was never in the present moment.

Kathy's scans: Take a look at Kathy's "before meditation" brain scan in Figure 10.9. These delta-to-theta ratio measurements represent her ability to maintain focus and concentration in order to process and deal with intrusive and extraneous thoughts. The first arrow in the back of her brain on the right side, where the larger red spot is located, shows that she is seeing pictures in her mind. The second arrow, near the smaller red area on the left side, indicates that Kathy is internally talking to herself about those pictures. The imagery and constant mind chatter are causing her brain to be stuck in a loop.

In the "after meditation" scan, taken at the end of the workshop, you can clearly see that Kathy's brain is more balanced, more whole, and more normal. She no longer has any brain chatter, because her brain is integrating and processing information more efficiently. She's in a state of coherence. And the change in her brain state is accompanied by much greater joy, clarity, and love.

Now let's look at her coherence measurements in Figure 10.10. At the beginning of the workshop, Kathy's brain was in high-range beta, a state of high arousal, high analysis, and high-emergency mode. The thick red lines in alpha and beta show that she's three SD above normal. Her brain is hyperactive, out of balance, and highly incoherent—and she's having trouble controlling her anxiety.

Now take a look at the "after meditation" scan, taken on the last day of the February event. You should, by now, be able to recognize a more normal and balanced brain, which has much fewer high-range beta brain waves and far more coherence.

Kathy still had some work to do, so we set up an experiment after the workshop, because she lives in the Phoenix area and could visit Dr. Fannin's clinic. Dr. Fannin showed her a picture of a healthy, balanced, and normal brain on a QEEG scan (in green) and told her that this was where she needed to focus her attention. He suggested that when she moved into a new state of being every day in her meditation, she should select that potential outcome for the next 29 days. Since she then could assign more meaning to the placebo, she held a greater degree of intention about the benefits of the outcome.

It worked. If you look at Figure 10.11, which shows the scan dated April 8, 2013, about six weeks later, you'll see an even more normal brain, with no evidence of anxiety (seen in red). In addition, check out Figure 10.12. Can you see the progression from February 20, 2013, where Kathy's brain scan is red in the higher brain-wave frequencies (21 to 30 Hz), to the end of the February event, where her brain scan has changed to green in the second image (and so is much more normal)? The red areas represented show very high levels of anxiety (high-range beta) and over-analysis because her brain waves in the higher frequencies (21 to 30 Hz) are hyperactive—her brain was working too hard. By the beginning of April (shown in Figure 10.13), Kathy's brain is balanced, coherent, and much more synchronized. Kathy has a much different brain today and reports truly feeling like a different person.

Kathy's new self: Kathy reports that she has seen numerous positive changes in her career, her daily life, and her relationships. She meditates daily, and when she thinks she doesn't have time to meditate, that's when she makes sure to *find* the time to do it. She understands that the attitude that created her out-of-balance mind and brain is related to time and the conditions in her external environment. Kathy says that the answers to her questions come more easily and with far less of a struggle. She listens to her heart more often, and she catches herself before she moves into cycles of vigilance. She rarely gets caught up in those loops, and she finds herself acting in a kinder and more patient manner. Kathy is happier from the inside out.

Healing Fibroid Tumors by Changing Energy

Bonnie's old self: In 2010, Bonnie developed significant pain and excessive bleeding during her menstrual cycle. She was diagnosed with excessive estrogen production and was encouraged to begin bioidentical hormones. At age 40, she found this solution to her diagnosis to be extreme.

Bonnie remembered that her mother had had the same symptoms at her age. Her mother had taken hormone pills and eventually died of bladder cancer. While there may be no specific connection between the hormone therapy and bladder cancer, what caught Bonnie's attention was that she was having the same physical symptoms as her mother. She didn't want to develop the same outcome.

Her vaginal bleeding began to last even longer (sometimes up to two weeks), and Bonnie became anemic and lethargic, and gained about 20 pounds. She would lose an average of two liters of blood each month during her menstrual cycle. A pelvic sonogram confirmed fibroid tumors. Bonnie went through myriad blood tests and was told she was perimenopausal and most likely had an ovarian cyst. Her specialist who recommended the hormone therapy told Bonnie that fibroids don't go away and that the severe bleeding would continue for the rest of her life.

I randomly selected Bonnie for one of the extra brain maps during our Englewood, Colorado, event in July 2013; she was mortified when I pointed at her to indicate she was selected for the scan. Bonnie's menstrual cycle had started the evening before the workshop, and she typically had to wear a large diaper to capture the amount of blood she lost during her period. When, after several meditations, I instructed the students to lie down, Bonnie was concerned that she would bleed all over herself and the floor.

Because of the extreme pain that accompanied Bonnie's periods, even sitting was uncomfortable. Even so, she was determined to continue practicing the meditation techniques every day for her own peace of mind. During the first meditation in which she was being brain mapped, Bonnie had an experience that she can only describe as mystical. She felt her heart open and expand. Her head pushed back, and her breathing changed. Bonnie saw light flood into her body, and she experienced a tremendous sense of peace. She also heard the words: "I am loved, blessed, and not

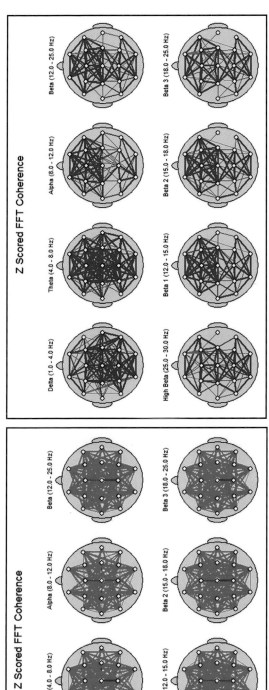

HYPOACTIVITY
OR
HYPO-AROUSAL

Z Scored FFT Coherence

HYPERACTIVITY
OR
HYPER-AROUSAL

Z Scored FFT Coherence

Represented in Standard Deviations (SD)
Red = ABOVE Normal   Blue = BELOW Normal

‒ Z-Score ≥ 1.98 +   ‒ Z-Score ≥ 2.58 +   ‒ Z-Score ≥ 3.09 +

Figure 10.2

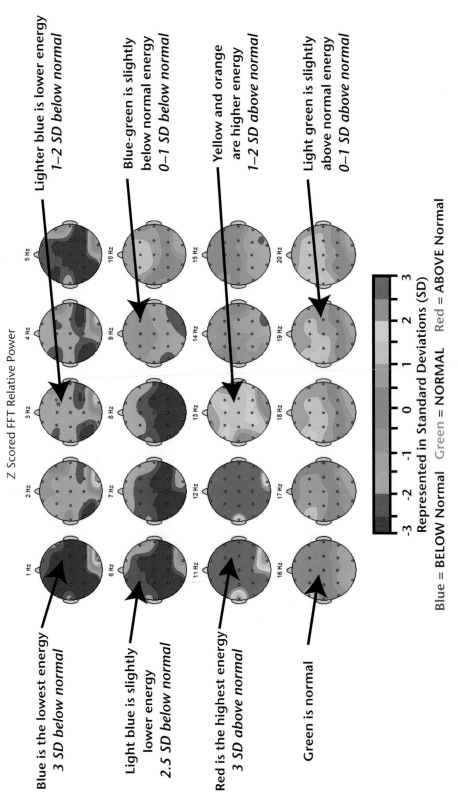

Z Scored FFT Relative Power

Blue is the lowest energy
3 SD below normal

Lighter blue is lower energy
1–2 SD below normal

Light blue is slightly
lower energy
2.5 SD below normal

Blue-green is slightly
below normal energy
0–1 SD below normal

Red is the highest energy
3 SD above normal

Yellow and orange
are higher energy
1–2 SD above normal

Green is normal

Light green is slightly
above normal energy
0–1 SD above normal

Represented in Standard Deviations (SD)

Blue = BELOW Normal   Green = NORMAL   Red = ABOVE Normal

Figure 10.3

CHANGES IN COHERENCE IN MEDITATION

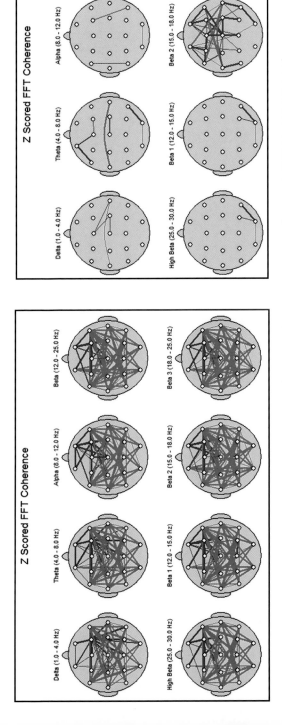

Figure 10.4

CHANGES IN PARKINSON'S DISEASE AFTER MEDITATION

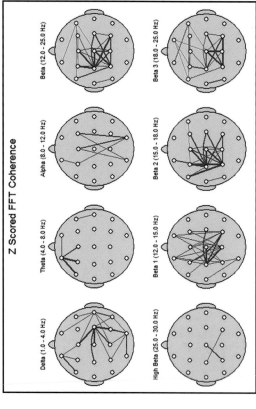

Figure 10.5

CHANGES IN PARKINSON'S DISEASE AFTER MEDITATION

February 20, 2013

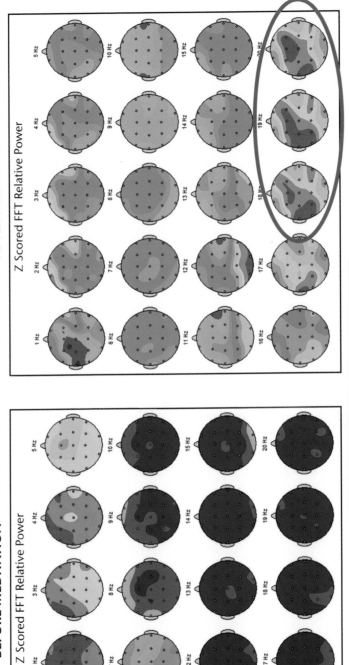

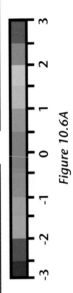

Figure 10.6A

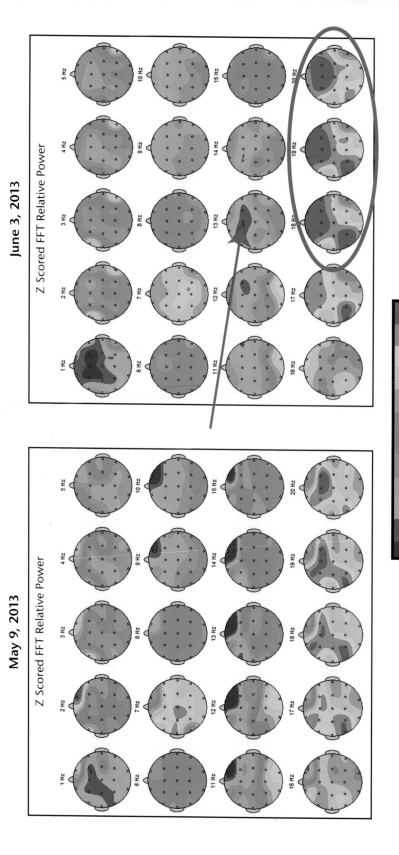

Figure 10.6C

Figure 10.6B

June 27, 2013

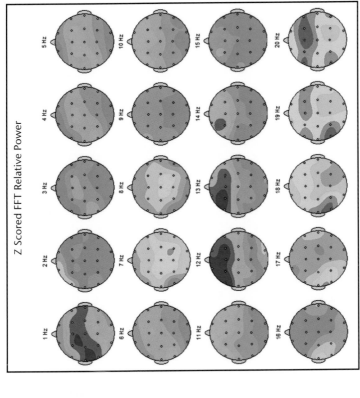

Figure 10.6D

July 13, 2013

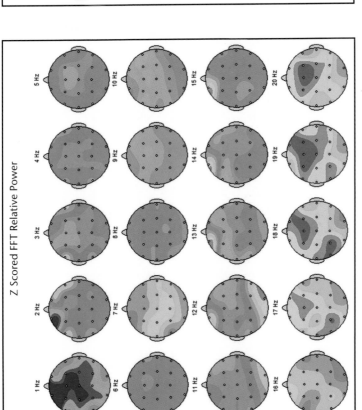

Figure 10.6E

CHANGES IN TRAUMATIC BRAIN INJURY AFTER MEDITATION

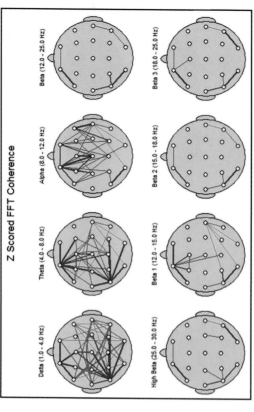

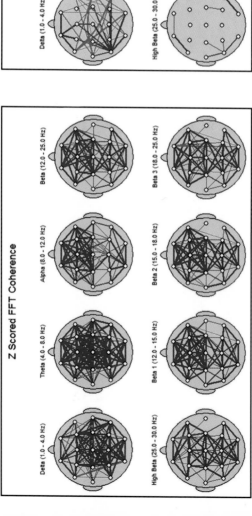

Figure 10.7

CHANGES IN TRAUMATIC BRAIN INJURY AFTER MEDITATION

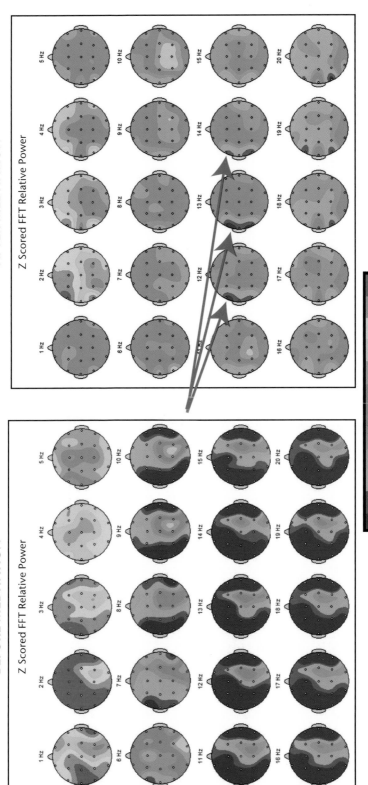

Figure 10.8

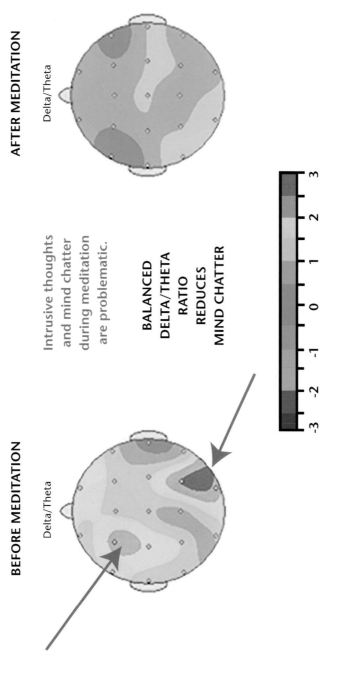

Figure 10.9

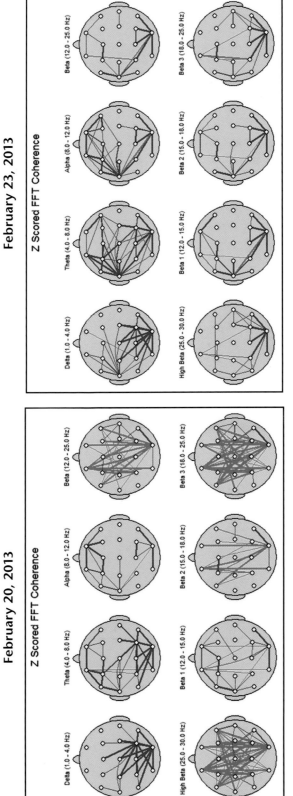

Figure 10.10

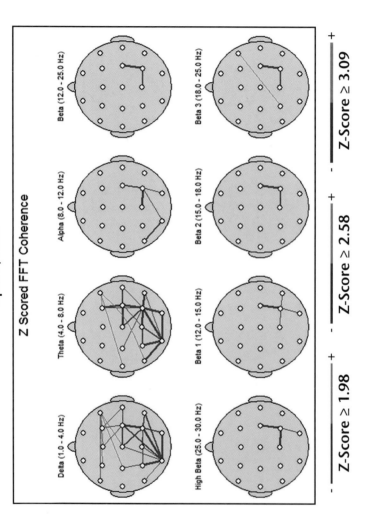

April 8, 2013

Z Scored FFT Coherence

Figure 10.11

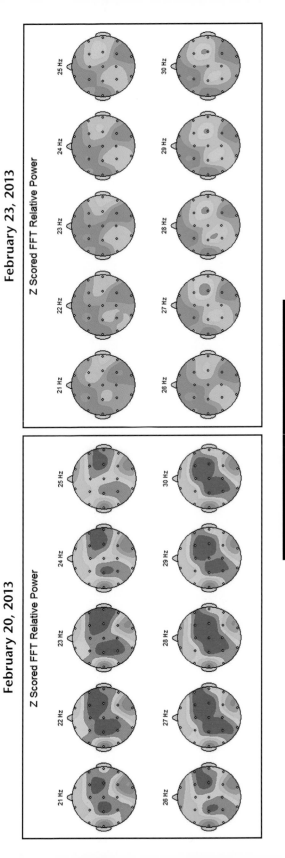

Figure 10.12

April 8, 2013

Z Scored FFT Relative Power

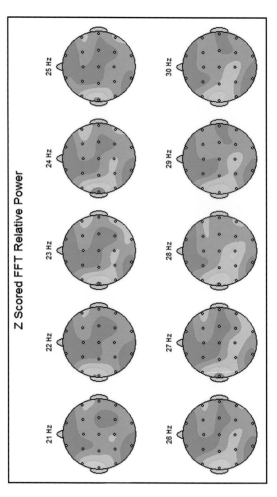

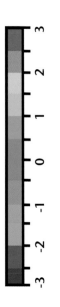

Figure 10.13

NORMAL EEG SCAN

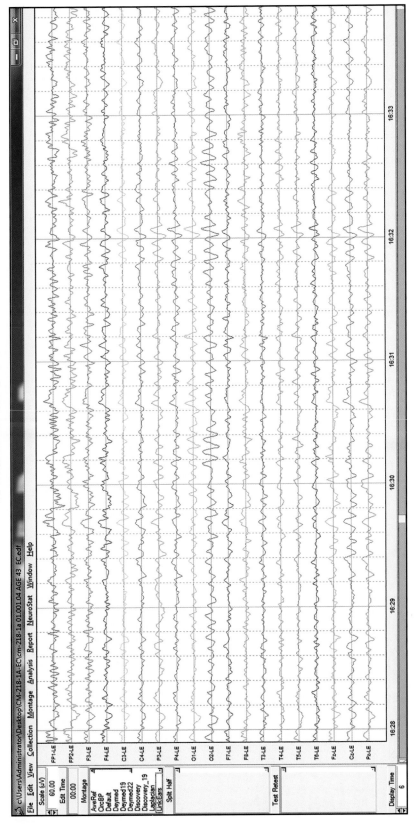

Figure 10.14

HEIGHTENED ACTIVITY IN THE FRONTAL LOBE

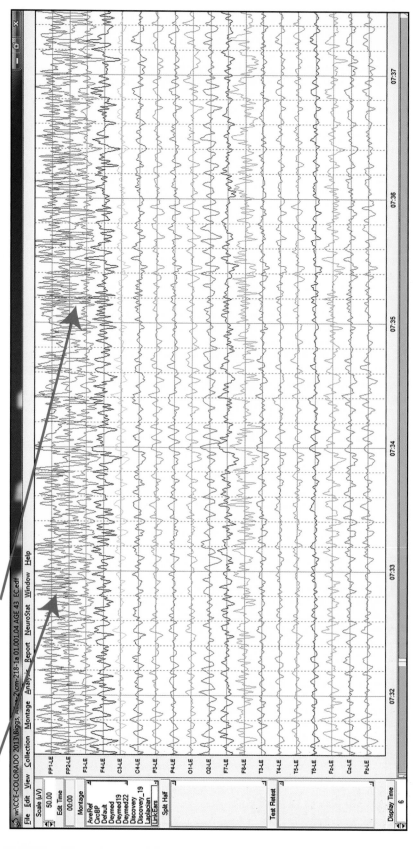

Figure 10.15A

HEIGHTENED ACTIVITY IN THE FRONTAL LOBE

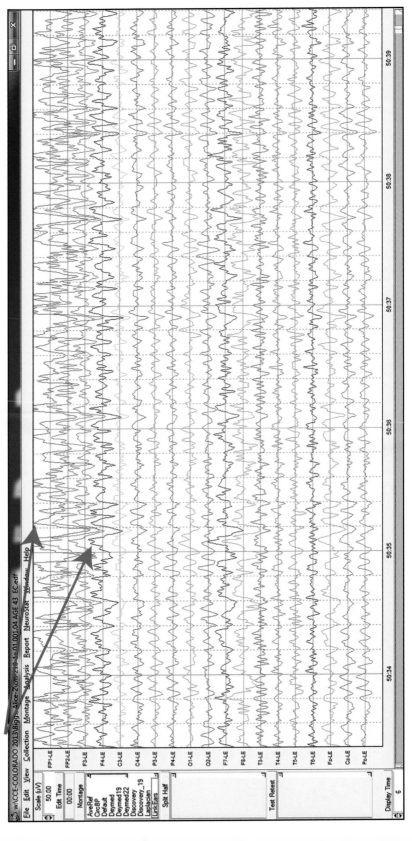

Figure 10.15B

HEIGHTENED ACTIVITY IN THE FRONTAL LOBE

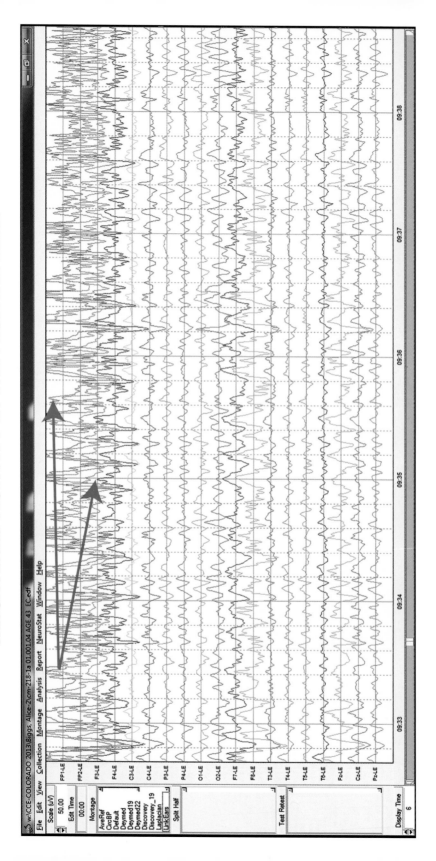

Figure 10.15C

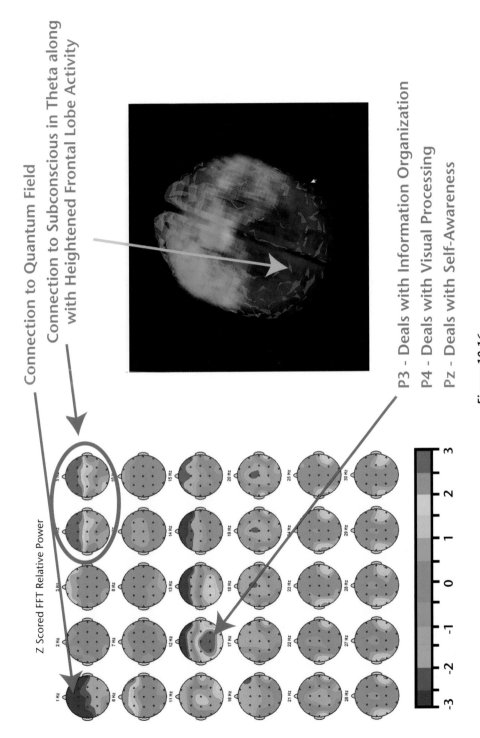

Connection to Quantum Field

Connection to Subconscious in Theta along with Heightened Frontal Lobe Activity

Z Scored FFT Relative Power

P3 - Deals with Information Organization
P4 - Deals with Visual Processing
Pz - Deals with Self-Awareness

Figure 10.16

EXPERIENCING ECSTACY DURING MEDITATION

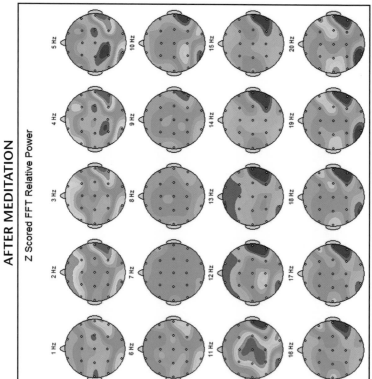

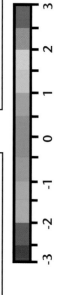

Figure 10.17

EXPERIENCING FULL OUT ECSTACY DURING MEDITATION

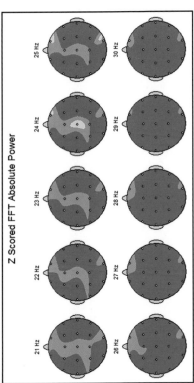

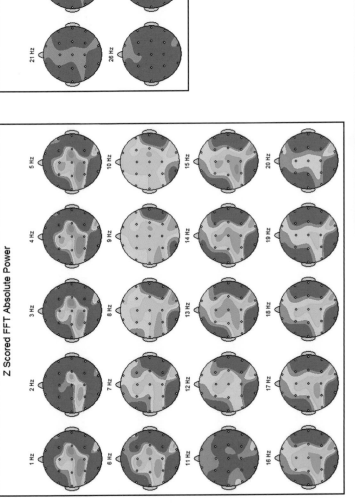

Figure 10.18

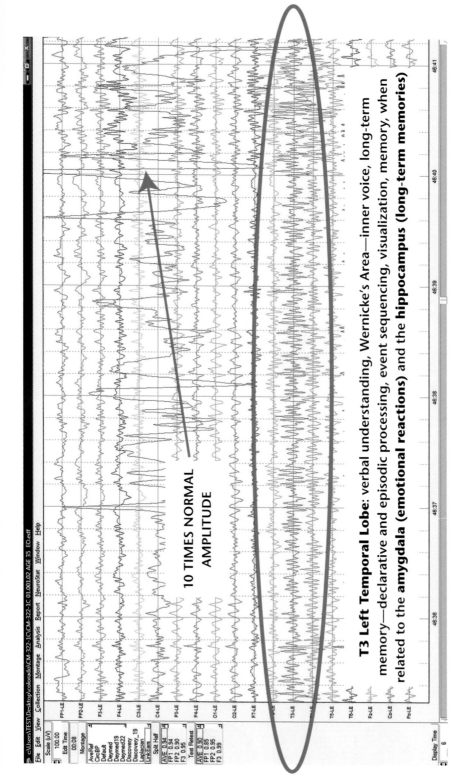

T3 Left Temporal Lobe: verbal understanding, Wernicke's Area—inner voice, long-term memory—declarative and episodic processing, event sequencing, visualization, memory, when related to the **amygdala (emotional reactions)** and the **hippocampus (long-term memories)**

Figure 10.19

February 20, 2013–Carefree, AZ

Z Scored FFT Absolute Power

July 11, 2013–Englewood, CO

Z Scored FFT Absolute Power

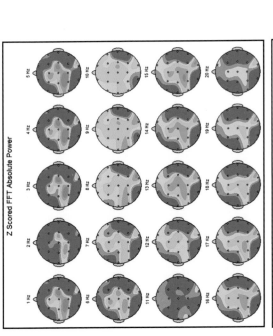

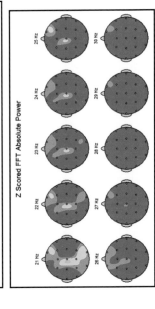

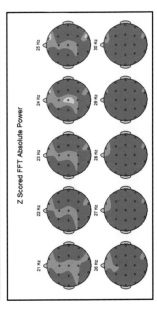

Figure 10.20

NORMAL BRAIN-WAVE ACTIVITY

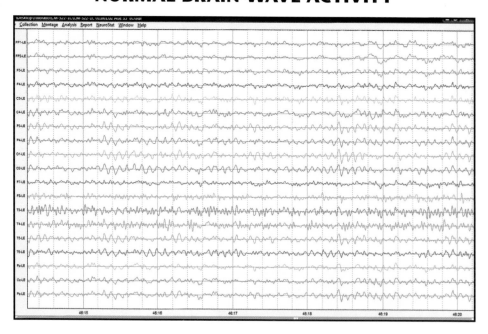

KUNDALINI–ECSTACY EXPERIENCE

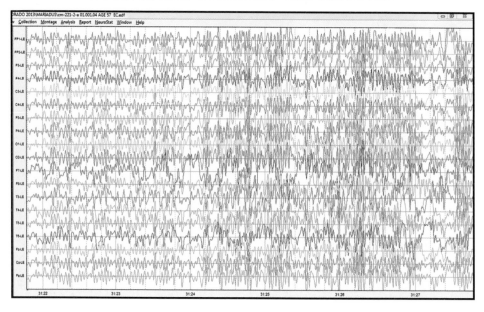

Figure 10.21

forgotten." Bonnie burst into tears during the meditation, and her brain scan showed that she was in a state of bliss.

Bonnie's scans: Take a look at Bonnie's EEG scan in Figure 10.14. We were lucky enough to catch the whole experience in real time. The first graphic shows normal brain-wave activity. Everything is in balance and quiet. If you review Bonnie's three scans in Figure 10.15, which capture what was happening to her at different times during her meditation, you can see elevated energy and amplitude in her frontal lobes, which represents her processing quite a bit of information and emotion. She's in an expanded state of consciousness and is experiencing peak moments at different intervals. Most of the activity is happening in the theta brain waves, and it signifies that she is in her subconscious mind. The inner experience is very real to her in that moment. She's so completely focused on the thought that it becomes the experience. The emotional quotient is represented by the amount of energy (amplitude) her brain is processing. Take a look at the vertical length of the lines where the arrows are pointing. That's very coherent energy. Bonnie is in a heightened state of awareness.

Now glance at Figure 10.16. Bonnie's QEEG scan in real time has an arrow pointing to 1 Hz in delta brain waves, illustrating her connection to the quantum field (shown in blue). Bonnie also has heightened energy in her frontal lobe in theta brain waves (demonstrated in red) to match exactly what was happening in her EEG scan. Look at the red circle that is highlighting her frontal lobes as well as the arrow pointing to a top view of the brain's frontal lobe immediately below. The image you are seeing is a snapshot of a motion picture of Bonnie's brain activity during her entire meditation. Because one of the functions of the frontal lobe is to make thoughts real, what she is experiencing in theta with her eyes closed is very real to her. We could say that Bonnie's inner experience was like a very vivid, lucid dream. The red arrow at 12 Hz alpha—isolating the red spot in the center of her brain—shows Bonnie's attempt to make sense of her inner experience and then process what she was seeing in her mind's eye. The rest of her brain is healthy and balanced (shown in green).

Bonnie's new self: Bonnie's experience that day changed her for good. The amplitude of energy related to the inward experience was greater than any past experience from her external environment, and thus her past was biologically removed. The energy of the momentous peak of her meditation superseded the hard-wired programs in her brain and the emotional conditioning in the body—and her body instantly responded to a new mind, to a new consciousness. Bonnie had changed her state of being. In less than 24 hours, her bleeding stopped completely. She had no symptoms of pain and instinctively knew that she was healed. In the months since the event, Bonnie has experienced only normal menstrual cycles. She hasn't had any excessive bleeding or pain since the workshop.

Experiencing Ecstasy

Genevieve's old self: Genevieve, a 45-year-old artist and musician, currently resides in Holland and travels quite a bit because of her vocation. During the February event, I was watching her brain scan with Dr. Fannin during her meditation. We started to notice some significant changes in her energy during the middle of her inward journey. When we both saw a particular reading on her scan at the same time, we looked at each other, knowing something was about to happen. Within moments, when we turned to look at her, we saw tears of joy running down her face. Genevieve was in ecstasy. She was in utter pleasure, and her body was responding quite readily. We'd never seen anything like this before.

Genevieve's scans: If you look at Figure 10.17, you'll see a relatively normal brain scan before Genevieve's meditation. The areas of green spread throughout the brain signify a healthy, well-adjusted woman with a balanced brain. The blue areas of lessened sensory-motor activity before she begins, in alpha 13 to 14

Hz, where you see the arrows, probably indicate jetlag, because she'd just arrived from Europe that day. If you observe Genevieve's brain during the meditation, you see an overall increase in balance. What happens next is off-the-chart amazing. When we saw her reach this peak moment at the end of her meditation, we knew from watching her scans that she had quite a bit of energy in her brain.

Now take a peek at Figure 10.18. This type of red activity, showing high amounts of energy in all brain-wave range frequencies, suggests that Genevieve is in a highly altered state. Someone who didn't know that she was meditating and who just saw the brain scan would say that she was experiencing an extreme level of anxiety or psychosis. But because her personal testimonial described her being in sheer ecstasy, we know that all of the red represents a lot of energy in her brain. Her brain is at 3 SD above normal. It's energy, in the form of emotion stored in her body as the mind, that is being released and is traveling back to her brain.

Figure 10.19, which shows her EEG reading, validates this position. If you review the purple lines where the arrow is, you'll see that this part of the brain is processing ten times the normal amounts of energy. The area that's circled in red tells us that the experience is so emotionally profound that it's being stored in Genevieve's long-term memory. At the same time, she is also trying to verbally understand and make sense of what's happening to her in that moment. She might be saying something to herself like, *Oh my God! This is amazing. I feel so great! What is this feeling?* Her inner experience is as real as any outward event, and she's not trying to make it happen—it's just happening to her. She's not visualizing; she's experiencing a profound moment.

Interestingly, we scanned Genevieve again in July, at the event in Colorado, and she still displayed the same energy changes. When we handed her the microphone during both events, all she could say was that she was so in love with life that her heart was fully open and that she felt connected to something greater than herself. She was in a state of grace, and she felt so great that she wanted to stay in the present moment. If you look at Figure 10.20, you'll see that her brain had the same patterns and effects at the July event as it had at the February event. The experience was still happening to her months later. She was truly altered from her personal transformation.

Genevieve's new self: I spoke with Genevieve several weeks after the July event. She told me that she's not the same person she was at the beginning of the year. Her mind has deepened, and she's more present and much more creative. She feels profound love for all things, and most important, she feels so lifted that she no longer feels as if she needs or wants anything. She feels whole.

Bliss: Moving the Mind Out of the Body

Maria's old self: Maria is a highly functional woman with normal brain activity. During the first meditation of the day, a 45-minute exercise, she experienced a significant change in her brain waves within moments.

Maria's scans: Look at Figure 10.21 and notice the difference between Maria's normal brain waves and her state of ecstasy. I watched her as she went into a heightened state of increased energy, and it appeared as though she were having an orgasm in her brain. Her scan shows a fully active brain having a full-on kundalini experience (kundalini is a latent energy stored in the body, which, when aroused, brings on higher states of consciousness and energy in the brain). If you look at Maria's scans, you can see that *all* areas of her brain were experiencing a very heightened energy. When the kundalini energy is awakened, it can rise from the lower spine to reach the top of the brain, at which point it can produce an extremely profound mystical experience. Many students in the workshops have these brain orgasms. In Maria's scan, all areas of the brain are fully engaged with energy, and her brain waves show three to four times the normal amplitude. Her brain is coherent and very synchronized. If you look at the scans, you'll see that the ecstasy comes in waves, just like an orgasm. She was not trying to do any of this. It was actually just happening *to* her. Her entire brain was engaged in the inner event, and as a result, she was filled with profound energy.

Maria's new self: Today, Maria continues to have similar mystical experiences. Each time they occur, she reports feeling more relaxed, more conscious, more aware, and more whole. She welcomes the next unknown moment.

Now It's Your Turn

These few examples (out of many that were documented) prove that it is indeed possible to *teach* the placebo effect. Now that you've received all of the information, stories, and proof of what's possible, it's time for you to learn the "how-to" so that you can experience your own transformation. The next two chapters will outline the steps you can take to begin your personal meditation process. It's my desire for you to put into practice all of the knowledge you've learned so far so that you experience the truth of your efforts. Once you receive the tools that you need to cross the river of change, I hope to see you on the other side.

Part II

TRANSFORMATION

Chapter Eleven

Meditation Preparation

Now that you've read and absorbed all the information in Part I, you're ready to move to transformation. In this chapter, I'll go over what you need to know to get ready to meditate so that when you get to the next chapter, you'll be ready for me to walk you through the actual meditation. All of the participants in this book who changed something about themselves had to first go inward and change their state of being. So think of your meditation practice as a way for you to take the placebo every day. But instead of taking a pill, you'll be going inward. In time, your meditation will become like your belief in taking medication.

When to Meditate

There are two times a day that are the most conducive to meditation: right before you go to bed at night and right after you get up in the morning. That's because when you fall asleep, you naturally shift though the entire spectrum of brain-wave states, going from your waking, beta state to the slower alpha state, when you close your eyes, to the slower-still theta state, when you're half-asleep and half-awake, all the way down to the deep-sleep delta brain-wave state. And when you wake up in the morning, you do the same thing in reverse: rising from delta to theta to alpha to beta, where you're fully awake and conscious.

So if you meditate when you're getting ready for sleep or just coming out of sleep, it's easier to slip into alpha or theta brain waves; you're more primed for being in an altered state, because it's the direction you either have just come from or are slipping into. You could say that the door to the subconscious mind is open during these two times. I personally prefer to meditate in the morning, but either time is fine. Pick what will work best for you, and then stick with it. If you can meditate every day, it will become a good habit and will be something you look forward to doing daily.

Where to Meditate

The most important consideration in selecting a place to meditate is to choose a place where you won't be distracted. Because you'll be unplugging from the external, physical world, pick a quiet place where you can be alone and uninterrupted (either by other people or by pets)—a place that you can return to every day and use as your regular, sacred meditation spot.

I don't recommend that you meditate in bed, because you associate bed with sleep. (For the same reason, I don't recommend that you lie down or use a recliner when you meditate.) Pick a chair to sit in, or arrange a spot on the floor where you'll be able to sit for up to an hour—a spot away from any drafts and in a room where the temperature is comfortable.

If you prefer to meditate to music, choose soft, relaxing, trance-inducing instrumentals or chants without lyrics. (In fact, a little music works well to cover background noise if you aren't in an environment that's completely quiet.) Definitely don't play music that brings up associative memories of some past event or that would be distracting in any way. Also, be sure to turn off your computer and your phone if they're in the room. And try to avoid the aroma of coffee brewing or food cooking. You may even want to use a blindfold or earplugs to enhance the effect of sensory deprivation, since the goal in your preparation is to eliminate as much external stimuli as possible.

Making Your Body Comfortable

Dress in comfortable, loose clothing and remove your watch or any jewelry that might be distracting. If you wear glasses, take them off, too. Drink a little water before you sit down, and have a glass within reach in case you need it. Use the bathroom before you begin, and try to take care of any similar issues so that you won't be distracted during your meditation.

Whether you're sitting in a chair or on the floor cross-legged, sit up straight and keep your spine erect. Your body should be relaxed, but your mind needs to stay focused, so don't be so relaxed that you fall asleep. If your head begins to nod during meditation, it's a sign that you're moving into a slower brain-wave state, so don't worry too much about that. With some practice, your body will become conditioned and won't want to doze off.

As you begin the meditation, close your eyes and take a few slow, deep breaths. Soon you should drop from a beta brain-wave state into an alpha state. This more restful, but still focused, state activates your frontal lobe, which as you read, lowers the volume on the circuits in your brain that process time and space. Although at first you might not be able to slip easily into the next slower brain-wave state, theta, with practice you'll be able to slow your brain waves down even further. Theta is the brain-wave state where the body is asleep but the mind is awake, and it's where you can more readily change your body's automatic programs.

How Long to Meditate

While your meditation will generally last between 45 minutes and an hour, allow yourself plenty of time, if possible, to settle your mind before you begin. If you need to finish by a certain time, set an alarm to go off ten minutes before you have to end the meditation, to give you an opportunity to finish the session without having to come to an abrupt stop. Don't let time be a distraction though. Remember, just as you're getting away from sensory input, you're also getting away from being conscious of time, so if you're constantly worried about what time it is, you'll be completely defeating your purpose. If you need a few more minutes in your day to be able to meditate without this distraction, consider waking up earlier or going to bed later.

Mastering Your Will

I want to warn you about a very common stumbling block for people who are starting a meditation practice. Any time you start to change something in your life, your body, as the mind, will signal your brain to be in control again. The next thing you know, you might start to hear negative voices in your head like, *Why don't you start tomorrow? You're too much like your mother! What's wrong with you? You'll never change. This doesn't feel right.* That's the body trying to unseat you so that it can be the mind again. You may have unconsciously conditioned it to be impatient, frustrated, unhappy, victimized, or pessimistic, to name a few examples. So that's how it wants to subconsciously behave.

The moment you respond to that voice as if what it's saying is true, your consciousness immerses itself back into the automated program, so you return to thinking the same thoughts, performing the same actions, and living by the same emotions—but still expecting something to change in your life. If you use feelings and emotions as a barometer for change, you'll always talk yourself out of possibility. When you instead free the body of the chains of these emotions, you are then able to relax into the present moment (more on that later in this chapter), and you'll be liberating energy from the body—going from particle to wave—so that it becomes available to create new destiny. To get to that place, to teach your body a new way of being, you have to sit your body down and let it know who the master is.

We have a ranch with 18 horses, and mastering the will to stay focused in meditation reminds me of what it's like to ride a favorite stallion after I haven't been on him in a while. When I first climb up into the saddle, that stallion couldn't care less about me. He smells the mares on the other side of the property, and that's where his attention goes. It's as though he's saying to me, "Where have you been for the last eight months? I got into some bad habits while you were away, the girls are over there, and I'm not concerned about what you want to do, so I'm going to throw you off. I'm in charge here." He gets mad, temperamental, and controlling, and he tries to run me into the side of the arena. But I pay attention to him, and when his head starts to turn toward those mares, I take control of him.

So the moment I see him start to move away from my lead, I slowly but firmly grab the reins and pull them in, and I just wait. And before long, he stops and lets out this big snort, and I stroke him on the side and tell him, "That's right." And we take two steps and then I see his head starting to turn just slightly again, and I stop him—and wait. And he lets out another big snort, and once he knows I'm in charge, we start to move forward again. I just keep following the same procedure until he ultimately surrenders to me.

That kind of gentle but firm refocusing is exactly the same approach to use with your body when you sit down to meditate. Think of your body as the animal that you, as consciousness, are training. Every time you become conscious that your attention has wandered and you bring it back like that, you're reconditioning your body to a new mind. You are mastering yourself and your past.

So let's say you wake up in the morning and have a list of people to call, a list of errands to run, 35 texts to respond to, and all these e-mails to answer. If the first thing you do every morning is start thinking about all of those things that you have to do, your body is already in the future. When you sit down to meditate, your mind may naturally want to go in that direction. And if you allowed it, then your brain and body would be in that same predictable future, because you'd be anticipating an outcome based on your same past experience from yesterday.

So the moment you start to notice your mind wanting to go in that direction, you just pull the reins in, settle your body down, and bring it back to the present moment—just as I do when I ride my stallion. And then, in the next moment, if you start thinking, *Yeah, but you have to do this, you forgot about that, and you need to do the thing you didn't get to yesterday,* just bring your mind back to the present moment again. And if it keeps happening and that brings up the emotions of frustration, impatience, worry, and so on, just remember that whatever emotion you're experiencing is merely part of the past. So you just notice it; you become aware: *Ah, my body-mind wants to go to the past. All right. Let's settle down and relax back into the present.*

Just as your mind will try to distract you, your body may do the same. It may want to get nauseated, create pain, or make that spot in the middle of your back itch, but if that happens, remember that it's just the body trying to be the mind. So as you master it, you are becoming greater than your body. If you can master it during your meditation each time, then when you walk back into your life, you're going to be more present, more aware, and more conscious—and less unconscious.

Sooner or later, just as my stallion surrenders to me and follows my commands without letting the mares or anything else distract him, your body will also acquiesce to your mind during your meditation without getting hijacked by any stray thoughts. And when the horse and rider are one, when the mind and body are working together, there's simply no greater feeling—you're in a new state of being. It's incredibly empowering.

Moving into an Altered State

The meditation I'm going to walk you through in the next chapter begins with a technique the Buddhists call *open focus.* It's very helpful for getting into the altered state we're trying to achieve, because in our normal day-to-day existence, living in survival mode and marinating in stress hormones, we're naturally very narrow focused. We put all our attention on things and people and problems (focusing on the particle or matter, not on the wave or energy), and we define reality by our senses. We can call that type of attention *object focused.*[1]

With all our attention on the outer world, which in this state appears more real to us than the inner world, our brains pretty much stay in a higher-range beta brain-wave state—the most reactive, unstable, and volatile of all the different brain-wave patterns. Because we're on high alert, we aren't in a position to create, daydream, solve problems, learn new things, or heal. It's certainly not a state that's conducive to meditating. The electrical activity in our brains increases, and thanks to the fight-or-flight response, our heart rate and respiration naturally increase. Our bodies can't spend much, if any, of their resources for growth and optimal health, because they're always on the defensive, trying to protect us, just trying to help us make it through the day.

Under these less-than-favorable conditions, our brains tend to compartmentalize, meaning that some regions of the brain begin to work separately from the others instead of working together, and some even work in opposition to each other—like stepping on the brake and the gas at the same time. It's a house divided against itself.

In addition to the parts of the brain not communicating well with each other, the brain no longer communicates with the rest of the body in an efficient, orderly manner. Because the brain and the central nervous system control and coordinate all the other systems of our bodies—keeping our hearts beating and our lungs breathing, digesting food and eliminating waste, controlling our metabolism, regulating the immune system, balancing our hormones, and keeping countless other functions working—we become unbalanced. Our brains send very disorderly messages and "dis-integrated" signals down the spinal cord to the rest of the body. As a result, none of the body's systems gets a clear message. Instead, the message is very incoherent.

Picture the immune system responding, "I don't know how to make a white blood cell out of that instruction." And then picture the digestive system saying, "I can't tell if I should secrete acid in my stomach first or if I should secrete it in my small intestine. These orders are pretty mixed up."

At the same time, the cardiovascular system laments, "I can't tell if my heart should be in rhythm or out of rhythm, because the signal I'm getting is pretty out of rhythm itself. Is there really a lion around the corner again?"

This state of imbalance keeps us out of homeostasis or equilibrium, and it's easy to see then how it sets us up for disease, producing arrhythmias or high blood pressure (unbalanced cardiovascular system); indigestion and acid reflux (unbalanced digestive system); and a preponderance of colds, allergies, cancer, rheumatoid arthritis, and other conditions (unbalanced immune function)—to name just a few examples.

That state—with our brain waves becoming scrambled and filled with static—is what I referred to in the last chapter as a state of incoherence. There's no rhythm or order to our brain waves or to the messages the brain sends the body—it's total cacophony.

In the open-focus technique, on the other hand, we close our eyes, take our attention off the outer world and its trappings, and instead open our focus to pay attention to the space around us (on the wave instead of the particle). The reason it works is that when we're *sensing* this space, we're not giving our attention to anything material and we're not *thinking.* Our brain-wave patterns shift to the more restful and creative alpha (and eventually theta as well). In this state, our inner world now becomes more real to us than the outer world, which means we're in a much better position to make the changes we want to make.

Research shows that when we use the open-focus technique properly, the brain starts to become more organized and more synchronized, with the different compartments working together in a more orderly fashion. And what syncs together links together. In this level of coherence, the brain can now send more coherent signals throughout the entire nervous system to the rest of the body, and everything starts to move in rhythm, working together. Instead of cacophony, now our brains and our bodies are playing a beautiful symphony. The end result is that we feel more whole, integrated, and balanced. My colleagues and I saw this type of consistent brain changes in the majority of the students we scanned in our workshops, so we *know* this technique works.

The Sweet Spot of the Present Moment

After walking you through open focus, the meditation you'll do will move you into the practice of finding the present moment. Being present gives us access to possibilities on the quantum level that we didn't have access to before. Remember how I said that in the quantum field, the subatomic particles exist simultaneously in an infinite array of possibilities? In order for that to be true, the quantum universe can't have only one line of time. It must have an *infinite* number of timelines, simultaneously containing all of these possibilities stacked on top of one another. In fact, every experience—past, present, and future—of every single thing from the smallest microorganism to the most advanced culture in the universe exists within the field of unlimited information called the "quantum field." I said the quantum world has no time, but the truth is that it has *all* time simultaneously—it just doesn't have *linear* time, which is the way we usually think of time.

As the quantum model of reality says, all possibilities exist in the present moment. But if you're waking up every morning and doing the same sequence of events—making the same choices that lead to the same behaviors that create the same experiences that produce the same emotional payoff—then you aren't open to any of those other possibilities and you aren't going anywhere new.

Take a look at Figure 11.1. The circle represents you in the present moment on a particular line of time. The line to the left of that represents your past, and the line to the right represents your future. Let's say that every day, you wake up, go to the bathroom, brush your teeth, take the dog out, drink your coffee or tea, have the same breakfast, get dressed in the same routine way, drive to work along a familiar route, and so on. Each of these events is represented by a point on the timeline of your immediate future.

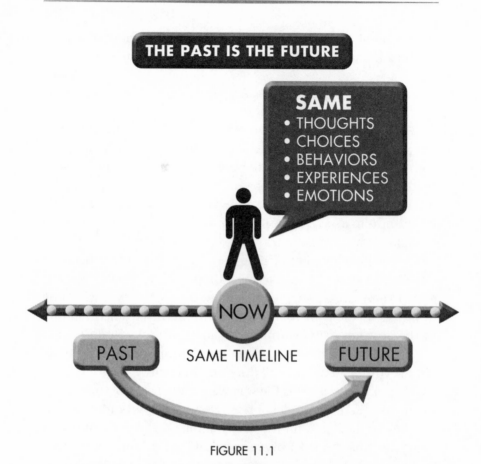

FIGURE 11.1

Each dot on the timeline represents the same thought, choice, behavior, experience, and emotion from past days, weeks, months, and even years. Therefore, the past becomes the future. Since a habit is a redundant set of automatic thoughts, actions, and feelings that is acquired through frequent repetition—that is, when the body becomes the mind—then for most, our bodies are already programmed to be in the same predictable future based on our state of being from the past. And if we memorize emotions that keep us connected to the past, and those feelings drive our thoughts, then our bodies are literally living in the past. We are rarely in the present moment.

So let's say you've gone through pretty much that same sequence every day for ten years. Your body is then already programmed by habit to be in the future, based on your past, because as you emotionally begin to anticipate each of those events on your timeline, your body (as the unconscious mind) believes it's in that same predictable reality. And the same emotion signals the same genes in the same way, and now you're in that predictable future line of time. In fact, you could take that timeline from your past and just lift it up and set it into your future, because in this scenario, your past *is* your future. You're like the piano players who installed the circuitry in their brains just by thinking about playing the same sequence of keys over and over again and like the finger exercisers who changed their bodies by thought alone; you're priming your brain and conditioning your body into the same future as you mentally rehearse the same predictable daily scenario in your mind from yesterday.

We can never find the present moment, because our brains and bodies are already living in a known future reality based on the past. Now take a look at all of those points on your timeline that represent the choices, habits, actions, and experiences that create the same emotions in order to remind you of the feeling of you. There's no room for something new or unknown, something uncommon or miraculous, to show up in your life, because those points are so closely knit together. It would be too inconvenient, and frankly, it would disrupt your routine. How upsetting it would be for something new to show up in the life of a personality that's unconsciously anticipating the future based on the past!

I should warn you here that when you begin a meditation practice, if you just insert your meditation as another event on your timeline, there's a danger that you'll merely be adding another item to your to-do list. And if that's how you approach it, you still won't be able to find the present moment. To accomplish what you're after here, healing and making lasting changes, you have to be fully in the present moment, not thinking about what the next predictable event is on your timeline.

That's true because wherever you place your attention is where you're placing your energy. So if you're paying even the smallest bit of attention to things, people, places, or events in your external environment, then you're reaffirming that reality. And if you're in the habit of obsessing about time—thinking about either the past (the known) or the future, which is based on your past (and so is also the known)—then you're missing the present moment, where all possibility exists. When you focus on the known, you, as the quantum observer, can only get more of exactly that. You'll be collapsing all those possibilities in the quantum field into the same patterns of information called your life.

In order to access the unlimited potential that's waiting for you in the quantum field, you have to forget about the known (your body, your face, your gender, your race, your profession, and even your concept of what you have to do today) so that you can remain for a while in the *unknown*—where you are no *body,* no *one,* no *thing,* and in no *place* and in no *time.* You have to become pure consciousness (nothing but a thought or an awareness that you're aware in a void of potentials) so that your brain can recalibrate.

And when the body wants to distract you, but you keep mastering it and settling it back into the present moment over and over again until it acquiesces, the way you read about earlier, then that line that goes into the future no longer exists because the body is no longer living in that predictable destiny. You've disconnected from it or unplugged your energy circuits from it.

Similarly, if your body is conditioned and addicted to emotions you've memorized that keep you connected to the past, but you manage to bring your body back and settle it down every time you feel angry or frustrated until your body finally surrenders into the present moment, then that line that goes into that past no longer exists either. You've unplugged from that line, too. And when both your past and your future lines disappear, your predictable genetic destiny vanishes as well.

In this moment, there's no longer any past to drive the future, and there's no longer any predictable future based on the past. You're solely in the present, where you have access to all those potentials and possibilities. And the longer you're invested in the unknown by unplugging from those timelines and lingering in those possibilities, the more energy you liberate from your body and make available for creating something new. Figure 11.2 demonstrates how the past and the future no longer exist when the brain and the body are totally in the present moment. The predictable reality of knowns does not exist, therefore you're in the unknown realm of possibilities.

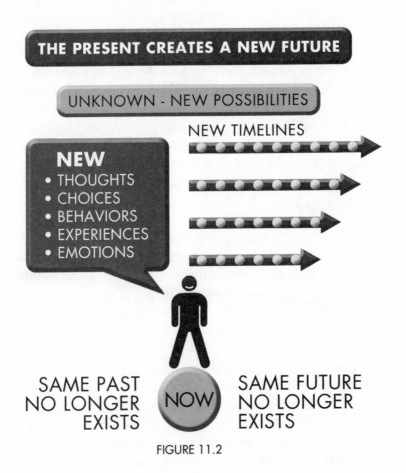

FIGURE 11.2

When you find the sweet spot of the present moment and you forget about yourself as the same personality, you have access to other possibilities that already exist in the quantum field. That's because you are no longer connected to the same body-mind, to the same identification with the environment, and to the same predictable timeline. In the moment, the same familiar past and future literally no longer exist, and you become pure consciousness—a thought alone. That is the moment that you can change your body, change something in your environment, and create a new timeline.

The meditation outlined in the next chapter includes a period where you get to linger in this potent unknown, in the blackness of possibility, and invest your energy into the void of potentials that exist in the present moment. Remember that even though it may look as if there's nothing there, it really isn't just empty blackness; it's the quantum field, and it's just bursting with energy and possibility.

When my colleagues and I examined our advanced-workshop students who were able to become pure consciousness—a thought separate from this known reality—we saw the greatest strides in their ability to change their brains, their bodies, and their lives. If the placebo is about changing the body by thought alone, then a very important step is to become a thought—alone.

Seeing Without Eyes

Here's one of my favorite examples of what can happen when you focus on the unknown in meditation. Not long ago, I was doing a workshop in Sydney, Australia, in which I was leading a meditation where I'd asked the participants to be no *body,* no *one,* no *thing,* and to be in no *place* and in no *time*—to become pure consciousness, lingering in the unknown (just as you're about to do in the next chapter).

As I was watching the group meditate, I happened to notice a woman, named Sophia, sitting in the third row, meditating with her eyes closed, just like everyone else. And all of a sudden, I saw her energy change. Something just told me to wave to her, so I did, and still with her eyes closed, Sophia waved back! I motioned for two of my trainers who were at the other end of the room to come over. When they got to me, I pointed directly at Sophia, and she waved back at me again—without ever opening her eyes.

"What's going on?" my trainers whispered.

"She's seeing without eyes," I told them. As I said, when you focus on the unknown, you get the unknown. After we finished the event in Sydney, we had a more advanced workshop in Melbourne one week later, and Sophia came to that workshop as well.

"Hey, I saw you, and I saw the trainers," she told me, proceeding to describe everything that had happened in the room during the meditation when she'd had her eyes closed. She was extremely accurate. After the workshop, Sophia decided to apply to become one of my corporate trainers, and I selected her because of her ability. So she came to a training just a few months later.

At the end of every day of my trainings, I always have the new trainers close their eyes while I run through the entire day's lessons in 30 minutes, just to reactivate the new circuits in their long-term memories. So as I was doing that, Sophia was sitting there with her eyes closed, and all of a sudden, she opened her eyes, shook her head, closed her eyes again, turned around to look behind her, and then turned back around and looked straight at me with an amazed expression on her face. After she repeated this a few times, I motioned for her to just stay with the meditation, and we spoke afterward.

Not only could Sophia see in front of her with her eyes closed in meditation, she told me, but now she could see a full 360-degree view. She could see what was in front of her, what was behind her, and what was all around her at the same time. Because Sophia had been in the habit of seeing with her eyes open for her whole life, she kept opening her eyes and closing them again in a reflexive attempt to see what she was already seeing.

I happened to have Dr. Fannin at that training, and we were scanning some of the trainers' brains just so that we could plan what patterns of brain waves we'd be measuring in our students for our first advanced workshop in Arizona. When it was Sophia's turn, I didn't say anything to Dr. Fannin about her. So he hooked her up to the EEG machine, and then with her back to us, we sat down about seven feet away to watch her scan on the monitor. All of a sudden, the back of Sophia's brain, which is the visual cortex, lit up on the computer screen.

"Oh, look!" Dr. Fannin whispered to me. "She's visualizing!"

"No," I said softly, shaking my head. "She's not visualizing."

"What do you mean?" he mouthed.

"She's *seeing*," I quietly responded.

"What do you mean?" he repeated, confused. So I waved at her. And still sitting with her back to me, she reached above her head, turned her hand backward, and waved back. It was amazing. The proof was right on the scan: Sophia was seeing without eyes. Her visual cortex was processing information, just as though she were seeing, but it was her *brain* that was doing the seeing—not her eyes.

As I said, if you focus on the unknown, you get the unknown. Ready to see for yourself?

Chapter Twelve

Changing Beliefs and Perceptions Meditation

In this chapter, I'm going to walk you through a guided meditation designed to help you change some beliefs or perceptions about yourself or your life. I recommend meditating while playing a recording, either of this meditation (which helps you change two beliefs or perceptions and lasts about an hour) or of a slightly shorter version (which helps you change one belief or perception and lasts 45 minutes). Both meditations are available for purchase on audio CDs or MP3 files from my website (www.drjoedispenza .com). The one-hour version is called *You Are the Placebo Book Meditation: Changing Two Beliefs and Perceptions,* and the 45-minute version is called *You Are the Placebo Book Meditation: Changing One Belief and Perception.* Or you can make a recording of yourself reading the text of either version of the meditation (both of which you will find in the Appendix).

Remember that beliefs and perceptions are subconscious states of being. They start with thoughts and feelings that you think and feel over and over, until they ultimately become habituated or automatic—at which point they form an attitude. Attitudes strung together become beliefs, and related beliefs strung together become perceptions. Over time, this redundancy creates a view of the world and of yourself that's largely subconscious. It affects your relationships, your behaviors, and really everything in your life.

So if you want to change a belief or perception, you have to first change your state of being. And changing your state of being means changing your energy, because in order for you to affect matter, you have to become more energy and less matter, more wave and less particle. That requires you to combine a clear intention and an elevated emotion—those are the two ingredients.

As you've read, this process involves making a decision with a high-enough level of energy that your thought about the new belief becomes an experience that carries a strong emotional signature, which alters you on some level in that moment. That's how you change your biology, become your own placebo, and make your mind matter. We all have had experiences that have affected our biology to some degree or another. Remember the Cambodian women, from Chapter 7, who developed vision problems because of the horrors they were forced to witness when the Khmer Rouge was in power? That's an extreme example, of course, but you can use the same principle to make a *positive* change.

In order for this to work, the new experience has to be greater than the past experience. In other words, the internal experience you have when you meditate has to have a greater amplitude—greater energy—than the external past experience that created the belief and perception that you want to change. *The body must respond to a new mind.* So you have to put your heart into that elevated emotion; you really have to get goose bumps. You have to feel lifted, inspired, invincible, and empowered.

I'll be giving you the opportunity to change two beliefs and perceptions about yourself in this meditation. So before you begin, decide which two you want to change. You can select one of the common limiting beliefs listed in Chapter 7, or you can come up with something else on your own—such as, *I'll always have this pain or condition, Life is too hard, People are unfriendly, Success takes a lot of work,* or *I'll never change.*

Once you decide, get a piece of paper and draw a vertical line down the middle. On the left side, write down the two beliefs and perceptions you want to change, one on top of the other.

Then think for a minute: If you don't want to believe and perceive these things anymore, then what *do* you want to believe and perceive about yourself and your life? And if you *did* believe and perceive those new things, how would that make you feel? Write down the new beliefs and perceptions that you want to have on the right side of the paper.

As you'll soon see, this meditation is in three parts:

— The **first** part is the induction, in which you will use the open-focus technique you read about in the last chapter to get you into more coherent alpha or theta brain-wave states where you're more suggestible. This is vital, because the only way you can truly influence your heath and become the placebo is when your own suggestibility is enhanced.

— In the **second** part, you'll find the present moment and linger in the quantum void, where all possibilities exist.

— And in the **third** part, you'll change your beliefs and perceptions. Here, to walk you through what you'll be doing when you actually sit down to meditate, I'll give you some direction at the beginning of each part, and then the text of the meditation will follow in italics.

If you're an experienced meditator, feel free to do the entire meditation the whole way through during your first time. If you're new to meditation, you may want to practice the first part every day for a week, then add the second part the second week, and progress to all three parts the third week. Either way, keep doing this same meditation on a daily basis, until you see some changes happening in your life.

If you are already practicing the meditation that I outlined in *Breaking the Habit of Being Yourself,* I want to point out that the meditation in this book is entirely different, even though you'll find some similarities in the way in which both meditations begin (the induction phase). If you can do only one meditation per day, I recommend trying this new meditation for a few months so that you can fully reap the benefits. Then you can decide which meditation you want to continue with, or you can switch back and forth between the two as you wish.

Induction: Creating Brain Coherence and Slower Brain Waves with Open Focus

When you move into the open-focus meditation, you'll be going from particle to wave, from the narrow focus you usually have on people, places, and things in the outer world to a more open focus—where you'll be concentrating not on any physical *thing*, but on space. After all, if an atom is approximately 99.9 percent energy and we're always focusing on the particle, maybe it's time we paid some attention to the wave, because our awareness and our energy are intrinsically combined—putting attention on our energy is what amplifies our energy.

When you use this technique, your brain naturally recalibrates, because to do it correctly, you have to let go of your analytical mind (which is very busy thinking in high beta as an identity). That identity, who you know yourself to be, is connected to the external environment, to your emotional addictions and habits, and to time. The moment you get beyond those elements, you're nothing but pure consciousness, and as you read earlier, the different compartments of your brain begin to communicate better and your brain waves become very orderly—they start sending a coherent signal to the rest of the body, just as you saw in the workshop participants.

Stay present during this meditation; don't try to figure anything out and don't try to visualize. Just sense and feel. If you can sense where your left ankle is, if you can feel where your nose is, and if you can sense where the space between your sternum and your chest is, then you're resting your awareness, your consciousness, and your attention in those places. You might get a picture or an image in your head (say, of your chest or of your heart), but you don't have to strive for that; you just have to become aware of the space within and around your body in space.

This first part of the meditation should last for approximately 10 to 15 minutes.

Meditation: Part One

Now . . . can you rest your awareness . . . in the space . . . between your eyes . . . in space?

And can you sense . . . the energy of space . . . between your eyes . . . in space?

And now . . . can you become aware . . . of the space . . . between your temples . . . in space?

And can you sense . . . the volume of space . . . between your temples . . . in space?

And now . . . can you become aware . . . of the space . . . that your nostrils . . . occupy in space?

And can you sense . . . the volume of space . . . that the inside of your nose occupies . . . in space?

And now . . . can you become aware . . . of the space . . . between your tongue and the back of your throat . . . in space?

And can you sense . . . the volume of space . . . that the back of your throat occupies . . . in space?

And now . . . can you sense . . . the energy of space . . . around your ears . . . in space?

And can you feel . . . the energy of space . . . beyond your ears . . . in space?

And can you become aware . . . of the space . . . below your chin . . . in space?

And can you feel . . . the volume of space . . . around your neck . . . in space?

And now . . . can you sense . . . the space . . . beyond your chest . . . in space?

And can you feel . . . the energy of space . . . around your chest . . . in space?

And now . . . can you become aware . . . of the volume of space . . . beyond your shoulders . . . in space?

And can you sense . . . the energy of space . . . around your shoulders . . . in space?

And now . . . can you become aware . . . of the space . . . behind your back . . . in space?

And can you feel . . . the energy of space . . . beyond your spine . . . in space?

And now . . . can you rest . . . your awareness . . . in the space . . . between your thighs . . . in space?

And can you sense . . . the energy of space . . . connecting your knees . . . in space?

And now . . . can you sense . . . the volume of space . . . around your feet . . . in space?

And can you feel . . . the energy of space . . . beyond your feet . . . in space?

And can you become aware . . . of the space . . . around your entire body . . . in space?

And can you sense . . . the energy of space . . . beyond your body . . . in space?

And now . . . can you become aware . . . of the space between your body and the walls of the room . . . in space?

And can you sense . . . the volume of space . . . that the entire room occupies . . . in space?

And now . . . can you become aware . . . of the space . . . that all of space occupies . . . in space?

And can you sense . . . the space . . . that all of space takes up . . . in space?

Becoming Possibility: Finding the Present Moment and Lingering in the Void

In this next part of the meditation, you'll find the sweet spot of the present moment, where all things are possible. To do that, you must lay down your identity and disconnect from your body, the environment, and time, because the longer you linger in the unknown, the more you draw the unknown to you. And if nerve cells that no longer fire together no longer wire together, you'll be silencing the circuits in your brain that are connected to the old self. As you've read, those circuits maintain a hardwired program, so if you successfully disconnect from them, you'll also be disconnecting from the program. You'll no longer be emotionally signaling the same genes in the same way. And then as your body moves into a more balanced and harmonious state, you'll find yourself in the sweet spot of the present moment, and that's where all possibility exists.

If you find your mind drifting to thoughts about people you know, various problems you have, events that happened in the past or that are coming up in your future, your body, your weight, your pain, your hunger, or even how long this meditation will go on, simply become aware of those thoughts and then bring your consciousness back to the blackness or the quantum void of possibility. And then, once more, surrender into nothing.

This second part of the meditation should last for approximately 10 to 15 minutes.

Meditation: Part Two

And now . . . it's time . . . to become no body . . . no one . . . no thing . . . no where . . . in no time . . . to become . . . pure consciousness . . . to become an awareness in the infinite field of potentials . . . and to invest your energy into the unknown. . . . And the longer you linger in the unknown . . . the more you draw a new life to you. . . . Simply become a thought in the blackness of infinity . . . and unfold your attention—into no thing . . . into no body . . . into no time. . . .

And if you . . . as the quantum observer . . . find your mind returning to the known . . .to the familiar . . . to people . . . to things . . . or places in your known familiar reality . . . to your body . . . to your identity, to your emotions . . . to time . . . to the past . . . or the predictable future . . . simply become aware that you are observing the known . . . and surrender your consciousness back into the void of possibilities . . . and become no one . . . no body . . . no thing . . . no where . . . in no time. . . . Unfold into the immaterial realm of quantum potentials. . . The more you become awareness in possibility . . . the more you create possibility and opportunity in your life. . . . Stay present. . . .

[Allow 10 to 15 minutes here for you to linger.]

Changing Beliefs and Perceptions about Yourself and Your Life

In the final section of the meditation, it's time to bring up that first belief or perception about your life that you want to change. I'll ask you if you want to continue believing and perceiving in that way. If your answer is no, then you'll be invited to make a decision with such firm intention that the amplitude of energy related to that decision is greater than the hardwired programs in your brain and the emotional addictions in your body. Your body will then respond to a new mind, to a new consciousness.

Next I'll ask you, "What do you want to believe and perceive about yourself and your life, and how would that feel?" Then your task will be to move into a new state of being. You'll have to change your energy by marrying a clear intention with an elevated emotion—and lift matter to a new mind. You should get up feeling different from when you sat down. If so, then you changed biologically.

At that point, the past will no longer exist, because that higher-amplitude experience will have just overwritten the program of the old experience. That's why making that choice becomes an experience that you never forget, because now it's a long-term memory. You'll be making an unknown possibility known, which takes you out of the past-now and puts you into the future-now, where the event has already happened. Remember, it's not your job to figure out when or where or how it's going to happen. Your job is merely to move into a new state of being and then see the future you're creating.

Then you'll be guided to change the second belief or perception, so you'll repeat the same process all over again.

This final part of the meditation will last for approximately 20 to 30 minutes.

Meditation: Part Three

Now . . . what was that first belief . . . or perception . . . that you wanted to change about yourself and your life?

Do you want to continue to believe and perceive in this way?

If not . . . I want you to make a decision . . . with such firm intention . . . that the amplitude of that decision . . . carries a level of energy that's greater than the hardwired programs in your brain . . . and the emotional addictions in your body . . . and allow your body to respond to a new mind. . . .

And allow the choice to become an experience that you'll never forget . . . and let the experience . . . produce an emotion with such energy . . . that it rewrites the programs . . . and changes your biology. . . . Come out of your resting state and change your energy . . . so that your biology is altered by your own energy. . . .

Now it's time to surrender the past back into possibility . . . and allow the infinite field of possibilities to resolve it in a way that's right for you. . . . Give it up.

Now . . . what do you want to believe and perceive about yourself and your life . . . and how would that feel?

Come on . . . it's time to move into a new state of being . . . and allow your body to respond to a new mind . . . change your energy by combining a clear intention with an elevated emotion so that matter is lifted to a new mind. . . .

And let the choice . . . carry an amplitude of energy . . . that's greater than any experience of the past . . . and let your body be altered by your consciousness, by your own energy. . . . and shift into a new state of being . . . and make this moment define you . . . and let this intentional thought become such a powerful internal experience . . . that it carries an elevated emotional energy, which becomes a memory that you never forget . . . replacing the past memory with a new memory in your brain and body. . . . Come on! Become empowered. . . . Be inspired. . . . Make the choice a decision that you'll never fail to remember. . . .

Now . . . give your body a taste of the future by showing it how it will feel to believe this way . . . and let your body respond to a new mind. . . .

And how would you live from this state of being? . . . What choices will you make? . . . How will you behave? . . . What experiences are in your future? . . . How will you live? . . . How would it feel? . . . How will you love? . . . and allow infinite waves of possibility to collapse into an experience in your life. . . .

And can you teach your body emotionally what it is to be in this new future? . . . Come on . . . open your heart . . . and believe in possibility. . . . Be lifted . . . fall in love with the moment . . . and experience that future now. . . .

And now, surrender your creation to a greater mind . . . for what you think and experience in this realm of possibility . . . if it is truly felt . . . it will manifest in some future time . . . from waves of possibilities to particles in reality . . . from the immaterial to the material . . . from thought to energy into matter. . . .

Now . . . surrender your new belief into a field of consciousness that already knows how to organize the outcome in a way that's perfect for you . . . planting a seed in possibility. . . .

Now . . . what was that second belief or perception that you wanted to change about yourself and your life? . . . And does it serve you to continue believing and perceiving . . . in this way?

If not, it's time to make a decision with such firm intention . . . that the amplitude of that decision . . . carries a level of energy that causes your body to respond to a new mind . . . and that the choice that you make is final . . . and that your decision becomes an experience that you never forget. . . . Come out of your familiar resting state and change your energy so that matter is lifted to a new mind. . . . Go on! Become empowered. . . . Be moved by your own energy. . . .

And let the energy of the choice . . . rewrite the subconscious programs neurologically in your brain . . . and emotionally and genetically in your body . . . and make the choice be greater than the past . . . and let your biology be changed by your energy. . . . Be inspired. . . .

And now . . . surrender that belief to a greater intelligence . . . simply let go . . . and give it up . . . to the field of possibilities . . . returning it back to energy. . . .

Now . . . what do you want to believe and perceive about yourself and your life? . . . And how would that feel?

Come on, move into a new state of being . . . and allow your body to be lifted to a new mind . . . and let the energy of this choice . . . rewrite the circuits in your brain . . . and the genes in your body . . . and allow your body to be liberated into a new future. . . . You must feel a new energy . . . to become some thing greater than your body, your environment, and time . . . so that you have dominion over your body, your environment, and time. . . . Become a thought that affects matter. . . .

And can you teach your body emotionally . . . what it would feel like to believe in this way . . . to be empowered . . . to be moved by your own greatness . . . to have courage . . . to be invincible . . . to be in love with life . . . to feel unlimited . . . to live as if your prayers are already answered? . . . Come on, give your body, as the unconscious mind, a taste of your future . . . signaling new genes in new ways. . . . Your energy is the epiphenomenon of matter . . . change your energy and change your body . . . Come on, make your mind matter. . . .

And how will you live, from this state of being? . . . And if you believe this, what choices would you make? . . . What behaviors could you demonstrate? . . . And what experiences can you observe from this state of being? . . . And how will they feel . . . to be healed, to be free, to believe in yourself and possibility? . . . Let yourself go. . . .

Bless this future with your own energy. . . . Then it means . . . you're connected to a new destiny . . . for wherever you place your attention is where you place your energy. . . . Investing in your future . . . and being defined by your future instead of your past. . . . Open your heart and allow your body to become moved by your own inward experience . . . and remember that whatever you truly experience in the unknown . . . and emotionally embrace . . . will ultimately slow down in frequency as energy . . . into three dimensions as matter. . . .

And now let go and give it up . . . and allow it to be executed by a greater intelligence in a way that's right for you. . . .

And now . . . take your left hand and place it over your heart . . . and I want you to bless your body . . . that it be lifted to a new mind . . . and bless your life . . . that it be an extension of your mind . . . to bless your future . . . that it never be your past . . . to bless your past . . . that it turns to wisdom . . . to bless the adversity in your life . . . that it initiates you into greatness . . . and that you see the hidden meaning behind all things . . . to bless your soul . . . that it wake you up from this dream . . . and to bless the divine in you . . . that it moves in you . . . that it moves through you . . . and that it moves all around you . . . that it shows cause in your life. . . .

And finally . . . I want you to give thanks for a new life before it's made manifest . . . so that your body, as the unconscious mind, begins to experience that future now. . . . For the emotional signature of gratitude means the event has already happened. . . . For gratitude is . . . the ultimate state of receivership. . . .

And just memorize this feeling . . . bring your awareness . . . back to a new body . . . to a new environment . . . and to a whole new time . . . and when you are ready, you can open your eyes.

AFTERWORD

Becoming Supernatural

Some critics may categorize this body of work as faith healing. I'm actually fine with that accusation at this point in my life, because what is faith but when we believe in thought more than anything else? Isn't it when we accept a thought—independent of the conditions in our environment—and then surrender to the outcome to such a degree that we live as if our prayers were already answered? Sounds like a formula for the placebo. We've always been the placebo.

Maybe it's not so important that we pray rigorously every day to have our prayers answered, but that we instead get up from our meditations as if our prayers have *already* been answered. If we accomplish this daily, we are at a level of mind where we're truly living in the unknown and expecting the unexpected. And this is when the mysterious knocks on our door.

The placebo response is about being healed by thought alone. Thought by itself, however, is unmanifested emotion. Once we embrace that thought emotionally, it begins to become real—that is, it becomes reality. A thought without an emotional signature is void of experience, and thus it is latent, waiting to be made known from the unknown. As we initiate a thought into an experience and then into wisdom, we are evolving as human beings.

When you look into the mirror, you see your reflection and know that whom you are seeing is the physical you. But how do the true self, the ego, and the soul see themselves? Your life is a mirror image of your mind, your consciousness, and who you really are.

There are no schools of ancient spiritual wisdom sitting high on mountaintops in the Himalayas waiting to initiate us into becoming mystics and saints. Our *lives* are our initiation into greatness. Maybe you and I should see life as an opportunity to reach greater and greater levels of self so that we can overcome our own limitations with more expanded levels of consciousness. That's how a pragmatist, instead of a victim, sees it.

To abandon the familiar ways in which we've grown accustomed to thinking about life in order to embrace new paradigms will feel unnatural in the beginning. Frankly, it takes effort—and it's uncomfortable. Why? Because when we change, we no longer feel like ourselves. My definition of *genius,* then, is to be uncomfortable and to be okay with being uncomfortable.

How many times in history have admirable individuals who struggled against outdated beliefs, living outside of their comfort zones, been considered heretics and fools, only to later emerge as geniuses, saints, or masters? In time, they became supernatural.

But how do you and I become supernatural? We have to begin to do what's unnatural—that is, *to give* in the midst of crisis, when everyone is feeling lack and poverty; *to love* when everyone is angry and judging others; *to demonstrate courage and peace* when everyone else is in fear; *to show kindness* when others are displaying hostility and aggression; *to surrender to possibility* when the rest of the world is aggressively pushing to be first, trying to control outcomes, and fiercely competing in an endless drive to get to the top; *to knowingly smile* in the face of adversity; and *to cultivate the feeling of wholeness* when we're diagnosed as sick.

It seems so unnatural to make these types of choices in the midst of such conditions, but if we repeatedly succeed, in time we'll transcend the norm—and we, too, become supernatural. And most important, by *your* being supernatural, you give *others* permission to do the same. Mirror neurons fire when we observe someone else performing an action. Our neurons mirror the neurons of that other person, as though we were performing the same action. For example, when you see a professional dancer dancing the salsa, *you* will dance the salsa better than you did before. If you watch Serena Williams hit a tennis ball, *you* will hit the ball better than you did before. If you observe someone leading a community with love and compassion, you'll lead in your life in the same way. And if you witness someone self-healing from a disease by changing his or her thought processes, you'll be more prone to do the same.

It's my hope that after reading this book, you'll realize that the ultimate belief is the belief in yourself and in the field of infinite possibilities—and when you merge the belief in yourself as a subjective consciousness with your belief in an objective consciousness, then you're balancing intention and surrender. It's tricky, though. If you overintend (that's called "trying"), you'll get in your own way and always fall short of your vision. If you oversurrender, you'll become too lazy, apathetic, and uninspired. But if you combine a clear intention with an uncompromising trust in possibility, then you'll step into the unknown, and that's when the supernatural starts to unfold. I think that you and I are at our best when we're in this state of being.

When these two states merge, I believe that we drink from a deeper well. And when wholeness, self-satisfaction, and self-love truly come from within, because you've ventured beyond what you believed was possible and you overcame your own self-imposed limitations, that's when the uncommon occurs. To be happy with yourself in the present moment while maintaining a dream of your future is a grand recipe for manifestation.

When you feel so whole that you no longer care whether "it" will happen, that's when amazing things materialize before your eyes. I've learned that being whole is the perfect state of creation. I've seen this time and time again in witnessing true healings in people all over the world. They feel so complete that they no longer want, no longer feel lack, and no longer try to do it themselves. They let go, and to their amazement, something greater than they are responds—and they laugh at the simplicity of the process.

This book and my research are, hopefully, a beginning and not the end. I'll certainly be the first to raise my hand to confess that I don't know it all. My greatest joy, though, is when I've contributed to someone's personal growth in some way. I've seen transformation on many faces, and I can say that independent of culture, race, or gender, we all look the same when we're freed from the bonds of our own self-limiting beliefs.

There's a principle that I adore in biology called *emergence.* Have you ever seen a school of fish all breaking in the same direction at the same time? Or a flock of hundreds of birds in flight, all moving together as one consciousness—as one mind? When you look at this phenomenon, you might think that all the individuals in the group are following one leader who's showing the way. It appears that the synchronistic movements of hundreds or even thousands of individual organisms all doing the same thing at the same time is a top-down phenomenon. But that's not what's really happening.

It turns out that this level of unity takes place as a bottom-up phenomenon. The group actually has no leader; everyone is leading. They're all part of the same collective consciousness, doing the same thing at the same time. It's as if the whole is connected in a field of information beyond space and time. One community is presenting as one mind. One organism is created from each individual becoming one. There's power in numbers.

We've been programmed and conditioned into a subconscious belief that if we lead with too much passion and change the world, we'll surely be assassinated. Most great leaders who've altered the course of history with a profound message "get it" in the end. Whether we're talking about Martin Luther King, Jr.; Mahatma Gandhi; John Lennon; Joan of Arc; William Wallace; Jesus of Nazareth; or Abraham Lincoln, an unconscious stigma exists that suggests that all visionary leaders must give their lives for the truth. But maybe we've finally arrived at the time in history when it's more important to *live* for the truth than to die for it.

If hundreds, thousands, or even millions of human beings embrace a new consciousness based on possibility; align their actions with their intentions; and live by greater universal laws of love, kindness, and compassion, a new consciousness will emerge—and we'll experience true oneness. Then, we might just have too many leaders to remove.

So if, on a daily basis, you're committed to demonstrating your personal best and you're overcoming selfish states of mind driven by stress hormones—and I'm doing the same—then together, we're changing the world by changing ourselves. And if enough of us are tempering ourselves into more whole human beings, then as the individual communities we live in emerge around the world, they'll eventually consume the present mindset of reality based on fear, competition, lack, hostility, greed, and deception. In time, the old will be completely consumed by the new. A particular concern of mine is that we now live in a world where scientific research is commingled with self-interest and often influenced by profits, so I question whether we're being told the truth about the way things really are. It's up to us, then, to discover the truth for ourselves.

Imagine a world inhabited by billions of people, just like a school of fish, living as one—where everyone is embracing similar uplifting thoughts connected to unlimited possibility, and these thoughts allow people to make more inspired choices, demonstrate more altruistic behaviors, and create more enlightening experiences. People would then no longer be living by the survival-based emotions we're so familiar with now: feeling more like matter than energy, separate from possibility. Instead, they'd be living by more expanded, selfless, heartfelt emotions—feeling more like energy than matter, connected to something greater.

If we could do this, then an entirely different world would *emerge,* and we would be living by a new credo based on the open heart. That's what *I* see when I close my eyes to meditate.

— **Dr. Joe Dispenza**

APPENDIX

Script of the *Changing Beliefs and Perceptions Meditation*

If you want to make your own guided-meditation recording, instead of purchasing one of the prerecorded audio CDs or MP3 versions from my website, feel free to record yourself reading one of the following two scripts. The first script is for the hour-long meditation, which involves changing two beliefs or perceptions, and the second is a 45-minute meditation that involves changing just one belief or perception.

If you are recording your own meditation, pause for a second or two at each set of ellipses, and pause for at least five full seconds between sentences. As you'll see, I've added a note after the second part of each meditation, reminding you to include a period of silence on your recording so that you can linger in the unknown before you begin the last part of the meditation, where you'll change either one or two beliefs or perceptions.

Hour-long Version of Meditation
(changing two beliefs and perceptions)

Now . . . can you rest your awareness . . . in the space . . . between your eyes . . . in space?

And can you sense . . . the energy of space . . . between your eyes . . . in space?

And now . . . can you become aware . . . of the space . . . between your temples . . . in space?

And can you sense . . . the volume of space . . . between your temples . . . in space?

And now . . . can you become aware . . . of the space . . . that your nostrils . . . occupy in space?

And can you sense . . . the volume of space . . . that the inside of your nose occupies . . . in space?

And now . . . can you become aware . . . of the space . . . between your tongue and the back of your throat . . . in space?

And can you sense . . . the volume of space . . . that the back of your throat occupies . . . in space?

And now . . . can you sense . . . the energy of space . . . around your ears . . . in space?

And can you feel . . . the energy of space . . . beyond your ears . . . in space?

And can you become aware . . . of the space . . . below your chin . . . in space?

And can you feel . . . the volume of space . . . around your neck . . . in space?

And now . . . can you sense . . . the space . . . beyond your chest . . . in space?

And can you feel . . . the energy of space . . . around your chest . . . in space?

And now . . . can you become aware . . . of the volume of space . . . beyond your shoulders . . . in space?

And can you sense . . . the energy of space . . . around your shoulders . . . in space?

And now . . . can you become aware . . . of the space . . . behind your back . . . in space?

And can you feel . . . the energy of space . . . beyond your spine . . . in space?

And now . . . can you rest . . . your awareness . . . in the space . . . between your thighs . . . in space?

And can you sense . . . the energy of space . . . connecting your knees . . . in space?

And now . . . can you sense . . . the volume of space . . . around your feet . . . in space?

And can you feel . . . the energy of space . . . beyond your feet . . . in space?

And can you become aware . . . of the space . . . around your entire body . . . in space?

And can you sense . . . the energy of space . . . beyond your body . . . in space?

And now . . . can you become aware . . . of the space between your body and the walls of the room . . . in space?

And can you sense . . . the volume of space . . . that the entire room occupies . . . in space?

And now . . . can you become aware . . . of the space . . . that all of space occupies . . . in space?

And can you sense . . . the space . . . that all of space takes up . . . in space?

And now . . . it's time . . . to become no body . . . no one . . . no thing . . . no where . . . in no time . . . to become . . . pure consciousness . . . to become an awareness in the infinite field of potentials . . . and to invest your energy into the unknown. . . . And the longer you linger in the unknown . . . the more you draw a new life to you. . . . Simply become a thought in the blackness of infinity . . . and unfold your attention—into no thing . . . into no body . . . into no time. . . .

And if you . . . as the quantum observer . . . find your mind returning to the known . . . to the familiar . . . to people . . . to things . . . or places in your known familiar reality . . . to your body . . . to your identity, to your emotions . . . to time . . . to the past . . . or the predictable future . . . simply become aware that you are observing the known . . . and surrender your consciousness back into the void of possibilities . . . and become no one . . . no body . . . no thing . . . no where . . . in no time. . . . Unfold into the immaterial realm of quantum potentials. . . . The more you become awareness in possibility . . . the more you create possibility and opportunity in your life. . . . Stay present. . . .

[Allow anywhere from 5 minutes to 20 minutes here for you to linger, depending on how long you have to meditate.]

Now . . . what was that first belief . . . or perception . . . that you wanted to change about yourself and your life?

Do you want to continue to believe and perceive in this way?

If not . . . I want you to make a decision . . . with such firm intention . . . that the amplitude of that decision . . . carries a level of energy that's greater than the hardwired programs in your brain . . . and the emotional addictions in your body . . . and allow your body to respond to a new mind. . . .

And allow the choice to become an experience that you'll never forget . . . and let the experience . . . produce an emotion with such energy . . . that it rewrites the programs . . . and changes your biology. . . . Come out of your resting state and change your energy . . . so that your biology is altered by your own energy. . . .

Now it's time to surrender the past back into possibility . . . and allow the infinite field of possibilities to resolve it in a way that's right for you. . . .Give it up.

Now . . . what do you want to believe and perceive about yourself and your life . . . and how would that feel?

Come on . . . it's time to move into a new state of being . . . and allow your body to respond to a new mind . . . change your energy by combining a clear intention with an elevated emotion so that matter is lifted to a new mind. . . .

And let the choice . . . carry an amplitude of energy . . . that's greater than any experience of the past . . . and let your body be altered by your consciousness, by your own energy . . .

and shift into a new state of being . . . and make this moment define you . . . and let this intentional thought become such a powerful internal experience . . . that it carries an elevated emotional energy, which becomes a memory that you never forget. . . . replacing the past memory with a new memory in your brain and body. . . . Come on! Become empowered. . . . Be inspired. . . . Make the choice a decision that you'll never fail to remember. . . .

Now . . . give your body a taste of the future by showing it how it will feel to believe this way . . . and let your body respond to a new mind. . . .

And how would you live from this state of being? . . . What choices will you make? . . . How will you behave? . . . What experiences are in your future? . . . How will you live? . . . How would it feel? . . . How will you love? . . . And allow infinite waves of possibility to collapse into an experience in your life. . . .

And can you teach your body emotionally what it is to be in this new future? . . . Come on . . . open your heart . . . and believe in possibility. . . . Be lifted . . . fall in love with the moment . . . and experience that future now. . . .

And now, surrender your creation to a greater mind . . . for what you think and experience in this realm of possibility . . . if it is truly felt . . . it will manifest in some future time . . . from waves of possibilities to particles in reality . . . from the immaterial to the material . . . from thought to energy into matter. . . .

Now . . . surrender your new belief into a field of consciousness that already knows how to organize the outcome in a way that's perfect for you . . . planting a seed in possibility. . . .

Now . . . what was that second belief or perception that you wanted to change about yourself and your life? . . . And does it serve you to continue believing and perceiving . . . in this way?

If not, it's time to make a decision with such firm intention . . . that the amplitude of that decision . . . carries a level of energy that causes your body to respond to a new mind . . . and that the choice that you make is final . . . and that your decision becomes an experience that you never forget. . . . Come out of your familiar resting state and change your energy so that matter is lifted to a new mind. . . . Go on! Become empowered. . . . Be moved by your own energy. . . .

And let the energy of the choice . . . rewrite the subconscious programs neurologically in your brain . . . and emotionally and genetically in your body . . . and make the choice to be greater than the past . . . and let your biology be changed by your energy. . . . Be inspired. . . .

And now . . . surrender that belief to a greater intelligence . . . simply let go . . . and give it up . . . to the field of possibilities . . . returning it back to energy. . . .

Now . . . what do you want to believe and perceive about yourself and your life? . . . And how would that feel?

Come on, move into a new state of being . . . and allow your body to be lifted to a new mind . . . and let the energy of this choice . . . rewrite the circuits in your brain . . . and the genes in your body . . . and allow your body to be liberated into a new future. . . . You must feel a new energy . . . to become some thing greater than your body, your environment, and time . . . so that you have dominion over your body, your environment, and time. . . . Become a thought that affects matter. . . .

And can you teach your body emotionally . . . what it would feel like to believe in this way . . . to be empowered . . . to be moved by your own greatness . . . to have courage . . . to be invincible . . . to be in love with life . . . to feel unlimited . . . to live as if your prayers are already answered? . . . Come on, give your body, as the unconscious mind, a taste of your future . . . signaling new genes in new ways. . . . Your energy is the epiphenomenon of matter . . . change your energy and change your body. . . . Come on, make your mind matter. . . .

And how will you live, from this state of being? . . . And if you believe this, what choices would you make? . . . What behaviors could you demonstrate? . . . And what experiences can you observe from this state of being? . . . And how will they feel . . . to be healed, to be free, to believe in yourself and possibility? . . . Let yourself go. . . .

Bless this future with your own energy. . . . Then it means . . . you're connected to a new destiny . . . for wherever you place your attention is where you place your energy. . . . Investing in your future . . . and being defined by your future instead of your past. . . . Open your heart and allow your body to become moved by your own inward experience . . . and remember that whatever you truly experience in the unknown . . . and emotionally embrace . . . will ultimately slow down in frequency as energy . . . into three dimensions as matter. . . .

And now let go and give it up . . . and allow it to be executed by a greater intelligence in a way that's right for you. . . .

And now . . . take your left hand and place it over your heart . . . and I want you to bless your body . . . that it be lifted to a new mind . . . and bless your life . . . that it be an extension of your mind . . . to bless your future. . . . that it never be your past . . . to bless your past . . . that it turns to wisdom . . . to bless the adversity in your life . . . that it initiates you into greatness . . . and that you see the hidden meaning behind all things . . . to bless your soul . . . that it wake you up from this dream . . . and to bless the divine in you . . . that it moves in you . . . that it moves through you . . . and that it moves all around you . . . that it shows cause in your life. . . .

And finally . . . I want you to give thanks for a new life before it's made manifest . . . so that your body, as the unconscious mind, begins to experience that future now. . . . For the emotional signature of gratitude means the event has already happened. . . . For gratitude is . . . the ultimate state of receivership. . . .

And just memorize this feeling . . . bring your awareness . . . back to a new body . . . to a new environment . . . and to a whole new time . . . and when you are ready, you can open your eyes.

45-Minute Version of Meditation
(changing one belief or perception)

Now . . . can you rest your awareness . . . in the space . . . between your eyes . . . in space?

And can you sense . . . the energy of space . . . between your eyes . . . in space?

And now . . . can you become aware . . . of the space . . . between your temples . . . in space?

And can you sense . . . the volume of space . . . between your temples . . . in space?

And now . . . can you become aware . . . of the space . . . that your nostrils . . . occupy in space?

And can you sense . . . the volume of space . . . that the inside of your nose occupies . . . in space?

And now . . . can you become aware . . . of the space . . . between your tongue and the back of your throat . . . in space?

And can you sense . . . the volume of space . . . that the back of your throat occupies . . . in space?

And now . . . can you sense . . . the energy of space . . . around your ears . . . in space?

And can you feel . . . the energy of space . . . beyond your ears . . . in space?

And can you become aware . . . of the space . . . below your chin . . . in space?

And can you feel . . . the volume of space . . . around your neck . . . in space?

And now . . . can you sense . . . the space . . . beyond your chest . . . in space?

And can you feel . . . the energy of space . . . around your chest . . . in space?

And now . . . can you become aware . . . of the volume of space . . . beyond your shoulders . . . in space?

And can you sense . . . the energy of space . . . around your shoulders . . . in space?

And now . . . can you become aware . . . of the space . . . behind your back . . . in space?

And can you feel . . . the energy of space . . . beyond your spine . . . in space?

And now . . . can you rest . . . your awareness . . . in the space . . . between your thighs . . . in space?

And can you sense . . . the energy of space . . . connecting your knees . . . in space?

And now . . . can you sense . . . the volume of space . . . around your feet . . . in space?

And can you feel . . . the energy of space . . . beyond your feet . . . in space?

And can you become aware . . . of the space . . . around your entire body . . . in space?

And can you sense . . . the energy of space . . . beyond your body . . . in space?

And now . . . can you become aware . . . of the space between your body and the walls of the room . . . in space?

And can you sense . . . the volume of space . . . that the entire room occupies . . . in space?

And now . . . can you become aware . . . of the space . . . that all of space occupies . . . in space?

And can you sense . . . the space . . . that all of space takes up . . . in space?

And now . . . it's time . . . to become no body . . . no one . . . no thing . . . no where . . . in no time . . . to become . . . pure consciousness . . . to become an awareness in the infinite field of potentials . . . and to invest your energy into possibility. . . . And the longer you linger in the unknown . . . the more you draw the unknown to you. . . . Simply become a thought in the blackness of infinity . . . and unfold your awareness into no thing . . . into no body . . . into no time. . . . The more you focus on the unknown . . . the more you bring a new life to you.

Allow your awareness to move from particle to wave . . . from matter to consciousness . . . from the material to the im-material . . . from space and time to no time and to no space . . . from a world of the senses . . . to a world beyond the senses . . . from the known to the unknown. . . . And if you . . . as the quantum observer . . . find your mind returning to the known . . . to familiar people . . . to things . . . or places in your known reality . . . to your body . . . to your habits, your identity, your emotions . . . to time . . . to the past . . . or the predictable future . . . simply become aware that you are observing the known . . . and surrender your consciousness back into the void of possibilities . . . and become no one . . . no body . . . no thing . . . no where . . . in no time. . . . Unfold your awareness back into the immaterial realm of all quantum potentials . . . into the blackness of eternity. . . . And the more you become an awareness in possibility . . . the more you create possibility and opportunity in your life. . . . Stay present. . . .

[Allow anywhere from 5 minutes to 10 minutes here for you to linger, depending on how long you have to meditate.]

Now what was that belief or perception that you wanted to change about yourself in your life? . . . And do you want to continue to believe and perceive in this way? . . . If not . . . it's time to make a decision with such firm intention . . . that the amplitude of that decision carries a level of energy that's greater than the hardwired programs in your brain and the emotional addictions in your body . . . and allow your body to respond to a new mind . . . and allow the choice to become an experience that you never forget . . . and allow the inward experience to produce an emotion with such energy that it rewrites the programs and changes your biology. . . .

Come out of your resting state and change your energy so that your biology is altered by your own energy. . . . Come on! Become inspired and make the choice to be greater than your past. Become inspired, become empowered! Be moved by your own energy . . . and now surrender that belief to a greater intelligence . . . to a greater mind . . . just let go and give it up to the field of possibilities, returning it back to energy. . . .

Now what do you want to believe and perceive about yourself and your life . . . and how would that feel? . . . Come on . . . move into a new state of being . . . and allow your body to be lifted to a new mind . . . and let the energy of this choice rewrite the circuits in your brain and change the genes in your body . . . and allow your body to be liberated from the past into a new future. . . . Change your energy by combining a clear intention with an elevated emotion so that matter is lifted to a new mind . . . and let the choice carry an amplitude of energy that's greater than any past experience . . . and let your body be altered by your consciousness, by your energy . . . and shift into a new state of being . . . and make this moment define you . . . and let this internal process, this experience, carry such an elevated emotional energy that it becomes a memory that you never forget. . . .

And can you teach your body emotionally what it would feel like to believe in this way . . . to be empowered . . . to be moved by your own greatness . . . to be invincible . . . to have courage . . . to be in love with life . . . to feel unlimited . . . to live as if your prayers are already answered? . . . Give your body a taste of the future, signaling new genes in new ways. Your energy is what affects matter, and when you change your energy, you change your body. . . . Come on, make your mind matter . . . and from this new state of being, how will you live . . . what choices will you make . . . what behaviors will you demonstrate, and what experiences can you observe from this state of being, and how will it feel . . . to believe in possibility . . . to believe in yourself . . . to be healed . . . to be free . . . to be moved by the spirit? . . . Come on, love your future into life. . . . It's your creation; fall in love with it. From the state of being, nurture it with your attention . . . for wherever you place your attention is where you place your energy. . . . Invest in your future by observing it . . . and be defined by a new future instead of the familiar past. . . . Open your heart and allow your body to become moved by your own inward experience . . . for whatever you truly experience in possibility and emotionally embrace . . . will ultimately find you in some future time. . . . From thought . . . into energy . . . into matter . . . and now let go and give it up . . . to a greater intelligence . . . and allow it to be executed in a way that's right for you.

And take your left hand and place it over your heart . . . and I want you to bless your body . . . that it be lifted to a new mind . . . to a new energy. . . . And to bless your life . . . that it be an extension of your mind . . . that your state of being . . . be reflected in your world. . . . And to bless your future . . . that it never be your past. . . . and to bless your past . . . that it turn to wisdom . . . and to bless the challenges in your life . . . that they initiate you into greatness . . . and to bless your soul . . . that it wakes you up from this dream and that it be your guide . . . and to bless the unseen in you . . . that the energy move in you . . . that it stirs in you . . . that it moves through you . . . and that it moves all around you . . . that its mind become your mind . . . that its nature . . . become your nature . . . that its will . . . become your will . . . and its love for life . . . become your love for life . . . and that it shows cause by signaling you . . . in your life in some way . . . to let you know that it's real. . . . And now if the thought sends the signal out . . . and the feeling draws the event back to you . . . I want you to move into a state of gratitude . . . and to give thanks . . . for a new life before it's made manifest. . . . For the emotional signature of gratitude means . . . the event has already happened . . . and the longer you linger in gratitude . . . the more you draw your new life to you . . . for gratitude is the ultimate state of receivership. . . . And now bring your awareness back to a new body . . . to a new life . . . and to a whole new future time . . . and when you're ready . . . you can open your eyes.

ENDNOTES

Chapter One

1. C. K. Meador, "Hex Death: Voodoo Magic or Persuasion?" *Southern Medical Journal*, vol. 85, no. 3: pp. 244–247 (1992).

2. R. R. Reeves, M. E. Ladner, R. H. Hart, et al., "Nocebo Effects with Antidepressant Clinical Drug Trial Placebos," *General Hospital Psychiatry*, vol. 29, no. 3: pp. 275–277 (2007); C. K. Meador, *True Medical Detective Stories* (North Charleston, SC: CreateSpace, 2012).

3. A. F. Leuchter, I. A. Cook, E. A. Witte, et al., "Changes in Brain Function of Depressed Subjects During Treatment with Placebo," *American Journal of Psychiatry*, vol. 159, no. 1: pp. 122–129 (2002).

4. B. Klopfer, "Psychological Variables in Human Cancer," *Journal of Protective Techniques*, vol. 21, no. 4: pp. 331–340 (1957).

5. J. B. Moseley, Jr., N. P. Wray, D. Kuykendall, et al., "Arthroscopic Treatment of Osteoarthritis of the Knee: A Prospective, Randomized, Placebo-Controlled Trial. Results of a Pilot Study," *American Journal of Sports Medicine*, vol. 24, no. 1: pp. 28–34 (1996).

6. Discovery Health Channel, Discovery Networks Europe, Discovery Channel University, et al., *Placebo: Mind Over Medicine?* directed by J. Harrison, aired 2002 (Princeton, NJ: Films for the Humanities & Sciences, 2004), DVD.

7. J. B. Moseley, Jr., K. O'Malley, N. J. Petersen, et al., "A Controlled Trial of Arthroscopic Surgery for Osteoarthritis of the Knee," *New England Journal of Medicine*, vol. 347, no. 2: pp. 81–88 (2002); also note, the following independent study showed similar results: A. Kirkley, T. B. Birmingham, R. B. Litchfield, et al., "A Randomized Trial of Arthroscopic Surgery for Osteoarthritis of the Knee," *New England Journal of Medicine*, vol. 359, no. 11: pp. 1097–1107 (2008).

8. L. A. Cobb, G. I. Thomas, D. H. Dillard, et al., "An Evaluation of Internal-Mammary-Artery Ligation by a Double-Blind Technic," *New England*

Journal of Medicine, vol. 260, no. 22: pp. 1115–1118 (1959); E. G. Diamond, C. F. Kittle, and J. E. Crockett, "Comparison of Internal Mammary Artery Ligation and Sham Operation for Angina Pectoris," *American Journal of Cardiology*, vol. 5, no. 4: pp. 483–486 (1960).

9. T. Maruta, R. C. Colligan, M. Malinchoc, et al., "Optimism-Pessimism Assessed in the 1960s and Self-Reported Health Status 30 Years Later," *Mayo Clinic Proceedings*, vol. 77, no. 8: pp. 748–753 (2002).

10. T. Maruta, R. C. Colligan, M. Malinchoc, et al., "Optimists vs. Pessimists: Survival Rate Among Medical Patients over a 30-Year Period," *Mayo Clinic Proceedings*, vol. 75, no. 2: pp. 140–143 (2000).

11. B. R. Levy, M. D. Slade, S. R. Kunkel, et al., "Longevity Increased by Positive Self-Perceptions of Aging," *Journal of Personality and Social Psychology*, vol. 83, no. 2: pp. 261–270 (2002).

12. I. C. Siegler, P. T. Costa, B. H. Brummett, et al., "Patterns of Change in Hostility from College to Midlife in the UNC Alumni Heart Study Predict High-Risk Status," *Psychosomatic Medicine*, vol. 65, no. 5: pp. 738–745 (2003).

13. J. C. Barefoot, W. G. Dahlstrom, and R. B. Williams, Jr., "Hostility, CHD Incidence, and Total Mortality: A 25-Year Follow-Up Study of 255 Physicians," *Psychosomatic Medicine*, vol. 45, no. 1: 59–63 (1983).

14. D. M. Becker, L. R. Yanek, T. F. Moy, et al., "General Well-Being Is Strongly Protective Against Future Coronary Heart Disease Events in an Apparently Healthy High-Risk Population," Abstract #103966, presented at American Heart Association Scientific Sessions, Anaheim, CA, (November 12, 2001).

15. National Cancer Institute, "Anticipatory Nausea and Vomiting (Emesis)" (2013), www.cancer.gov/cancertopics/pdq/supportivecare/nausea/HealthProfessional/page4#Reference4.2.

16. J. T. Hickok, J. A. Roscoe, and G. R. Morrow, "The Role of Patients' Expectations in the Development of Anticipatory Nausea Related to Chemotherapy for Cancer," *Journal of Pain and Symptom Management*, vol. 22, no. 4: pp. 843–850 (2001).

17. R. de la Fuente-Fernández, T. J. Ruth, V. Sossi, et al., "Expectation and Dopamine Release: Mechanism of the Placebo Effect in Parkinson's Disease," *Science*, vol. 293, no. 5532: pp. 1164–1166 (2001).

18. C. R. Hall, "The Law, the Lord, and the Snake Handlers: Why a Knox County Congregation Defies the State, the Devil, and Death," *Louisville Courier Journal* (August 21, 1988); also see http://www.wku.edu/agriculture/thelaw.pdf.

19. K. Dolak, "Teen Daughters Lift 3,000-Pound Tractor Off Dad," ABC News (April 10, 2013), http://abcnews.go.com/blogs/headlines/2013/04/teen-daughters-lift-3000-pound-tractor-off-dad.

20. See note 1.

Chapter Two

1. H. K. Beecher, "The Powerful Placebo," *Journal of the American Medical Association*, vol. 159, no. 17: pp. 1602–1606 (1955).

2. W. B. Cannon, "Voodoo Death," *American Anthropologist*, vol. 44, no. 2: pp. 169–181 (1942).

3. The term *placebo* was first used in the part of Psalm 116 that opens the Catholic vespers for the dead. During the Middle Ages, the deceased's family often hired mourners to sing these verses, and because their fake grieving was sometimes over the top, the word *placebo* came to mean "flatterer" or "toady." In the early 19th century, doctors began giving inert tonics, pills, and other treatments to pacify patients whom they couldn't help or who sought medical attention for imagined ills; these doctors borrowed the term *placebo* and gave it its current meaning.

4. Y. Ikemi and S. Nakagawa, "A Psychosomatic Study of Contagious Dermatitis," *Kyoshu Journal of Medical Science*, vol. 13: pp. 335–350 (1962).

5. T. Luparello, H. A. Lyons, E. R. Bleecker, et al., "Influences of Suggestion on Airway Reactivity in Asthmatic Subjects," *Psychosomatic Medicine*, vol. 30, no. 6: pp. 819–829 (1968).

6. J. D. Levine, N. C. Gordon, and H. L. Fields, "The Mechanism of Placebo Analgesia," *Lancet*, vol. 2, no. 8091: pp. 654–657 (1978); J. D. Levine, N. C. Gordon, R. T. Jones, et al., "The Narcotic Antagonist Naloxone Enhances Clinical Pain," *Nature*, vol. 272, no. 5656: pp. 826–827 (1978).

7. R. Ader and N. Cohen, "Behaviorally Conditioned Immunosuppression," *Psychosomatic Medicine*, vol. 37, no. 4: pp. 333–340 (1975).

8. H. Benson, *The Relaxation Response* (New York: Morrow, 1975).

9. N. V. Peale, *The Power of Positive Thinking* (New York: Prentice-Hall, 1952).

10. N. Cousins, "Anatomy of an Illness (as Perceived by the Patient)," *New England Journal of Medicine*, vol. 295, no. 26: pp. 1458–1463 (1976).

11. N. Cousins, *Anatomy of an Illness as Perceived by the Patient: Reflections on Healing and Regeneration* (New York: W. W. Norton and Company, 1979).

12. T. Hayashi, S. Tsujii, T. Iburi, et al., "Laughter Up-Regulates the Genes Related to NK Cell Activity in Diabetes," *Biomedical Research (Tokyo, Japan)*, vol. 28, no. 6: pp. 281–285 (2007).

13. N. Cousins, *Anatomy of an Illness as Perceived by the Patient: Reflections on Healing and Regeneration* (New York: Norton, 1979), p. 56.

14. B. S. Siegel, *Love, Medicine, and Miracles: Lessons Learned About Self-Healing from a Surgeon's Experience with Exceptional Patients* (New York: Harper and Row, 1986).

15. I. Kirsch and G. Sapirstein, "Listening to Prozac but Hearing Placebo: A Meta-analysis of Antidepressant Medication," *Prevention and Treatment*, vol. 1, no. 2: article 00002a (1998).

16. I. Kirsch, B. J. Deacon, T. B. Huedo-Medina, et al., "Initial Severity and Antidepressant Benefits: A Meta-analysis of Data Submitted to the Food and Drug Administration," *PLOS Medicine*, vol. 5, no. 2: p. e45 (2008).

17. B. T. Walsh, S. N. Seidman, R. Sysko, et al., "Placebo Response in Studies of Major Depression: Variable, Substantial, and Growing," *Journal of the American Medical Association*, vol. 287, no. 14: pp. 1840–1847 (2002).

18. R. de la Fuente-Fernández, T. J. Ruth, V. Sossi, et al., "Expectation and Dopamine Release: Mechanism of the Placebo Effect in Parkinson's Disease," *Science*, vol. 293, no. 5532: pp. 1164–1166 (2001).

19. F. Benedetti, L. Colloca, E. Torre, et al., "Placebo-Responsive Parkinson Patients Show Decreased Activity in Single Neurons of the Subthalamic Nucleus," *Nature Neuroscience*, vol. 7, no. 6: 587–588 (2004).

20. F. Benedetti, A. Pollo, L. Lopiano, et al., "Conscious Expectation and Unconscious Conditioning in Analgesic, Motor, and Hormonal Placebo/ Nocebo Responses," *Journal of Neuroscience*, vol. 23, no. 10: pp. 4315–4323 (2003).

21. F. Benedetti, H. S. Mayberg, T. D. Wager, et al., "Neurobiological Mechanisms of the Placebo Effect," *Journal of Neuroscience*, vol. 25, no. 45: pp. 10390–10402 (2005).

22. F. Benedetti, M. Amanzio, S. Baldi, et al., "Inducing Placebo Respiratory Depressant Responses in Humans via Opioid Receptors," *European Journal of Neuroscience*, vol. 11, no. 2: pp. 625–631 (1999).

23. T. J. Kaptchuk, E. Friedlander, J. M. Kelley, et al., "Placebos Without Deception: A Randomized Controlled Trial in Irritable Bowel Syndrome," *PLOS ONE*, vol. 5, no. 12: p. e15591 (2010).

24. A. J. Crum and E. J. Langer, "Mind-Set Matters: Exercise and the Placebo Effect," *Psychological Science*, vol. 18, no. 2: pp. 165–171 (2007).

25. R. Desharnais, J. Jobin, C. Côté, et al., "Aerobic Exercise and the Placebo Effect: A Controlled Study," *Psychosomatic Medicine,* vol. 55, no. 2: pp. 149–154 (1993).

26. B. Blackwell, S. S. Bloomfield, and C. R. Buncher, "Demonstration to Medical Students of Placebo Responses and Non-drug Factors," *Lancet,* vol. 299, no. 7763: pp. 1279–1282 (1972).

27. I. Dar-Nimrod and S. J. Heine, "Exposure to Scientific Theories Affects Women's Math Performance," *Science,* vol. 314, no. 5798: p. 435 (2006).

28. C. Jencks and M. Phillips, eds., *The Black-White Test Score Gap* (Washington, D.C.: Brookings Institution Press, 1998).

29. C. M. Steele and J. Aronson, "Stereotype Threat and the Intellectual Test Performance of African Americans," *Journal of Personality and Social Psychology,* vol. 69, no. 5: pp. 797–811 (1995).

30. A. L. Geers, S. G. Helfer, K. Kosbab, et al., "Reconsidering the Role of Personality in Placebo Effects: Dispositional Optimism, Situational Expectations, and the Placebo Response," *Journal of Psychosomatic Research,* vol. 58, no. 2: pp. 121–127 (2005); A. L. Geers, K. Kosbab, S. G. Helfer, et al., "Further Evidence for Individual Differences in Placebo Responding: An Interactionist Perspective," *Journal of Psychosomatic Research,* vol. 62, no. 5: pp. 563–570 (2007).

31. D. R. Hamilton, *How Your Mind Can Heal Your Body* (Carlsbad, CA: Hay House, 2010), p. 19.

32. D. Goleman, B. H. Lipton, C. Pert, et al., *Measuring the Immeasurable: The Scientific Case for Spirituality* (Boulder, CO: Sounds True, 2008), p. 196; B. H. Lipton and S. Bhaerman, *Spontaneous Evolution: Our Positive Future (and a Way to There from Here)* (Carlsbad, CA: Hay House, 2009), p. 25.

Chapter Three

1. A. Vickers, *People v. the State of Illusion,* directed by S. Cervine (Phoenix, AZ: Exalt Films, 2012), film; see also Laboratory of Neuro Imaging, University of California, Los Angeles, http://www.loni.ucla.edu/About_Loni/education/brain_trivia.shtml.

2. L. R. Squire and E. R. Kandel, *Memory: From Mind to Molecules* (New York: Scientific American Library, 1999); see also D. Church, *The Genie in Your Genes: Epigenetic Medicine and the New Biology of Intention* (Santa Rosa, CA: Elite Books, 2007), p. 94.

3. Also known as Hebb's Rule or Hebb's Law; see D. O. Hebb, *The Organization of Behavior: A Neuropsychological Theory* (New York: John Wiley & Sons, 1949).

4. K. Aydin, A. Ucar, K. K. Oguz, et al., "Increased Gray Matter Density in the Parietal Cortex of Mathematicians: A Voxel-Based Morphometry Study," *American Journal of Neuroradiology,* vol. 28, no. 10: pp. 1859–1864 (2007).

5. V. Sluming, T. Barrick, M. Howard, et al., "Voxel-Based Morphometry Reveals Increased Gray Matter Density in Broca's Area in Male Symphony Orchestra Musicians," *NeuroImage,* vol. 17, no. 3: pp. 1613–1622 (2002).

6. M. R. Rosenzweig and E. L. Bennett, "Psychobiology of Plasticity: Effects of Training and Experience on Brain and Behavior," *Behavioural Brain Research,* vol. 78, no. 1: pp. 57–65 (1996); E. L. Bennett, M. C. Diamond, D. Krech, et al., "Chemical and Anatomical Plasticity Brain," *Science,* vol. 146, no. 3644: pp. 610–619 (1964).

Chapter Four

1. E. J. Langer, *Mindfulness* (Reading, MA: Addison-Wesley, 1989); E. J. Langer, *Counter Clockwise: Mindful Health and the Power of Possibility* (New York: Ballantine Books, 2009).

2. C. Feinberg, "The Mindfulness Chronicles: On the 'Psychology of Possibility,'" *Harvard Magazine* (September–October 2010), http://harvardmagazine.com/2010/09/the-mindfulness-chronicles.

3. J. Medina, *The Genetic Inferno: Inside the Seven Deadly Sins* (Cambridge, U.K.: Cambridge University Press, 2000), p. 4.

4. F. Crick, "Central Dogma of Molecular Biology," *Nature,* vol. 227, no. 5258: pp. 561–563 (1970).

5. M. Ho, "Death of the Central Dogma," Institute of Science in Society press release (March 9, 2004), http://www.i-sis.org.uk/DCD.php.

6. S. C. Segerstrom and G. E. Miller, "Psychological Stress and the Human Immune System: A Meta-analytic Study of 30 Years of Inquiry," *Psychological Bulletin,* vol. 130, no. 4: pp. 601–630 (2004); M. S. Kopp and J. Réthelyi, "Where Psychology Meets Physiology: Chronic Stress and Premature Mortality—The Central-Eastern European Health Paradox," *Brain Research Bulletin,* vol. 62, no. 5: pp. 351–367 (2004); B. S. McEwen and T. Seeman, "Protective and Damaging Effects of Mediators of Stress. Elaborating and Testing the Concepts of Allostasis and Allostatic Load," *Annals of the New York Academy of Sciences,* vol. 896: pp. 30–47 (1999).

7. J. L. Oschman, "Trauma Energetics," *Journal of Bodywork and Movement Therapies,* vol. 10, no. 1: pp. 21–34 (2006).

8. K. Richardson, *The Making of Intelligence* (New York: Columbia University Press, 2000), referenced by E. L. Rossi, *The Psychobiology of Gene*

Expression: Neuroscience and Neurogenesis in Hypnosis and the Healing Arts (New York: W. W. Norton and Company, 2002), p. 50.

9. E. L. Rossi, *The Psychobiology of Gene Expression: Neuroscience and Neurogenesis in Hypnosis and the Healing Arts* (New York: W. W. Norton and Company, 2002), p. 9.

10. D. Church, *The Genie in Your Genes: Epigenetic Medicine and the New Biology of Intention* (Santa Rosa, CA: Elite Books, 2007), p. 32.

11. See http://www.epigenome.org.

12. J. Cloud, "Why Your DNA Isn't Your Destiny," *Time Magazine* (January 6, 2010), http://content.time.com/time/magazine/article/0,9171,1952313,00.html#ixzz2eN2VCb1W.

13. M. F. Fraga, E. Ballestar, M. F. Paz, et al., "Epigenetic Differences Arise During the Lifetime of Monozygotic Twins," *Proceedings of the National Academy of Sciences USA,* vol. 102, no. 30: pp. 10604–10609 (2005).

14. D. Ornish, M. J. Magbanua, G. Weidner, et al., "Changes in Prostate Gene Expression in Men Undergoing an Intensive Nutrition and Lifestyle Intervention," *Proceedings of the National Academy of Sciences,* vol. 105, no. 24: pp. 8369–8374 (2008).

15. L. Stein, "Can Lifestyle Changes Bring out the Best in Genes," *Scientific American* (June 17, 2008), http://www.scientificamerican.com/article.cfm?id=can-lifestyle-changes-bring-out-the-best-in-genes.

16. T. Rönn, P. Volkov, C. Davegårdh, et al., "A Six Months Exercise Intervention Influences the Genome-Wide DNA Methylation Pattern in Human Adipose Tissue," *PLOS Genetics,* vol. 9, no. 6: p. e1003572 (2013).

17. D. Chow, "Why Your DNA May Not Be Your Destiny," *LiveScience* (June 4, 2013), http://www.livescience.com/37135-dna-epigenetics-disease-research.html; see also note 12 above.

18. M. D. Anway, A. S. Cupp, M. Uzumcu, et al., "Epigenetic Transgenerational Actions of Endocrine Disruptors and Male Fertility," *Science,* vol. 308, no. 5727: pp. 1466–1469 (2005).

19. S. Roy, S. Khanna, P. E. Yeh, et al., "Wound Site Neutrophil Transcriptome in Response to Psychological Stress in Young Men," *Gene Expression,* vol. 12, no. 4–6: pp. 273–287 (2005).

20. M. Uddin, A. E. Aiello, D. E. Wildman, et al., "Epigenetic and Immune Function Profiles Associated with Posttraumatic Stress Disorder," *Proceedings of the National Academy of Sciences,* vol. 107, no. 20: pp. 9470–9475 (2010).

21. S. W. Cole, B. D. Naliboff, M. E. Kemeny, et al., "Impaired Response to HAART in HIV-Infected Individuals with High Autonomic Nervous

System Activity," *Proceedings of the National Academy of Sciences,* vol. 98, no. 22: pp. 12695–12700 (2001).

22. J. Kiecolt-Glaser, T. J. Loving, J. R. Stowell, et al., "Hostile Marital Interactions, Proinflammatory Cytokine Production, and Wound Healing," *Archives of General Psychiatry,* vol. 62, no. 12: pp. 1377–1384 (2005).

23. J. A. Dusek, H. H. Otu, A. L. Wohlhueter, et al., "Genomic Counter-Stress Changes Induced by the Relaxation Response," *PLOS ONE,* vol. 3, no. 7: p. e2576 (2008).

24. M. K. Bhasin, J. A. Dusek, B. H. Chang, et al., "Relaxation Response Induces Temporal Transcriptome Changes in Energy Metabolism, Insulin Secretion, and Inflammatory Pathways," *PLOS ONE,* vol. 8, no. 5: p. e62817 (2013).

Chapter Five

1. S. Schmemann, "End Games End in a Huff," *New York Times* (October 20, 1996), http://www.nytimes.com/1996/10/20/weekinreview/end-games -end-in-a-huff.html.

2. J. Corbett, "Aaron Rodgers Is a Superstar QB out to Join Super Bowl Club," *USA Today* (January 20, 2011), http://usatoday30.usatoday.com/ sports/football/nfl/packers/2011-01-19-aaron-rodgers-cover_N.htm.

3. J. Nicklaus, *Golf My Way,* with K. Bowden (New York: Simon & Schuster, 2005), p. 79.

4. H. H. Ehrsson, S. Geyer, and E. Naito, "Imagery of Voluntary Movement of Fingers, Toes, and Tongue Activates Corresponding Body-Part-Specific Motor Representations," *Journal of Neurophysiology,* vol. 90, no. 5: pp. 3304–3316 (2003).

5. A. Pascual-Leone, D. Nguyet, L. G. Cohen, et al., "Modulation of Muscle Responses Evoked by Transcranial Magnetic Stimulation During the Acquisition of New Fine Motor Skills," *Journal of Neurophysiology,* vol. 74, no. 3: pp. 1037–1045 (1995).

6. V. K. Ranganathan, V. Siemionow, J. Z. Liu, et al., "From Mental Power to Muscle Power: Gaining Strength by Using the Mind," *Neuropsychologia,* vol. 42, no. 7: pp. 944–956 (2004); G. Yue and K. J. Cole, "Strength Increases from the Motor Program: Comparison of Training with Maximal Voluntary and Imagined Muscle Contractions," *Journal of Neurophysiology,* vol. 67, no. 5: pp. 1114–1123 (1992).

7. P. Cohen, "Mental Gymnastics Increase Bicep Strength," *New Scientist,* vol. 172, no. 2318: p. 17 (2001), http://www.newscientist.com/article/ dn1591-mental-gymnastics-increase-bicep-strength.html#.Ui03PLzk_Vk.

8. A. Guillot, F. Lebon, D. Rouffet, et al., "Muscular Responses During Motor Imagery as a Function of Muscle Contraction Types," *International Journal of Psychophysiology,* vol. 66, no. 1: pp. 18–27 (2007).

9. I. Robertson, *Mind Sculpture: Unlocking Your Brain's Untapped Potential* (New York: Bantam Books, 2000); S. Begley, "God and the Brain: How We're Wired for Spirituality," *Newsweek* (May 7, 2001), pp. 51–57; A. Newburg, E. D'Aquili, and V. Rause, *Why God Won't Go Away: Brain Science and the Biology of Belief* (New York: Ballantine Books, 2001).

10. Rossi, *The Psychobiology of Gene Expression.*

11. Yue and Cole, "Strength Increases from the Motor Program"; N. Doidge, *The Brain That Changes Itself* (New York: Viking Penguin, 2007).

12. K. M. Dillon, B. Minchoff, and K. H. Baker, "Positive Emotional States and Enhancement of the Immune System," *International Journal of Psychiatry in Medicine,* vol. 15, no. 1: pp. 13–18 (1985–1986); S. Perera, E. Sabin, P. Nelson, et al., "Increases in Salivary Lysozyme and IgA Concentrations and Secretory Rates Independent of Salivary Flow Rates Following Viewing of Humorous Videotape," *International Journal of Behavioral Medicine,* vol. 5, no. 2: pp. 118–128 (1998).

13. B. E. Kok, K. A. Coffey, M. A. Cohn, et al., "How Positive Emotions Build Physical Health: Perceived Positive Social Connections Account for the Upward Spiral Between Positive Emotions and Vagal Tone," *Psychological Science,* vol. 24, no. 7: pp. 1123–1132 (2013).

14. T. Yamamuro, K. Senzaki, S. Iwamoto, et al., "Neurogenesis in the Dentate Gyrus of the Rat Hippocampus Enhanced by Tickling Stimulation with Positive Emotion," *Neuroscience Research,* vol. 68, no. 4: pp. 285–289 (2010).

15. T. Baumgartner, M. Heinrichs, A. Vonlanthen, et al., "Oxytocin Shapes the Neural Circuitry of Trust and Trust Adaptation in Humans," *Neuron,* vol. 58, no. 4: pp. 639–650 (2008).

16. M. G. Cattaneo, G. Lucci, and L. M. Vicentini, "Oxytocin Stimulates in Vitro Angiogenesis via a Pyk-2/Src-Dependent Mechanism," *Experimental Cell Research,* vol. 315, no. 18: pp. 3210–3219 (2009).

17. A. Szeto, D. A. Nation, A. J. Mendez, et al., "Oxytocin Attenuates NADPH-Dependent Superoxide Activity and IL-6 Secretion in Macrophages and Vascular Cells," *American Journal of Physiology: Endocrinology and Metabolism,* vol. 295, no. 6: pp. E1495–501 (2008).

18. H. J. Monstein, N. Grahn, M. Truedsson, et al., "Oxytocin and Oxytocin-Receptor mRNA Expression in the Human Gastrointestinal Tract: A Polymerase Chain Reaction Study," *Regulatory Peptides,* vol. 119, no. (1–2): pp. 39–44 (2004).

19. J. Borg, O. Melander, L. Johansson, et al., "Gastroparesis Is Associated with Oxytocin Deficiency, Oesophageal Dysmotility with HyperCCKemia, and Autonomic Neuropathy with Hypergastrinemia," *BMC Gastroenterology,* vol. 9: p. 17 (2009).

Chapter Six

1. Discovery Channel, "Brainwashed," season 2, episode 4 of *Curiosity* series, aired October 28, 2012.

Chapter Seven

1. A. Mardiyati, "Kuda Lumping: A Spirited, Glass-Eating Javanese Game of Horse," *Jakarta Globe* (March 16, 2010), http://www.thejakartaglobe.com/archive/kuda-lumping-a-spirited-glass-eating-javanese-game-of-horse.

2. Two studies, in particular, demonstrate this well. In the first, subjects wore special goggles made so that if they looked to the left, everything appeared blue and if they looked to the right, everything appeared yellow. After a certain period of time, they no longer saw the blue and yellow tints; the world appeared the way it always had before, because they were seeing it not through their eyes but through their brains, which filled in reality based on their memories; see I. Kohler, *The Formation and Transformation of the Perceptual World* (New York: International Universities Press, 1964). In the other study, when depressives were shown two different pictures—one of a celebratory feast and one of a funeral—in rapid-fire fashion, they remembered the funeral scene more often than chance would allow, indicating that we tend to perceive the environment in a way that reinforces how we feel; see A. T. Beck, *Cognitive Therapy and The Emotional Disorders* (New York: International Universities Press, 1976).

3. D. P. Phillips, T. E. Ruth, and L. M. Wagner, "Psychology and Survival," *Lancet,* vol. 342, no. 8880: pp. 1142–1145 (1993).

4. P. D. Rozée and G. van Boemel, "The Psychological Effects of War Trauma and Abuse on Older Cambodian Refugee Women," *Women and Therapy,* vol. 8, no. 4: pp. 23–50 (1989); G. B. van Boemel and P. D. Rozée, "Treatment for Psychosomatic Blindness Among Cambodian Refugee Women," *Women and Therapy,* vol. 13, no. 3: pp. 239–266 (1992).

5. L. Siegel, "Cambodians' Vision Loss Linked to War Trauma," *Los Angeles Times* (October 15, 1989), http://articles.latimes.com/1989-10-15/news/mn-232_1_vision-loss.

6. A. Kondo, "Blinding Horrors: Cambodian Women's Vision Loss Linked to Sights of Slaughter," *Los Angeles Times* (June 4, 1989), http://articles.latimes.com/1989-06-04/news/hl-2445_1_pol-pot-khmer-rouge-blindness.

7. P. Cooke, "They Cried until They Could Not See," *New York Times Magazine,* vol. 140: pp. 24–25, 45–48 (June 23, 1991).

8. R. de la Fuente-Fernández, T. J. Ruth, V. Sossi, et al., "Expectation and Dopamine Release: Mechanism of the Placebo Effect in Parkinson's Disease," *Science,* vol. 293, no. 5532: pp. 1164–1166 (2001).

9. S. Siegel and B. M. C. Ramos, "Applying Laboratory Research: Drug Anticipation and the Treatment of Drug Addiction," *Experimental and Clinical Psychopharmacology,* vol. 10, no. 3: pp. 162–183 (2002).

10. S. L. Assefi and M. Garry, "Absolut Memory Distortions: Alcohol Placebos Influence the Misinformation Effect," *Psychological Science,* vol. 14, no. 1: pp. 77–80 (2003).

11. R. S. Ulrich, "View Through a Window May Influence Recovery from Surgery," *Science,* vol. 224, no. 4647: pp. 420–421 (1984).

12. C. W. F. McClare, "Resonance in Bioenergetics," *Annals of the New York Academy of Sciences,* vol. 227: 74–97 (1974).

13. B. H. Lipton, *The Biology of Belief: Unleashing the Power of Consciousness, Matter & Miracles* (Carlsbad, CA: Hay House, 2008), p. 111; A. R. Liboff, "Toward an Electromagnetic Paradigm for Biology and Medicine," *Journal of Alternative and Complementary Medicine,* vol. 10, no. 1: pp. 41–47 (2004); R. Goodman and M. Blank, "Insights into Electromagnetic Interaction Mechanisms," *Journal of Cellular Physiology,* vol. 192, no. 1: pp. 16–22 (2002); L. B. Sivitz, "Cells Proliferate in Magnetic Fields," *Science News,* vol. 158, no. 13: pp. 196–197 (2000); M. Jin, M. Blank, and R. Goodman, "ERK1/2 Phosphorylation, Induced by Electromagnetic Fields, Diminishes During Neoplastic Transformation," *Journal of Cellular Biochemistry,* vol. 78, no. 3: pp. 371–379 (2000); C. F. Blackman, S. G. Benane, and D. E. House, "Evidence for Direct Effect of Magnetic Fields on Neurite Outgrowth," *FASEB Journal,* vol. 7, no. 9: pp. 801–806 (1993); A. D. Rosen, "Magnetic Field Influence on Acetylcholine Release at the Neuromuscular Junction," *American Journal of Physiology,* vol. 262, no. 6, pt. 1: pp. C1418–C1422 (1992); M. Blank, "Na,K-APTase Function in Alternating Electrical Fields," *FASEB Journal,* vol. 6, no. 7: pp. 2434–2438 (1992); T. Y. Tsong, "Deciphering the Language of Cells," *Trends in Biochemical Sciences,* vol. 14, no. 3: pp. 89–92 (1989); G. P. A. Yen-Patton, W. F. Patton, D. M. Beer, et al., "Endothelial Cell Response to Pulsed

Electromagnetic Fields: Stimulation of Growth Rate and Angiogenesis in Vitro," *Journal of Cellular Physiology,* vol. 134, no. 1: pp. 37–46 (1988).

Chapter Eight

1. N. Bohr, "On the Constitution of Atoms and Molecules," *Philosophical Magazine,* vol. 26, no. 151: pp. 1–25 (1913).

2. F. A. Popp, "Biophotons and Their Regulatory Role in Cells," *Frontier Perspectives,* vol. 7, no. 2: pp. 13–22 (1998).

Chapter Ten

1. D. J. Siegel, *The Mindful Brain: Reflection and Attunement in the Cultivation of Well-Being* (New York: W. W. Norton and Company, 2007).

Chapter Eleven

1. L. Fehmi and J. Robbins, *The Open-Focus Brain: Harnessing the Power of Attention to Heal Mind and Body* (Boston: Trumpeter Books, 2007).

INDEX

L

L

S

T

ACKNOWLEDGMENTS

After I finished my second book, I was certain that I was done writing. The amount of sheer effort it takes just to make the time to write and research while running a very busy integrated health clinic and traveling almost every week—never mind time for family, staff meetings, and even sleeping or eating—doesn't leave me the leisure of staring out a picture window viewing nature while taking long pauses to reflect upon the next thought I'm about to type.

I've learned that bringing an immaterial idea into material reality requires a great deal of persistence, determination, focus, endurance, energy, time, creativity, and—most important—support. Personally, the only way I could pull any of this off is with the unconditional love, encouragement, assistance, and cooperation of my professional relationships, my staff, my friends, and my family. For them, I am forever grateful.

I would like to express my gratitude to the Hay House team for their belief in me again. I feel honored and blessed to be a part of such a nice family. Thank you, Reid Tracy, Stacey Smith, Shannon Littrell, Alex Freemon, Christy Salinas, and the rest of the team. I hope I have contributed to each of you in some way.

And every once in a while, an angel blesses us in our lives. These angels are usually humble, selfless, powerful, and very devoted. I have been fortunate to meet a true angel in writing this book. My dear editor and now friend, Katy Koontz, is the embodiment of excellence, magic, grace, and humility. Katy, I am deeply honored to have worked with you on this project. Thank you for being so tireless, wise, and sincere—and for giving so much.

Sally Carr, I appreciate your involvement with my manuscript. I feel so very blessed that you created time for me at a moment's notice to help me when I needed it. You were so generous.

I would also like to recognize Paula Meyer, my executive assistant and manager, who has become a true leader and a voice of reason in my life. Thank you for being so committed to the same cause. Your light is shining. I am so impressed with who you have become.

Dana Reichel is the office manager of our clinic and my personal assistant. Dana, I appreciate how instrumental you've been in overseeing the staff and making sure everyone is loved and taken care of. I can't acknowledge you enough for your emotional intelligence, your simple wisdom, your courage, and the joy you bring to so many—including me. Please keep going.

Thank you to Trina Greenbury. Never have I met a person who is so organized, professional, honest, and noble. Thank you for continuing the journey with me. I think you're amazing.

My sister-in-law, Katina Dispenza, has been instrumental in so many creative ways. Katina, I'm so fortunate that you care so much and that you work for me. All of the special details you put into representing me to the world have never gone unnoticed. You are stellar.

Also, a special thank-you goes to Rhadell Hovda, Adam Boyce, Katie Horning, Elaina Clauson, Tobi Perkins, Bruce Armstrong, Amy Schefer, Kathy Lund, Keren Retter, Dr. Mark Bingel, and Dr. Marvin Kunikiyo. You have all contributed to my life in so many wonderful ways, and I'm grateful to all of you.

John Dispenza, my brother and best friend, I'm always moved by your creative mind. Thanks for the cover design and the graphics, but most important, thanks for your love and guidance over my lifetime.

Jeffrey Fannin, Ph.D., is our quantum neuroscientist who has helped me in endless ways in measuring change. Jeffrey, it's because of you that we're making history. I respect all that you've done for me without limits.

Dawson Church, Ph.D., is a genius and a noble friend who's as passionate about science and mysticism as I am. Dawson, I'm honored by your beautiful words in writing the Foreword to this book. I hope we work together in the future.

Beth Wolfson is the manager of my trainers and a devoted corporate leader. Thank you, Beth, for creating the business model for transformation with me and for being so endlessly passionate about believing in this message. To the rest of my corporate trainers around the world, who work so diligently in becoming the living example of change and leadership for so many, I'm inspired by your commitment to this work.

Special acknowledgment goes to John Collinsworth and Jonathan Swartz, who have professionally consulted, advised, and counseled me to better understand the workings of business.

To my children, Jace, Gianna, and Shen, who are growing up to be respectable young adults, thank you for allowing me to be so weird.

And to my beloved Roberta Brittingham, you are my placebo.

ABOUT THE AUTHOR

Joe Dispenza, D.C., first caught the public's eye as one of the scientists featured in the award-winning film *What the Bleep Do We Know!?* Since that movie's release in 2004, his work has expanded, deepened, and spiraled in several key directions—all of which reflect his passion for exploring how people can use the latest findings from the fields of neuroscience and quantum physics to not only heal illness, but also enjoy a happier and more fulfilled life. Dr. Joe is driven by the conviction that each one of us has the potential for greatness and unlimited abilities.

As a teacher and lecturer, Dr. Joe has been invited to speak in more than 26 countries on 6 continents, educating thousands of people in his trademark, easy-to-understand, encouraging, compassionate style, detailing how they can rewire their brains and recondition their bodies to make lasting changes. In addition to offering a variety of online courses and teleclasses, he personally teaches three-day progressive workshops and five-day advanced workshops in the United States and abroad. Dr. Joe is also a faculty member at the International Quantum University for Integrative Medicine in Honolulu; the Omega Institute in Rhinebeck, New York; and Kripalu Center for Yoga and Health in Stockbridge, Massachusetts. He's also an invited chair of the research committee at Life University in Atlanta, Georgia.

As a researcher, Dr. Joe explores the science behind spontaneous remissions and how people heal themselves of chronic conditions and even terminal diseases. He has more recently begun partnering with other scientists to perform extensive research on the effects of meditation during his advanced workshops. He and his team conduct brain mapping with electroencephalograms (EEGs) and individual energy-field testing with a gas discharge visualization (GDV) machine, as well as measure both heart coherence with HeartMath monitors and the energy present in the workshop environment before, during, and after events with a GDVSputnik sensor. Soon, he plans to include epigenetic testing in this research as well.

As a corporate consultant, Dr. Joe gives on-site lectures and workshops for businesses and corporations interested in using neuroscientific principles to boost their employees' creativity, innovation, productivity, and more. His corporate program also includes private coaching for upper management. He has personally trained a group of 40 corporate trainers who teach his model of transformation to companies around the world. He recently began certifying independent coaches in using his model of change with their own clients.

As an author, Dr. Joe has written *Evolve Your Brain: The Science of Changing Your Mind* (Health Communications Inc., 2007), followed by *Breaking the Habit of Being Yourself: How to Lose Your Mind and Create a New One* (Hay House, 2012), both of which detail the neuroscience of change and epigenetics. *You Are the Placebo: Making Your Mind Matter,* which builds on his previous work, is his third book.

Dr. Joe received his doctor of chiropractic degree from Life University, graduating with honors. His postgraduate training covered neurology, neuroscience, brain function and chemistry, cellular biology, memory formation, and aging and longevity. When not lecturing and writing, Dr. Joe sees patients at his chiropractic clinic near Olympia, Washington. He can be contacted at www.drjoedispenza.com.

Hay House Titles of Related Interest

YOU CAN HEAL YOUR LIFE, the movie, starring Louise Hay & Friends
(available as a 1-DVD program and an expanded 2-DVD set)
Watch the trailer at: www.LouiseHayMovie.com

THE SHIFT, the movie,
starring Dr. Wayne W. Dyer
(available as a 1-DVD program and an expanded 2-DVD set)
Watch the trailer at: www.DyerMovie.com

ALL IS WELL: Heal Your Body with Medicine, Affirmations, and Intuition,
by Louise Hay and Mona Lisa Schulz, M.D., Ph.D.

FROM BIRTH TO BLISS: The Power of Conscientious Living,
by C. Norman Shealy, M.D., Ph.D.

*HELP ME TO HEAL: A Practical Guidebook for Patients, Visitors, and
Caregivers,* by Bernie S. Siegel, M.D., and Yosaif August

HOW YOUR MIND CAN HEAL YOUR BODY, by David R. Hamilton, Ph.D.

MIND OVER MEDICINE: Scientific Proof That You Can Heal Yourself,
by Lissa Rankin, M.D.

*ONE MIND: How Our Individual Mind Is Part of a Greater Consciousness
and Why It Matters,* by Larry Dossey, M.D.

TUNE IN: Let Your Intuition Guide You to Fulfillment and Flow,
by Sonia Choquette

THE TURNING POINT: Creating Resilience in a Time of Extremes,
by Gregg Braden

All of the above are available at your local bookstore,
or may be ordered by contacting Hay House (see next page).

We hope you enjoyed this Hay House book. If you'd like to receive our online catalog featuring additional information on Hay House books and products, or if you'd like to find out more about the Hay Foundation, please contact:

Hay House, Inc., P.O. Box 5100, Carlsbad, CA 92018-5100
(760) 431-7695 or (800) 654-5126
(760) 431-6948 (fax) or (800) 650-5115 (fax)
www.hayhouse.com® • www.hayfoundation.org

Published and distributed in Australia by:
Hay House Australia Pty. Ltd., 18/36 Ralph St., Alexandria NSW 2015
Phone: 612-9669-4299 • *Fax:* 612-9669-4144 • www.hayhouse.com.au

Published and distributed in the United Kingdom by:
Hay House UK, Ltd., Astley House, 33 Notting Hill Gate, London W11 3JQ
Phone: 44-20-3675-2450 • *Fax:* 44-20-3675-2451 • www.hayhouse.co.uk

Published and distributed in the Republic of South Africa by:
Hay House SA (Pty), Ltd., P.O. Box 990, Witkoppen 2068
Phone/Fax: 27-11-467-8904 • www.hayhouse.co.za

Published in India by: Hay House Publishers India,
Muskaan Complex, Plot No. 3, B-2, Vasant Kunj, New Delhi 110 070
Phone: 91-11-4176-1620 • *Fax:* 91-11-4176-1630 • www.hayhouse.co.in

Distributed in Canada by:
Raincoast Books, 2440 Viking Way, Richmond, B.C. V6V 1N2
Phone: 1-800-663-5714 • *Fax:* 1-800-565-3770 • www.raincoast.com

---

Take Your Soul on a Vacation

Visit www.HealYourLife.com® to regroup, recharge,
and reconnect with your own magnificence.
Featuring blogs, mind-body-spirit news, and
life-changing wisdom from Louise Hay and friends.

Visit www.HealYourLife.com today